D0925304

Practically
Perfect

Practically Perfect

KILLERS WHO GOT AWAY WITH MURDER ... FOR A WHILE

Dale Brawn

DUNDURN

TORONTO

Copyright © Dale Brawn, 2013

All rights reserved. No part of this publication may be reproduced, stored in a retrieval system, or transmitted in any form or by any means, electronic, mechanical, photocopying, recording, or otherwise (except for brief passages for purposes of review) without the prior permission of Dundurn Press. Permission to photocopy should be requested from Access Copyright.

Editor: Britanie Wilson
Design: Jesse Hooper
Printer: Webcom

Library and Archives Canada Cataloguing in Publication

Brawn, Dale, 1948-
    Practically perfect : killers who got away with murder-- for awhile / by Dale Brawn.

Includes bibliographical references and index.
Issued also in electronic formats.
ISBN 978-1-4597-0970-6

    1. Murder. 2. Murderers. I. Title.

HV6515.B73 2013   364.152'3   C2013-900822-5

1   2   3   4   5   17   16   15   14   13

We acknowledge the support of the **Canada Council for the Arts** and the **Ontario Arts Council** for our publishing program. We also acknowledge the financial support of the **Government of Canada** through the **Canada Book Fund** and **Livres Canada Books**, and the **Government of Ontario** through the **Ontario Book Publishing Tax Credit** and the **Ontario Media Development Corporation**.

Care has been taken to trace the ownership of copyright material used in this book. The author and the publisher welcome any information enabling them to rectify any references or credits in subsequent editions.

J. Kirk Howard, President

Printed and bound in Canada.

VISIT US AT
Dundurn.com | Definingcanada.ca | @dundurnpress | Facebook.com/dundurnpress

Dundurn
3 Church Street, Suite 500
Toronto, Ontario, Canada
M5E 1M2

Gazelle Book Services Limited
White Cross Mills
High Town, Lancaster, England
L41 4XS

Dundurn
2250 Military Road
Tonawanda, NY
U.S.A. 14150

Angela and Gary Brawn
— always there

Truth will come to light; murder
cannot be hid long.
— *Merchant of Venice*, Act II, Scene 2

Contents

Acknowledgements

Writing is essentially a lonely process, and there is only so much others can do to help an author overcome obstacles. In the case of this book, four individuals deserve special acknowledgement for their assistance. Charlotte Neff, of the Department of Law and Justice at Laurentian University, in Sudbury, Ontario, is an incredibly talented researcher, and gave unstintingly of her time. Without her, this project would not have been possible. Pauline Begin, also of the Department of Law and Justice, solved every problem thrust at her. Her presence was calming beyond measure. The patience of Britanie Wilson of Dundurn was often taxed, but her many considerations made this book all that I hoped it might be. And then, of course, Gloria.

"If once a man indulges himself in murder, very soon he comes to think little of robbing; and from robbing he next comes to drinking and Sabbath-breaking, and from that to incivility and procrastination." (*Murder Considered as One of the Fine Arts.*)

Introduction

In the years I have been writing about crime I have come to the conclusion that getting away with murder has more to do with luck than careful planning or attention to detail. Even now I am surprised by how many people actually commit the perfect crime, and then do something to attract attention to themselves. This book is about some of those individuals.

These stories contain a number of common themes. For example, with perhaps one or two exceptions, all of those I wrote about were poor. Most were uneducated, although in the late nineteenth and early twentieth centuries a lack of education among members of the working class was the rule rather than the exception. A surprisingly large number of killers were mentally challenged. Were they to experience our criminal justice system today, they would almost certainly have been treated in a different way. A case in point are two Quebec lovers, whose lawyers argued that they should not be hanged because the couple was too ignorant to realize that in poisoning the husband of one of them they actually committed a crime. When the federal cabinet of Conservative Prime Minister John Diefenbaker considered the clemency application of Mickey Feener, everyone agreed that the killer of three was mentally disabled, but the cabinet still refused to commute his sentence. Deep down, a majority of cabinet members were convinced that a man so popular with women could not possibly be as intellectually challenged as the experts alleged.

It probably will come as no surprise to most readers that a large number of the killers I write about were violent individuals, for whom murder was the culmination of a life of crime. Emerson Shelley was barely a teenager when he committed his first murder, and in the years between his killings he was in and out of jail more often than he was employed. The same could be said about William Jasper Collins, a young American who killed his benefactor after the lawyer managed to convince a Montana jury that his teenage client did not sexually assault his own sister.

Most of the thirty males and two females whose crimes I examine were hanged, or died before their death sentences could be carried out, and the majority were murdered for money or sex. Notable among the exceptions are a Manitoba farmer who killed his neighbour to the north because the man cut down his favourite tree, then killed his neighbour to the south for no reason whatsoever (although he did say that after you kill once, killing a second time is not so difficult). That seems to have been the case for more than half of the people whose stories are described in this book. One man killed (or helped his lover kill) all five of the babies born to the couple; a Saskatchewan farmer killed his brother-in-law before turning his attention to his brother; two Quebec men insured the lives of unwed day labourers, then killed them for the proceeds of their insurance; and a prairie farmer murdered his wife, and when no one came to arrest him, he killed the man with whom he suspected she was having an affair.

A number of other commonalities can be gleaned from my stories of murder and mayhem. One is that the "perfect" murder was more likely to be committed in a small, rural community than a city. That is likely no longer the case, but until well into the twentieth century the inhabitants of most subsistence-level farms were more concerned with their own welfare than the well-being of their neighbours. These women and men were not unaware of what went on around them, but they were not inclined to bring the authorities into their own troubled lives, even if it was to discuss murder.

Another theme readers cannot help but notice is that those who got away with murder were less often tripped up by good police work than by the suspicions of a family member of their victim. The father of one of the men murdered for insurance could not get it out of his head that his son died so soon after taking out a policy of insurance, just as the son of a neighbour had; the sister of a man poisoned by his wife was convinced that her brother had been murdered, despite the fact that his death was ruled natural. Her perseverance resulted in an exhumation, and a double execution.

The thing that perhaps surprised me most when I was researching these stories was that most killers wanted to be caught. An Ontario multiple-murderer drove around the country in the bright red sports car of his first victim, his name spelled out on the hood of the car, with photographs of his victims taped to the dashboard. A Quebecer asked his girlfriend to kill his wife, and after she did, he killed her. Within minutes of being picked up by the police, he confessed virtually without hesitation. One killer began telling his neighbours about his crime within days of the murder, and continued to confess right up until the day of his trial; and an Ontario man killed his wife while his children watched from their beds, for the next decade daring them to go to the police.

All of the women and men described in this book got away with murder, for a while. Most were very bad people, who did little to hide their crime. Nonetheless, that they were caught was most often a result of bad luck. In fact, that is the lesson to be learned from these stories: if you want to get away with murder, you better be lucky.

1

They Got Away With It Before

The three cases discussed in this chapter are about individuals who murdered openly, and got away with it because none of their neighbours wanted to interfere. Had any of the four killers been content to stop with their first crime, their stories almost certainly would not have become known. But as is so often the case with those who deceive, success encourages continued bad conduct; and in the annals of Manitoba murders, no one's conduct was worse than that of Fred Stawycznyk and Pauline Yatchuk.

Fred Stawycznyk and Pauline Yatchuk: Babies in Boxes

For awhile Fred Stawycznyk had it all. He was thirty, the married father of three healthy children, and worked hard enough on his small acreage to be considered one of his community's more successful farmers. Then in 1918 his young wife died, leaving him to raise the couple's three children on his own. For the next few years everyone pulled together, and the family continued to prosper. Things changed when Nicola Yatchuk and his family arrived in Angusville, a small, mostly Ukrainian farming community near the Manitoba-Saskatchewan border about two hours northwest of Brandon. It is hard to imagine that the difference in circumstances between the Stawycznyks and the Yatchuks could have been any greater. While Fred and his kids lived in relative luxury, Nicola, his wife Pauline, and their five children lived in a shack set back fifty feet from one of the region's busiest highways, about a kilometre from town.

Nicola was not cut out to be a farmer and three or four years after he and his family arrived in Canada he returned to the United States to pursue wage labour, leaving Pauline to fend for herself. It did not take long before Stawycznyk noticed the absence of his neighbour's husband. Soon gossip spread that the two were having an affair, and beginning in 1927 the rumours became reality.

The first obvious product of the Stawycznyk-Yatchuk relationship was a baby girl, born on September 1, 1929. The child lived less than an hour before it was strangled. The tiny body was then placed in an empty fruit box and buried in the Yatchuk yard. What is difficult to imagine is that no one asked what happened to the baby, but unfortunately that was the case. In a farm community as isolated as Angusville, people minded their own business. Almost everyone in the district was an immigrant, and most had more pressing concerns than worrying about what was happening next door. That could not be said for Pauline's husband though, and when he showed up it did not take him long to learn of the affair his wife was having with Stawycznyk. He packed his things, and with the three oldest of the five children he knew belonged to him, left.

Pauline was nothing if not fertile, and ten and a half months after producing her first illegitimate child, she gave birth to a second. On July 18, 1930, it joined its brother or sister in the Yatchuk garden, buried under two feet of soil. Again, no questions were asked. When they returned to their mother a month and a half later, even the children taken by their father to the United States appeared not to know about the latest birth. That could not be said of the twins born in June 1931. Although Pauline sent her children to the stable whenever Stawycznyk showed up, and it was there they waited while the couple carried on their affair and he delivered their mother's babies, the kids knew what was going on. One year after the birth of the twins Stawycznyk was away from his farm and Yatchuk delivered a fifth infant on her own. The result was the same, except this time Pauline just covered the body and put it under her bed. It remained there for three days until Stawycznyk buried the child.

The two lovers might have produced and murdered even more children had they not fought in the summer of 1932. A stable on Stawycznyk's farm burned earlier in the year, and just weeks after it was rebuilt, it was destroyed again. The first fire may have been an accident, but this time there was absolutely no doubt in Stawycznyk's mind who was responsible. The bloom, it seems, had withered in his relationship with Yatchuk, and Stawycznyk was convinced that his former lover burned his stable to get even. They fought until November, when Yatchuk put an end to things — literally. She wrote an anonymous letter to the Angusville justice of the peace, suggesting that the authorities might want to look into what happened to five children who, over a period of four years, disappeared from the home of Pauline Yatchuk.

From that point on events unfolded rapidly, and on November 28 the police arrived in force on the Yatchuk acreage. Officers later commented on how surprised they were that Pauline was so willing to talk. In fact, as soon as they asked about the missing babies, she started telling them about her relationship with Stawycznyk and what the two had done. She admitted that she was responsible for the death of one of her babies and accused Fred of killing the others. When she finished confessing, Yatchuk led investigators into her snow-covered yard. Officers with shovels followed her around and wherever she pointed, they dug. The first box was discovered about forty yards from the Yatchuk shack, near a well. The next was located in a garden a few feet away. Then the twins were brought up, and after them, the last victim. With a police officer standing nearby, Stawycznyk watched the digging, periodically complaining about the cold. At one point there was no body where Yatchuk pointed, and he told a policeman to dig a little to one side, through about three feet of snow. Instead, the officer handed the alleged killer a shovel and told him to get to it. It took Stawycznyk only a minute or two to uncover the spot where the body of the last baby was interred. There was not much left, and the district coroner could not confirm whether all, or indeed any, of the children died a violent death.

As soon as the police discovered the remains of the five infants, they took Stawycznyk and Yatchuk into custody and charged them with murder. Yatchuk had already confessed her part in the deaths of the babies, but Stawycznyk denied murdering anyone. He told investigators that he knew where the body of the fifth baby was buried only because he put it there, after he was told to do so by Yatchuk. Besides, he said, he was not the only man with whom she was carrying on.

Less than two weeks later preliminary hearings were held to determine if there was sufficient evidence to commit the pair to trial. Stawycznyk went first. The story Yatchuk told at his hearing was identical to the statement she gave police, and Stawycznyk was bound over for trial. At the end of Yatchuk's own preliminary, the presiding magistrate decided there was evidence that the fifth child was stillborn and not murdered, and he directed that the murder charges laid against Yatchuk be replaced with charges of concealing a birth. There is some doubt whether that was an appropriate decision. Sixteen days after her preliminary hearing ended, Yatchuk was overheard confessing that she killed her babies by herself.

Nonetheless, when Stawycznyk's murder trial got underway in early April 1933, he alone was charged with murder. In the months the Royal Canadian Mounted Police spent investigating the infant deaths, a number of evidentiary problems arose. As a result, the Crown decided to withdraw one of the five murder charges laid against Stawycznyk and replace it with a single count of concealing a birth. The Crown would proceed with one murder charge at a time and continue with separate trials until it obtained a conviction. If they did not obtain one, Stawycznyk would be tried on the charge of concealing a birth. Yatchuk would be prosecuted on just four charges of concealment.

As was the case during his preliminary hearing, the principal witness against Stawycznyk was the mother of the babies he was charged with killing. One of the few things to which Yatchuk testified that had not come out earlier was that although she was living from hand to mouth, not once did her lover provide her with financial assistance. In fact, in the five years Stawycznyk carried on his affair with Yatchuk, few people actually saw the couple together. The most neighbours could say was that they noticed Stawyscznyk at the Yatchuk shack "several" times, although a few admitted to being present on one occasion when the two fought and Yatchuk accused Stawycznyk of ruining her life. Even the woman's thirteen-year-old son was a reluctant witness. All the Crown was able to get him to admit was that his neighbour was a "frequent" visitor.

The jurors empanelled to decide the fate of Fred Stawycznyk sat through four days of testimony, including that given by the accused. He denied murdering the babies and said the only crime he committed was burying the last of Yatchuk's five illegitimate infants. Under cross-examination, however, he did admit to not wanting any more children, and testified that if his daughter and twin boys found out there was to be a new member of the family, they would leave him. Ninety minutes after it started deliberating, the jury returned with its verdict — Stawycznyk was to be hanged on July 12, in Manitoba's new indoor death chamber. It took a few moments before the convicted killer realized what he heard, and when he did, tears began streaming down his face. His voice shaking with emotion, he repeated that he did nothing wrong, that the court was ordering an innocent man to be hanged.

By a vote of two-to-one the Manitoba Court of Appeal turned down Stawycznyk's request for a new trial. The dissenting judge said that in his opinion an injustice had been done to the accused and he urged his colleagues to join him in ordering a new trial. That was not to be, nor was the condemned killer granted clemency, but by then the Angusville farmer seemed to have accepted his fate.

Author's photo.

Fred Stawycznyk was a rarity in the annals of Canadian executions; he helped his lover murder at least four of the children born to the couple. Because of the crime for which he died, Stawycznyk was not buried on consecrated grounds. Instead, he was interred in an area a few feet north of the cemetery.

The death cell in the Headingley jail, where Stawycznyk spent his last months, is separated from the gallows by a single door. The distance from the cell to the traps is no more than three metres, and Stawycznyk walked it unaided. He stood without moving while his executioner pinioned his legs, calmly looking around the small chamber. Just before the hood was pulled over his head, Stawycznyk was asked if he had any last words. He did, although not many. In Ukrainian he said, "I thank everybody here for the way they treated me, because I am innocent and prepared to meet my Maker."[1] His statement was translated into English by a prison guard, and seconds later the trapdoors on which Stawycznyk stood were opened. For the next twenty minutes his body was suspended over a shallow pit dug into the floor of the room below, to ensure that his feet did not make contact with the ground.

Fred Stawycznyk's body was claimed by his sons a few hours after he was executed, and it was returned to Augusville. There it was interred close to (but not quite in) a cemetery near the family farm.

William Bahrey: The Brothers in the Haystacks

William Bahrey had a confused sense of propriety when it came to women. On the one hand, he was fiercely protective of his two sisters, particularly Annie. When it turned out that the man she married in the summer of 1931 already had a wife, William killed him to preserve his wife's honour. Yet shortly after his older brother Alexander married Dora, he began an affair with his sister-in-law. After Alex began abusing her, William killed him too. Despite having the intelligence of a ten-year-old, and the subtlety of a hammer, he got completely away with the first murder; and if he had kept his mouth shut, he would never have been linked to his brother's death, either.

When the whole business started, Alexander and Dora Bahrey were no longer newlyweds. Although they were still in their twenties, they had a number of things going for them. Alexander was short, very heavy, and not much of a farmer, but he owned his own land, and in the Whitlow district of south-central Saskatchewan he was the go-to guy when it came to bootleg liquor or stolen wheat. William had a homestead next to his brother's, and helped Alex in his illegal endeavours whenever he could. Above all else, however, William was devoted to his sister-in-law. Alexander knew of the affair, and while it bothered him, he did nothing to bring it to an end. In the fall of 1931 circumstances dictated that the brothers temporarily put aside their squabbling over Dora. Annie Bahrey had been married only a few months when someone found out that her husband, Nestor Tereschuk, already had a wife in Poland. That did not sit well with the Bahreys, yet had Tereschuk not started abusing Annie, it was likely something the family was prepared to overlook. But after the couple separated, and Annie moved in with Alex and Dora, the wound festered.

For a while it looked like the federal government was going to preserve the honour of the Bahrey family for them. It started proceedings to deport Tereschuk to his native Poland, removing the problem without resorting to violence. But the government allowed the bigamist to remain in Canada until everything was concluded, provided Tereschuk reported in every month to the North Battleford detachment of the Royal Canadian Mounted Police. The wheels of government grind slowly, however, and in the fall of 1932 William decided it was time to take matters into his own hands. On October 31, Tereschuk showed up at Alexander's farm, where William was visiting, and during the ensuing conversation William learned that Alexander, Dora, and Annie were going to spend the night at his father's home, six miles away. Tereschuk was not invited. On his way home, William decided this was the perfect time to exact revenge for the dishonour Tereschuk brought on the Bahreys. With his .22 calibre rifle in hand, he walked to a nearby hill, and looked down at his brother's house. When he saw three people come out, he put his plan in action. William ran to Alex's barn, and waited. From his vantage point he was ideally positioned to shoot Tereschuk when he left Alexander's house; but instead of walking past the barn, as William thought he was going to do, Tereschuk went around it.

When he saw his brother-in-law holding a rifle, Nestor knew immediately what he was intending to do, and begged him not to shoot. William ignored him and hit the startled man with the butt of the gun, stunning him. He then picked up the hub of a buggy wheel, which was lying nearby, and beat him to death. Bahrey dragged Tereschuk's body to a flat area below the house, and as soon as it was dark, came back with his horse. Out of an abundance of caution he shot his brother-in-law in the head, from point-blank range. After that he looped a rope around the feet of the dead man and dragged Tereschuk's corpse four kilometres to the haystack of a neighbour. The homestead was vacant, and Bahrey had all the time he needed to bury the body in the hay and then set the stack on fire. On the way home he threw the rifle into a creek. At his brother's farm he found a cap, which apparently fell off the head of his victim when he dragged the man's body to the haystack. He shoved it down a gopher hole, and covered it with a rock.

In retrospect, it is unlikely that William murdered his brother-in-law without the consent of his father, or at least the knowledge of his family. Immediately after the murder he told his sister he killed her husband, and within days everyone in the district was aware of what happened. Everyone, that is, except Dora.

> All the Bahreys knew of the killing of Nestor Tereschuk ... the whole bunch knew before I did because they were talking between themselves. When someone said they were afraid that Nestor might come back, the Bahreys said he will never come back. If I would spread this [to the authorities], they would punish me. I am only one, they are a whole bunch. I was a stranger and they were no good to me.[2]

Until Bahrey confessed to the killing nearly a year later, no one in authority had a clue that Tereschuk was dead.

It is a little ironic that when William talked to Dora of murdering Nestor, he told her that "if Tereschuk don't know how to live properly with a wife here, we don't want him."[3] Five months after murdering his brother-in-law, William grew tired of the way his brother was treating Dora. Alex was a brutal man, with little affection and no respect for his wife. So William decided that he too must die.

Within months of their wedding, Alex started beating his new wife, causing her to complain in front of his family that she would rather hit herself with stones than have her husband continue striking her.[4] Over time Alexander's ill treatment progressed from cruelty to brutality. The day after Dora gave birth to the couple's first child Alex left for a day or two. Before he did, he barricaded the pathway from the couple's house to the woodpile, forcing Dora to walk through waist-high snow to gather kindling for a fire. When her husband returned she complained. "Don't you know that a woman will die if she goes out in the snow to get wood the day after a child is born?" He told her that was exactly what he had in mind. "I want it that way for you to die."[5] Despite the fact that most of their fights took place in front of family members, no one aside from William expressed any sympathy for what Dora was going through. After one particularly heated exchange, Alexander asked Nestor what he thought should be done with his wife. The men debated, in her presence, whether it would be better to put a stone around her neck and throw her into a well, or just kill her.[6]

William found this mistreatment profoundly upsetting, and he talked to his sister-in-law about what he should do. He later said that he "told Dora I would do something to him." He left her with no doubt about what that would be. "Dora knew I was going to kill him."[7] Which is precisely what William did.

On April 10, 1933, Dora and Annie decided to spend a couple of days visiting at the home of Annie's father. After they left, siblings John, William, and Alexander Bahrey played cards with a neighbour. Eventually everyone went home, except William and his older brother. Before they parted, Alec told William that he needed beer bottles for the moonshine he was making, and he was going over to their bother-in-law's farm to get some. It was about two kilometres away, and when Alexander headed out, William followed. As the elder brother entered a granary, William crept up to a nearby snow bank. When Alex stepped out with the bottles, William shot him with a .32-20 Winchester, a centre fire rifle used to kill small game. To be sure his brother was dead he climbed onto a haystack and shot him three more times. William left the body where it lay and went home. The next morning he returned, tied a piece of barbed wire to Alexander's arm, and dragged his body to the top of the same stack he stood on a few hours earlier. Then, just as he had done five months before, he started a fire.

The owner of the haystack noticed it go up in flames, but he lived some distance away, and it was not until April 16 that he went out to the field to investigate. Before he got there his dog was already nosing around what remained of the stack. Lying in the middle of the huge mound were bones of what clearly was once a human being. Because he did not have a telephone of his own, it was the next morning before the farmer contacted the local justice of the peace, who in turn telephoned the police.

On their way to the scene a contingent of officers from the North Battleford detachment of the Royal Canadian Mounted Police got stuck in a mud hole, and by the time they showed up news of the gruesome discovery had spread. What little remained of the body was considerably disturbed. Scattered around the field were parts of a man's overalls, braces, buttons, and bones. Included among the latter were parts of a skull, a human torso extending from the waist to the thighs, pelvic bones, some teeth, and numerous small bones. At the bottom of a half-metre pile of ashes investigators also found a short piece of barbed wire with a loop at one end. Lying near it were two shell casings.

William Bahrey brutally murdered both his brother and his brother-in-law. He was mentally challenged, although not sufficiently so to escape the noose. His lack of understanding of his circumstances can be seen in the letter he wrote seeking commutation of his death sentence. He wanted to be paroled from jail, he said, because he was "anxious to return to take care of my farm duties."

Courtesy of Library and Archives Canada.

After the remains were removed to a nearby church, the police encouraged people to view the body, in the hope that someone would see something that might help identify the person to whom the bones once belonged. Over the few days dozens of residents of the Whitlow district filed by, but many stayed away. John Bahrey was among the latter. He recalled being at home when his brother Harry stopped by. "We were talking about who it might be. It was said that it might be a tramp who had walked in there and slept in the straw pile."[8] William listened to the conversation, but said nothing. After four days Ambrose could no longer put off what he must have suspected from the beginning: the body was almost certainly that of his son Alex, who had been missing for nearly a week.

Once the patriarch of the Bahrey clan identified the remains, the police quickly began questioning other family members. On April 19, they got around to William. He told them that the last time he saw Alexander, his brother was riding away from home on a bay saddle horse. A week later the horse was located, tied to a tree two kilometres from its owner's homestead. It was obvious to investigators that in the preceding two weeks the animal had been well cared for.

The same day the police made their discovery, a coroner's inquest was convened to look into the circumstances surrounding the death of Alexander Bahrey. After jurors finished examining the remains, the bones were sent to Regina to be examined by the province's chief pathologist. She concluded that they belonged to "a fat, thick-set man of about 30 years of age and medium height."[9] The short, chubby Alexander fit the description to a T. Even before investigators received the pathologist's report, they concluded that if Alexander was murdered, his brother was the likely killer. In fact, from the time the police heard that Alexander was missing, officers kept William under surveillance. On April 25, they decided to increase the pressure on the Bahreys, and William was taken into custody on a coroner's warrant. Even at this late stage had he said nothing, there was little chance William would have been charged with murder, and even less that he would be convicted. But a little over two weeks after being picked up, he told his jailors that he was ready to confess. What surprised the police was not that he was prepared to talk about his brother, but that he wanted to tell them about a second murder as well.

May 9, the day after he confessed to the killings, Bahrey led officers to the scene of both crimes. First he directed them to the haystack where he burned the body of his brother-in-law. There was not much left, although investigators found a quantity of small bones, a pair of cufflinks, and articles of clothing. It was not until more than four months later that the dead man's skull was discovered a half kilometre away, and the remains were positively identified as those of Nestor Tereschuk.

From the haystack containing the bones of Nestor, William took his minders to the stream into which he threw the rifle he used to shoot his brother. Handed a rake, William went to the exact spot, and in no time pulled out the gun. After that he led the group to the gopher hole in which he stuffed Nestor's cap. Next he walked to his brother's farm. On the roof of a hen house officers found the dead man's watch and razor, hidden there after he was murdered. Then William showed investigators where he was standing when he shot Nestor.

On May 11, Bahrey appeared at a preliminary hearing, called to determine if there was enough evidence to bind him over for trial. The result was a foregone conclusion, but Dora made the proceedings memorable. She had to be carried into the room, and as soon as she was sworn in, she became unresponsive to questioning, almost comatose. Then she suddenly she sat up, and in a loud, hoarse voice called out "Give me the Bible, swear me in a second time, and I will tell you all I know."[10] With that she relapsed into her former state, and even questions posed by an obviously irate coroner did nothing to rouse her. Dora, however, was not to get off that easily. The police were aware that almost from the moment she learned that Alexander was murdered the grieving widow began living with her husband's killer. The next day Dora was recalled to the stand, and this time she was ready to talk. In the opinion of many onlookers, her story could have come from a Tolstoy novel, delivered in broken English, and punctuated with a plethora of eastern-European idioms. The essence of what she had to say was crystal clear: William murdered both her husband and his brother-in-law.

Bahrey's trial was scheduled to get underway the first week of October 1933, but before it did a specially empanelled jury was asked to determine whether the accused was mentally fit to stand trial. It was convened on October 2, and after deliberating for four hours, determined that William was sane enough to instruct counsel, and to appreciate the seriousness of what he was accused of doing. Bahrey's trial started the next day. One Bahrey after another took the stand. None made any attempt to deny, or even minimize, what William did. On the seventh, Chief Justice James Thomas Brown imposed the only sentence he could: William Bahrey was to hang. The Saskatchewan Court of Appeal heard arguments about whether the condemned prisoner was sane enough to stand trial. The three-member panel reserved its decision, but when the judgment came down it confirmed that William must hang. On February 13, the Governor General, on the advice of the federal cabinet, turned down his request for clemency. The man who could not keep a secret was to be hanged ten days later.

Two days before that was to happen, Arthur Ellis, Canada's busiest executioner, arrived in Prince Albert. He spent the next day making sure everything was in order, and just before 6:00 a.m. on February 23, 1934, Bahrey started on his last journey. Beside him, but ignored by the condemned killer, walked his spiritual adviser. William was hanged exactly as scheduled, and ten minutes later joined his two victims in the hereafter.

William Larocque and Emmanuel Lavictoire: Murders for Insurance

Fifty-seven-year-old William Larocque and his best friend and neighbour, fifty-one-year-old Emmanuel Lavictoire, were not subtle men. After they insured and murdered a young man who lived near them in southeastern Ontario, they realized they had a money-making scheme that worked. Their story is a saga of limitless greed, and illustrates how easy it was in the 1930s to get away with murder, at least for a while.

It all started with Athanase Lamarche. In October 1930, he drowned in a car accident while driving with Larocque and Lavictoire near Masson, Quebec. Shortly before his death, Larocque persuaded the dead man to take out a policy of life insurance, which paid double its face value if Lamarche were to die in an accident. Larocque and Lavictoire were the only witnesses to testify at the coroner's inquest convened following the drowning, and the jury quickly concluded that Lamarche died as a result of an accident. Shortly after the father of Lamarche was paid by his son's insurance company, Larocque and Lavictoire swindled him out of a large portion of the proceeds. The ease with which they were able to persuade their victim to insure himself, and then get away with killing him, seemed to inspire the two men.

Over the next several months they approached three other single men about insuring themselves. All refused to consider it, but when Larocque and his partner spoke to twenty-seven-year-old Léo Bergeron, the response was different. The young man supported himself by working for room and board, and was easily manipulated. He was, however, cautious enough to ask his father what he should do. The advice he got was blunt: "Don't go in that. They will do with you the same as they did with Lamarche."[11] A few weeks later Larocque showed up at the Bergeron farm, and said he was upset by what Leon said to his son, Léo. The father was unapologetic. He asked Larocque how much the policy cost. Told $55, he said his son could never afford it. Larocque insisted the issue was not money; it was about a smart business decision. "Larocque told me that Leo had no home and if he broke an arm or became ill he would be looked after. I insisted that Leo should not take out the policy. I did all I could to stop him, but after seeing that it was hopeless, I told Leo he could do as he pleased."[12]

When Léo was finally persuaded to buy the insurance, proceeds of the $2,500 policy were to be paid to his father, and if Léo died in an accident, the amount paid out would be double what his life was insured for. In early December 1931, Larocque made arrangements, presumably with Léo's consent, to have the value of the policy increased to $5,000, and he replaced the insured's father as sole beneficiary. Around the same time Lavictoire, who knew Bergeron only casually, tried to persuade the young man to take out a second policy of insurance, with Lavictoire as beneficiary. This time Léo refused. A little later Larocque asked an acquaintance cutting ice on the Ottawa River to hire Bergeron for the winter, but the man refused to consider it, suggesting the job was far too dangerous for a novice. The following month Léo was killed in an accident on Larocque's farm.

The day before the incident Larocque made arrangements for Léo to help him with some harvesting. For a reason never explained he wanted Léo to start work at 8:00 a.m., although everyone else hired for the day was told to show up at noon. Bergeron's first job of the morning was backing a team of horses into Larocque's barn. Something spooked the animals, and as Larocque and Lavictoire looked on, Léo was trampled to death.

At least that is the story the two men told on March 18, 1932. No one believed it — not the doctor who first arrived on the scene, not the police who followed, and certainly not the dead man's father, who rushed to the Larocque farm as soon as he heard that his son was hurt.

When Leon Bergeron arrived, Léo was lying on the barn floor, a buffalo robe covering his face. The distraught father immediately removed it, and as he did so he saw his son gasp for breath, and then stop breathing. Bergeron was devastated, but he was also angry, and he confronted Larocque. The farmer told the grief-stricken father that his son's death was an accident, that he was trampled after being knocked down by the horses. Bergeron said he did not believe it. He was certain Larocque murdered his son, just as he had Lamarche. Larocque told Bergeron that that was an odd thing to say: "It's queer. I never heard anything about it."[13]

An autopsy on Léo's body revealed that his head was crushed in two places. While those injuries may have been caused by a horse, the other injuries he suffered could not, which was why when the police began their investigation, they suspected that they were dealing with a murder. Ten days later they were certain. By then investigators were looking into the drowning of Lamarche, and on March 10, a spokesperson for the Ontario Provincial Police announced that his force was going to exhume his body, to determine whether he might have been murdered. Two days later a coroner's inquest was adjourned to give the police more time to gather evidence. From that point forward, things began going very badly for the farmer and the gardener.

On April 5, 1932, the two men were arrested and charged with defrauding Felix Lamarche out of proceeds from his son's life insurance policy. Later the same day the reconvened coroner's jury concluded that the death of Léo Bergeron was caused either by a horse, or by person or persons unknown. Within the week those persons were officially identified, and Larocque and Lavictoire were charged with murder. Their December trial lasted nine days, and featured a number of heated skirmishes between the lawyers for the two men and the prosecutor. In his opening statement the Crown Attorney made clear what was to come. He told jurors that the conniving and duplicity of the accused would soon become apparent:

Bergeron had been taken at the time by the accused men to persons who would insure him. Then they would kill him for the insurance money. This money could never be collected without careful planning and execution of the crime itself. Such crimes are never committed in public. One of the accused in this case was bolder, more subtle than the other who stayed in the background. No human eye saw the blows that struck down and killed Leo Bergeron. In this case the evidence is of a circumstantial nature but if direct evidence was all a jury could decide on, then all a man would have to do would be to commit a crime in secret. The Crown charges that there was on the part of these two men a direct system of murder to maintain for a very short time an insurance policy on the life of another and then take that life and reap the benefits.[14]

Before jurors heard testimony that Bergeron was murdered, rather than trampled to death, the Crown introduced evidence about the effort made by Larocque to insure the life of Lamarche. First to testify was an agent for Manufacturers Life Insurance Company, who told the court that in the summer of 1930, Larocque arranged for him to meet Lamarche to discuss insuring his life. That policy was soon issued, but the next witness, an agent with Northern Life Insurance, refused when asked to issue a second policy on the same life. Following them to the stand was one of the police officers who investigated the death of Bergeron. He told jurors that when he found a blood-covered pitchfork handle on the dusty rafters of Larocque's barn, the farmer denied having seen it before. The witness said Larocque also denied having any knowledge of the blood found on the door and walls of his barn.

A constable was the next to testify. He testified he hit one of the horses accused of trampling Bergeron on the rump, duplicating what Larocque said happened when the animals were being backed into the barn. Both horses jumped ahead less than a metre, then stopped, and calmly began eating hay. Some of the most compelling testimony heard by jurors was that of the several doctors who examined Bergeron's body. The first to testify was Dr. Martin Powers, who arrived at the scene of the accident just as the injured man expired. He said that while it was possible the injuries to the dead man's head could have been caused by a horse, the same could not be said for the puncture wounds on his hands, which almost certainly were inflicted by a pitchfork. Next up was Dr. David Irwin, who told the court that in his opinion the wounds on the body of Bergeron were likely caused by a blunt instrument, like the fork handle introduced into evidence. He said that he once saw the remains of someone trampled by a horse, and the person's bones were completely crushed by the weight of the animal. In the present case, except for his head and hand wounds, Bergeron's body was unblemished. The third doctor had a slightly different opinion about what caused the fatal wounds. It was his belief that they were inflicted by someone swinging a square-faced weapon.

Apart from describing Bergeron's wounds, Powers testified about a confrontation that took place in the barn between Larocque and the father of the young man lying on the ground. According to the doctor, Leon Bergeron said to Larocque: "You killed Lamarche for his insurance and now you have killed my son for his."[15] Asked if anyone talked about insurance before the verbal onslaught, Powers said yes, Larocque brought it up.

The testimony of two witnesses who were only slightly acquainted with the main players in this drama was revealing, less for what was actually said, than for what was implied. One was the owner of a boarding house in Buckingham, Quebec. She told the court that she knew both of the accused, and that they once brought Athanase Lamarche to her home. Bergeron, too, she said, visited. In fact, she was the beneficiary in a policy of life insurance she took out on the young man's life. Also testifying was a farmer who showed up at the Larocque farm for a pre-arranged appointment to buy a cow. When he arrived the farmer was told by Larocque that Bergeron had been killed a little earlier. The visitor was upset at the news, and suggested it would be best if they finalized their business another day. Larocque would have none of that, and insisted on selling the cow without delay.

The defence of Larocque and Lavictoire was badly damaged by the testimony of the various medical experts called by the Crown, and when it was time to address the jury, the lawyers for the accused men attacked those doctors with considerable vigour. Counsel for Larocque spoke first. "Let the gentlemen of the medical profession agree upon their fantastic theories" he said, "before they have the gall to enter a court of law and ask you to accept those theories." Then he shifted to the media: "I cannot help but feel some dismay over the publicity given to this case by the press."[16] And so it went for almost two hours. While his address appeared to make little impression on jurors, it moved the accused to tears. By the time the lawyer finished, both men were weeping openly. Lavictoire's lawyer was far less dramatic, made fewer arguments, and finished in a fraction of the time taken by the counsel for Larocque. He denied his client benefitted in any way from the death of Bergeron, and suggested that nothing the jurors heard connected Lavictoire to his murder. Then he ended with a flourish: "May He who guides the destiny of men from the cradle to the grave guide you in your decision."[17]

On December 15, Mr. Justice Patrick Kerwin, a future chief justice of the Supreme Court of Canada, began his own address to the jury. Kerwin was presiding over his first criminal trial, but he made it clear what he thought of the evidence, and the guilt of the men in the prisoner's box.

> You may ask yourselves why Bergeron was asked to be at the Larocque farm at eight o'clock in the morning while other men asked to help with threshing were told not to be there until noon. In conjunction with the motive and the opportunity you may consider what means there were. You will have to consider the evidence in regard to the fork-handle which was found on a dusty beam. You will remember that while the beam was dirty, the fork-handle was clean. If that handle was not put on that beam by human agency then how did it get there? Consider Leon Bergeron who went to the barn and saw his boy breathing his last. The father turned to Larocque and accused him of having murdered his son. Ask yourselves if the reply of Larocque was consistent with the answer of an innocent man accused openly of murder. Were or were not all these wounds caused by the horses. If not, how did Bergeron receive them? You may take it from the evidence that some of the wounds were caused by horses. May I suggest to you that all of those wounds were not caused by horses. [and] How did the blood get on the walls of the barn? Was it as the result of some human agency attacking Bergeron? The accused are not obliged to show how Bergeron came

to his death, but if they gave an explanation which you think is not true then you will find them guilty as charged. If you conclude that Bergeron came to his death at the hands of both the accused, then they are both guilty of murder. If you think Bergeron came to his death at the hands of one of the accused but with the other aiding or abetting him, then they are both still guilty of murder.[18]

According to the official trial record, the jury deliberated just under four hours, but that is not quite true. Jurors decided in thirty minutes that Larocque and Lavictoire were guilty, but before they could announce their verdict, the court recessed. By the time the supper break ended and everyone was reassembled, more than three hours passed. When the accused killers heard the verdict neither showed any emotion, but after Justice Kerwin sentenced them to hang, they broke down. Lavictoire was the first to react. As the judge finished sentencing him to death, he bowed his head and cried. Larocque stared at the bench a moment longer, and then he too wept. The next day things were no better for the prisoners. For hours on end they paced back and forth across their separate but adjoining cells, crying inconsolably. Around 9:00 p.m. they were so exhausted from their ordeal they fell onto the bunks and slept.

The families of the killers either had no desire to appeal their sentences, or they lacked the resources to do so, and after their request for clemency was denied there was nothing to do but wait. On March 15, 1933, the ordeal of the killers came to an end. Lavictoire was led from his cell first, and at 1:00 a.m. he was hanged. A little over fourteen minutes later it was the turn of Larocque. He stepped on to the trap doors at 1:25 a.m., and after a bit of a delay, was dropped without incident. Five minutes later his body was cut down. When the inquests into the deaths of the two men ended, their families claimed their respective bodies. Seven months later the company that insured the life of Léo Bergeron refused to pay the proceeds of the policy to his father.

In a morbid postscript to this saga of greed and murder, it was later learned that not all of Athanase Lamarche or Léo Bergeron was buried following the police investigation into their deaths. The doctor who conducted the post-mortem on the two men kept their skulls, and for years they were displayed prominently on the mantle of his Toronto home.

2
Murdering Neighbours

Few relationships are subject to as much stress as that of neighbours. Even the smallest irritation can fester over time, and occasionally what may have started out as a slight can grow to become something akin to provocation. Usually, someone knows when she or he is on the outs with a neighbour, as was the case with Michael Farrell, who twice killed men living next door. But it is also the case that a victim of violence often has no forewarning of what a neighbour is about to do, which was the situation for the men Emerson Shelley and Larry Hansen murdered. The three people whose crimes are described in this chapter have one thing in common. Not only did each murder a neighbour, they all did it twice.

Michael Farrell: Fifteen Years between Murders

Michael Farrell was born and raised near Quebec City in the farming community of Sainte Catherine. He was a hard worker, but it was a struggle to make ends meet for a family that numbered nearly a dozen. Making things worse were his wild mood swings, suggestive that the insanity that hospitalized his brother could occasionally be seen in the actions of the highly emotionally Michael. Or maybe Farrell was just one of those individuals destined to experience more than his share of bad luck.

A case in point was his relationship with neighbours. In 1862, David Meagher and his father were two such individuals. No one knows why they did not get along with Farrell, but on at least one occasion the younger

Meagher threatened to kill his volatile neighbour. Things came to a head in March, when all three men were returning from Quebec City to their respective farms on the same road. The Meaghers were ahead of Farrell, but instead of turning down their own side road, they walked on, and waited by Farrell's turnoff. When Farrell drew near, the father and son waylaid him, but in the ensuing struggle David was struck several times by Farrell's axe. One blow hit his liver, mortally wounding the young man. Although a coroner's jury directed that Farrell be charged with manslaughter, his jurors believed that he had acted in self-defence, and acquitted him. The affair cost Farrell a significant amount of money, and fifteen years later likely was instrumental in his conviction for murdering Francis Conway, and in the denial of his subsequent request for commutation of his death sentence.

Until about 1875, Michael Farrell was, if not a close friend of Francis Conway, at least on good terms with his neighbour. Their relationship began to cool, however, when Conway started to abuse his right to pass through Farrell's property on the Gosford Railway right-of-way. The tracks ran across fifteen acres of Farrell's land. As more and more people began travelling to and from Quebec City into the countryside, they increasingly damaged crops growing alongside the road allowance. Worse, at least from Farrell's perspective, was the damage caused by cattle walking along the track, which often stopped to feed in his fields. To prevent that from happening, Farrell erected a fence and gate. Travellers were expected to take down the gate when they passed, and put it back up before they continued on their way. The Conways, however, refused to play by the rules. They used the road, and took down the gate when they passed Farrell's land, but they refused to put it back up. In fact, on the morning of his murder, Conway and his brother used the right-of-way, and, as usual, left the gate down when they moved on to their own fields.

As if this disagreement had not damaged the relationship of the neighbours sufficiently, they almost came to blows during a public meeting called to discuss financing a community school. Farrell asked his one-time friend to sign a form agreeing to pay his share of the school costs, and Conway refused.

On the last Sunday in August 1878, Conway left his house with his brother, a friend, and two of his young children. They were going to visit his father, who lived nearby. As they walked along the rail track, the group was confronted by Farrell, who demanded to know what they were doing on his land. Conway told him that they were on the right-of-way, not his property, and they had every right to be there. Farrell disagreed. "It is my land. Don't you come back here anymore, or you won't go off the same as you came."[1] With that he turned and left, while Conway and his party continued on their way.

When he was ready to return home, Francis asked his brother and a friend to walk with him a while, in case Farrell tried to do something. The trio had gone but a short way when they met up with the Conway children. As they walked along the track they soon noticed Farrell running parallel to them, about a kilometre away. In no time at all Farrell reached the roadway to his house, but he ran on towards the Conway farm. As he drew closer, narrowing the gap that separated them, everyone could see a rifle in one of his hands. In a matter of minutes they met at a crossroad. Farrell was now walking, and when he was about a metre and a half away, he told Conway to go back. He repeated the command two more times. Conway agreed to leave. "I will go back, but allow me to say a few words."[2] Then, with no warning whatsoever, Farrell raised the rifle to his shoulder and shot Conway in the head.

Conway's brother was standing fairly near Farrell, and when he heard the gun go off he rushed at the shooter and tried to grab his rifle. Farrell pulled it away and struck his adversary across the arm with the barrel. As he started to swing a second time he shouted, "God damn you, you will never hang me."[3]

With that the Conway brother took off running, Farrell in pursuit. "He followed me for about four acres; he stopped then, and I stopped, and he did something with the gun, I thought he was loading the gun; when he had it fixed he ran after me as hard as he could."[4] By the time the surviving Conway reached the home of a man he knew, Farrell was nowhere to be seen. As soon as Conway calmed down, he and his friend returned to the murder scene in a wagon. They found Francis lying where he fell. They loaded his body into the wagon, and then made their way to the home of the patriarch of the Conway clan.

While the Farrell-Conway confrontation was being played out, Reverend Father Leclaire, the parish priest, was visiting with the wife of Francis Conway. The two were talking when Michael McLaughlin came in. He was sent to advise Mrs. Conway that her husband had been killed, but when he got to the dead man's home all he managed to get out was that Frank was badly hurt in a shooting accident. That message delivered, he asked Father Leclaire to follow him outside, where he told the priest the truth. Leclaire then returned to Mrs. Conway.

> I told the wife of the deceased that I would go over to him and give her news of him. She answered that she felt strong enough to go over herself and that with medical assistance from Quebec she would try and bring him to. We then went to the house of the deceased's father. On entering the house Mrs. Conway saw the body of her husband and threw herself on the body almost frantic. I had the body removed from the floor where it was lying, and had his face washed, which was full of blood. It [Conway's body] was then put on a bed. I was present when inquest took place the day after the murder.[5]

About nine hours later Constable Paquet was on duty at Quebec City's Central Station. Around 3:00 a.m. on the morning of August 26, Farrell knocked on the station door, and identified himself. When the officer asked if he was from Sainte Catherine, Farrell admitted he was, and wondered whether the officer heard about a shooting. "I answered, yes, that we had had some information about an hour before; I said it was a bad affair, to which he answered, yes; he said it was about a fence; he said he had come to give himself up; I put him in a cell."[6]

Well before Farrell's trial got underway, someone, or some group, embarked on a campaign to build community resentment against him through a series of anonymous letters sent to area newspapers. Farrell's lawyer later used the program of letter-writing to support an application to have the accused killer's death sentence commuted to life imprisonment. Some "occult influence was at work" he said in the application, "in obtaining newspaper articles exciting prejudice against my client."[7] And he argued the campaign extended to local politicians. According to the lawyer:

> a month after the death of Conway, the Municipal Council of the Parish of Sainte Catherine passed resolutions of

condolence with Conway's family; the publication of those resolutions was delayed purposely, I believe, and produced by the Chronicle [newspaper] a week only before the trial, with the view, I verily believe, of prejudicing the public mind against Farrell. [A] deranged inebriate whose name I desire to suppress by reason of his respectable connections has been regularly subsidized to write several small squibs in the local papers against any indulgence whatever to Farrell; I cannot but believe that the money of the Conways has had the desired effect. The newspaper articles and correspondence so published had so thoroughly embittered the public mind here against Farrell, that I deemed it my duty to address to the Court an application for a change of venue to the District of Arthabaska, the nearest District to Quebec; But the Court rejected my application on the grounds that the prejudice against my client was a prejudice which would follow him everywhere, the natural prejudice arising from the perpetuation of a coldblooded murder.[8]

It turned out there was substance to these claims. A Quebec City justice of the peace swore that he was present when a man admitted that he had written a letter that appeared in the *Quebec Morning Chronicle*, signed "A friend of the deceased." The letter was little more than a tirade of abuse directed against Farrell, and for writing it the author received $2.50. But this campaign of intimidation did not end with letter-writing. Farrell's lawyer noted that after his application for a change of venue was refused, "I noticed the two brothers of the late Francis Conway, and an uncle and other relations of the late David Meagher mixing with the Jurors, who afterwards tried the accused; and I suspected that the Jurors were being tampered with to the prejudice of my client."[9]

The murder trial of Michael Farrell got underway in the Quebec City on November 2, 1878. Farrell's lawyer argued that the murder of Conway resulted from the victim's attempt to deliberately provoke Farrell. The murder would never have occurred, he suggested, had not the victim provoked his killer by twice confronting him on the Gosford right-of-way. And, he argued, the confrontation was anything but accidental.

Conway, his brother, and their friend all carried weapons when they confronted the hot-tempered Farrell. In the case of the murdered man, the weapon was a loaded revolver; in the case of the other men, it was a supply of stones, which they intended throwing at Farrell to goad him into some kind of retaliatory response. Farrell's counsel argued that the Conway group easily could have avoided running into Farrell by not walking down the pathway that cut through his land, or at the very least, stopping when they saw Farrell pursuing them. Conway clearly saw Farrell when they were almost a kilometre away from the spot where the deadly meeting took place, and even pointed Farrell out to his companions. As Farrell drew nearer, but well before the confrontation was unavoidable, everyone knew who the man running towards them was, and saw that he held a gun in his hand.

Farrell's lawyer later swore that he had available:

> a witness who had a conversation with the deceased, before he returned up the Gosford Railway track, and who had advised the deceased not to go back by the Gosford Railway track, but that the deceased rejected that warning and declared his determination to return, with his friends by the track; It is a well-known fact that the Meaghers and the Conways form a very wealthy, extensive, and turbulent connection, whose anger is not safe to incur.[10]

The problem for Farrell's lawyer was that the judge presiding over the murder trial was early on convinced of the guilt of the accused, and he was not inclined to admit into evidence any suggestion to the contrary.

Mr. Justice Samuel Cornwallis Monk made his position clear in the first few sentences of his charge to the jury. "The prisoner," he said, "stands charged with murder and there is no doubt of it being murder as it is a very clear case. All the witnesses concurred with each other in the evidence, the prisoner himself admitted having shot the deceased and merely that the deceased had brought it on himself."[11] Monk said that since there was no doubt Farrell was guilty of killing Conway, all that was left was for the jury to determine was whether the murder was premeditated. What he made clear was that it was his opinion that any suggestion that Farrell had not planned what he was going to do when he met Conway was pure poppy-cock. The jury agreed, and after deliberating for about an hour, returned with a verdict of guilty.

When the decision was announced the court clerk asked each juror in turn if he was in agreement with the verdict, and in every case the response was the same — an affirmative nod of a head. While the jury was being polled there was for a few moments of near absolute silence in the courtroom. Then, with startling suddenness, a loud sobbing broke out, growing as if someone was in great distress. Indeed, that proved to be the case. Mary Farrell somehow slipped unnoticed into the room, and sat in the back, hidden behind the men seated in front of her. Throughout the four day trial she managed to keep her emotions in check, though she feared the worse, and when the clerk began polling the jurors she could no longer contain her feelings. Her last faint hope that her life would return to normal was gone. In a moment, so too was she. By the time the polling was finished, Mrs. Farrell was nowhere to be seen.

Before formally pronouncing sentence, Monk asked the convicted murderer if there was any reason why the law should not take its course. Farrell did not have much to say, but he took what time he was allowed to lay the blame for the murder squarely on the victim.

> That man had liberty as well as any other to Pass by that "road, as long as he fastened up the gag [gate in the fence] after him." I met him on that day and told him to put it up, but he would not do it. If he had put up the fence after him he would "have been alive today." He told me that day, when I spoke to him about it, that "he would throw it into the ditch and me along with it." I can prove that he challenged me first to fight, and was willing to accept his challenge if he got two strange men with us, but he always had a crowd with him to back him.[12]

When Farrell concluded his remarks Justice Monk picked up the black, three-cornered hat worn by judges imposing a sentence of death, and spoke directly to the condemned man:

The case against you, prisoner, is sustained by evidence which leaves no alternative for a Court, but to perform the painful duty which the law requires of it. I cannot imagine how a man of your position and intelligence could possibly have conceived and carried out so terrible a crime. [If] there existed any provocation not disclosed by the evidence you cannot now advance it here, before this tribunal, but if the SEARCHER of all HEARTS, who, alone, can penetrate all secrets, can see anything in your crime unknown to the Court and the Jury, if there are any extenuating circumstances in the eyes of God in this "dark crime" you will profit from such, not here but hereafter. I would merely remind you that this sanguinary drama has been crowded by your own admission and that in the verdict of the Jury the court entirely concurs. You precipitated one, (we cannot call him your friend, but) your neighbor, to eternity, without a moment's notice. There is but one duty for this court to perform and that is to pronounce the sentence of the Law. It is right to say that you cannot expect the slightest mercy. On earth you can look on no mitigation of your sentence. You must prepare for your doom, for there is no hope for you on this side of the grave. You should avail yourself of all the means of repentance at your disposal, for there is no doubt that true contrition may always be awarded with salvation. The process may at first be difficult but spiritual assistance will be given you. Nothing now remains but for the Court to pronounce sentence upon you, which is, "That you" Michael Farrell, be taken from hence to the "common goal," and there, within its precincts on Friday, the 10th of January next, you be hanged according to the Provisions of the law, by the neck, until you are dead, and may the God Almighty have mercy upon your soul![13]

The death sentence imposed on her husband seemed to galvanize Mary Farrell, and she quickly launched a multi-pronged campaign for clemency.

She personally appeared before federal authorities in Ottawa, and when that failed to produce a commutation, she appealed to her friends and neighbours. One of the first to come onside was her municipal councillor, and through his efforts, the entire council announced its support for clemency. A petition was started, but the federal cabinet refused to commute the sentence, so she appealed to the wife of Canada's Governor General, who, according to tradition, had the final say in the matter of clemency.

December 27, 1878

May it please your Royal Highness.

Mary Farrell, humbly begs leave to approach Your Royal Highness, to lay at your feet, her Petition for mercy to her husband Michael Farrell, now under sentence of death in the Jail of Quebec. In her anguish she throws herself at the feet of Your Royal Highness, and tearfully implores Your Gracious Intercession, with the Most Noble The Marquis of Lorne, for his favorable consideration of the Petition, for His Executive Clemency, now before Him.

She prays Your Royal Highness, to forgive the boldness, begotten of her deep distress, which prompts her to approach Your Gracious Person, under the present circumstances, and she hopefully addresses her present supplication, and that of her helpless little children to Your Royal Highness; as to one upon whose kindly ear, the cry of the poor and the distressed, has never yet fallen in vain.

Mary Farrell[14]

While the petition of Mary Farrell was being considered, the condemned man's lawyer launched his own application for clemency. In an affidavit filed in support of it, he advanced two arguments not pursued at trial. The first was that when the murder occurred, Farrell was defending himself against a carefully constructed plot to kill him during a fight on the right-of-way. The lawyer said it was his belief "that, if the accused be reprieved for two months, I shall be able to establish that the deceased had a loaded pistol on his person, and that the two Conways and Landers had made up their minds, at the risk of losing of life by one of them, to take the life of Farrell."[15]

The lawyer's second argument was that when the murder occurred, Farrell was insane. In support of this suggestion, he filed an affidavit signed by a friend of Farrell's brother John, who died in a Quebec mental institution, and another sworn by neighbours of Farrell's mother. The friend of John Farrell swore that he knew John to be insane, and quick to resort to violence. It was his belief that Michael, "his brother now under sentence, when excited, or in passion, [was] subject to insanity."[16] In a similar vein, the neighbours swore that they were familiar with both Michael and John Farrell, and there was no doubt whatsoever that the late John Farrell had been insane for years before he was institutionalized. "We were sent for on many occasions to aid in preventing him from committing acts of violence on members of the family, on one occasion we found him quite naked chasing his mother round the stove, she having a piece of rope in her hand, endeavoring to beat him off. He had to be tied on one occasion to prevent him of committing an act of violence on the family."[17] Insanity, they suggested, ran in the Farrell family.

During the first eight of the nine weeks he spent waiting to be executed, the condemned man was convinced that his sentence would be commuted. Only in the last three days before his date with the hangman did Farrell show signs of weakness. The day before he was to hang a telegram from the federal minister of justice ended his hope for a reprieve:

> Department of Justice Ottawa, January 9th 1879 Time 4:40, Quebec: Governor General received your telegram asking for commutation of sentence of Farrell which he handed to me and commanded me to say that "His Excellency has not thought fit to change decision of Judge, Jury and Privy Council as reported to His Excellency by me."

> John A. Macdonald, Minister of Justice.[18]

The morning of his last day Farrell rose early, and admitted to inmates in cells nearby that he was nervous of what was to come. Shortly after daylight he was transferred to the cell reserved for those about to be executed. He realized all too well the significance of his new accommodations. To one of his guards he admitted, "I'm afraid this removal is a sure sign of my end."

When news of the telegram from Ottawa reached her, Mary Farrell rushed to her husband's cell. An observer described the meeting as a pitiful sight.

> Farrell had just sat at a table in his ward to partake of a cup of tea, when his wife rushed frantically to his side, and throwing her arms around his neck, clung to him. Her children wept, and in this state, they were assisted away after a great deal of heart-rendering scenes. Farrell bore up to the parting with great courage, but on seeing his wife and children take leave of him never again to meet on this earth, he broke down and sobbed bitterly.[19]

On Thursday, January 10, 1879, Farrell awoke after only a few hours of sleep. His two spiritual advisers were waiting, and the three men soon knelt in prayer. Farrell was nervous, although perhaps a little less anxious than he had been in the preceding two or three days. The black flag, a visible symbol of what was to come, was raised over the prison at 7:00 a.m., and the sheriff ordered spectators wandering the corridor in front of Farrell's cell out of the jail. When the time came for the condemned man to begin his last walk, the only non-officials allowed in the prison were his priests. At 8:00 a.m. the man who was to hang Farrell entered the prisoner's cell. At almost exactly the same time a Solemn Requiem Mass began in each of Quebec City's Roman Catholic churches. Although most cathedrals were thronged with celebrants, the silence was deafening. The least affected person in the city appeared to be the executioner. He was a short, thin man, and wore a long coat and a false beard and moustache. A local newspaper later told its readers that all that could be said of him was "that he showed signs of being a hardened wretch." Whether the executioner was hardened was pure speculation; that he was incompetent was a fact.

All of the officials involved with Farrell's execution were greatly affected by what was about to happen. The sheriff was pale, and his hands trembled. The jailor principally responsible for caring for the condemned murderer was so overcome with emotion that he could barely move, and the prison guards who were required to be in attendance looked despondent. Outside, however, the atmosphere was very different. More than two hundred spectators milled about in the prison yard. Among their number were doctors, shopkeepers, students, labourers, lawyers, and reporters. The hangman inspected the scaffold before the death walk began. It was an imposing structure, erected in the prison yard a short distance from the door through which Farrell was to exit the jail. During his first visit the executioner fastened the rope in its place, and then returned to the prison. There he tied Farrell's wrists behind his back, and pinioned his arms to his sides. That done, the once hot-headed farmer began his last journey, a priest on each side.

When he reached the scaffold Farrell looked around, and to those whom he recognized he said goodbye. Then, without making evident the emotion he must have felt, he walked to the trap doors, and knelt in silent prayer. The spectators standing below him joined in. After a moment or two Farrell rose, and the hangman moved in to bind his feet. He then started to adjust the noose under the prisoner's left ear, but could not get it right. His fumbling caught the attention of those standing in the yard, and almost in unison they began shouting. Throughout the turmoil Farrell stood quietly, staring intently at his priests. One of the spectators fainted, and several others turned away, perhaps anticipating what was to come.

When the hangman finally pulled the lever, opening the trap doors, one of Farrell's arms moved, and as he dropped, the rope caught on it, breaking his fall. Everyone watched in horror as the executioner rushed over and began shaking the rope. While he was doing that Farrell cried out, "Oh my God!" After what seemed an eternity the rope slipped off the poor man's arm, and the two-time killer dropped. But he fell only a few centimetres, a distance nowhere near great enough to break his neck. For minute after minute he struggled, more alive than dead, then his efforts grew weaker, and he seemed to give up his fight for life. Twice his hangman began to cut the rope, but on each occasion the prison doctor told him to stop, that Farrell's heart was still beating. After twenty minutes it stilled. The dead man's body was allowed to hang a further five minutes, out of an abundance of caution, and a coroner's inquest was immediately convened. Its verdict: death by strangulation.[20]

After most executions, those required to examine the body of the hanging victim were surprised by how peaceful the dead man or woman looked. Such was not the case for Farrell. The misplaced noose caused his neck to become badly twisted to one side, and where the rope had rubbed, his skin was nearly black. One man however, was not repulsed by what he witnessed. Farrell's body had not yet begun to cool when he pushed his way through spectators in an effort to take a picture. A few of Farrell's friends quickly interceded, and put an end to the photographer's plan to sell his execution photos on the streets of Quebec.

Before the execution of Michael Farrell was officially complete, one last telegram was sent to Ottawa.

Sheriff's Office

Quebec 20 January 1879

Sir,

I have the honor to report, that on the 10th of this month Michael Farrell was executed in my presence. I hereby certify that I, the undersigned attended the interment of Convict Michael Farrell at the Cholera Burying ground and saw his body buried in said Burying grounds on this Tenth Day of January 1879 in pursuant to order of the Government.

R. Mulholland, Assist. Keeper[21]

Emerson Shelley: A Neighbour Kills Again

Emerson Shelley was a violent man who spent very nearly his entire life in trouble with the law. Part of his problem may have been environmental.

His mother was charged with shooting her second husband during a domestic dispute, and the fact she was acquitted seemed to have inculcated in him the belief that it is not so much what you do that matters, but whether you are convicted. An early case in point was the way in which he treated his grade school classmates. One recalled that he was not yet a teenager when Shelley threw powdered medicine in his face, hurting his eyes. Another incident was more prophetic. Three of Shelley's school mates, the youngest of whom was about twelve, were walking to school when Shelley jumped from hiding, a rifle in hand, and shouted, "halt, hands up, money or your brains."[22] The youngest of the group immediately broke into tears, and Shelley's assurance that he was not really going to shoot them did little to make him feel better.

Shelley was barely fourteen when he took things further. During a heated argument with a female neighbour he took out a revolver and threatened to kill her. Others living near the Shelleys were subjected to similar abuse. A farmer who once hired the young man to help him around his acreage grew troubled by Shelley's conduct, and told the young rowdy that he was going to have to change his ways or he was going to be fired. Shelly did not want the farmer to tell his mother what he was up to. "He threatened to fill me up with lead if I told his mother about it, so I promised that I would not tell."[23] The farmer had good reason to be concerned. Shelley was widely known to skulk around area farms, firing bullets near unsuspecting neighbours. Many, including members of his own family, were concerned by his propensity to violence.

On August 16, 1909, that inclination became something much more. The incident started when a week earlier a rifle left with a local blacksmith went missing. The gun's owner used .22 calibre "long" shells, which substantially increased the power of bullets fired from the gun. This contributed to Shelley's first killing. Michael Hall, partially blind and physically disabled, lived with his wife on the farm next to Shelley's. The couple were both in their seventies, and from time to time they hired Shelley to help out. Occasionally Hall had words with the teenager, and in one heated exchange he called Shelley a liar. When Hall was found dead, shot in the head with a .22 calibre rifle, it came as a surprise to no one that within hours of the shooting the police took Shelley into custody. It was even less surprising that the gun he used was the one that went missing a week earlier.

The fifteen-year-old was charged with murder, but the coroner's inquest convened to look into the particulars of Hall's death concluded that while there was no doubt that Shelley fired the shot that killed the elderly farmer, there was no evidence that he actually meant to kill Hall. With that finding, the Crown had little choice but to release Shelley from custody, and withdraw the murder charge.

Between the shooting of Hall and the killing of Christian Shoup in 1915, Shelley kept busy. Less than four months after he was found not to be criminally responsible for causing the death of Hall, Shelley received a suspended sentence for stealing a gun. He was not yet twenty when he burned down a neighbour's house, after stealing most of what was inside it. Although charged and acquitted of arson, he was convicted of taking the contents. This time he was sentenced to two years in jail. Within weeks of his release he again acquired a gun, and recommenced his life of crime.

Shelley and an accomplice broke into a general store, and after threatening to kill the store owner, took a couple of cases of eggs and some agricultural feed. Before the day ended the police in a nearby town issued a warrant for his arrest on suspicion of raping a thirteen-year-old young woman. Shelley made no attempt to deny responsibility. On May 6, he and a group of acquaintances were standing on a Simcoe Street corner when a man he knew stopped to chat. In no time at all Shelley told him that he was in trouble over having sex with a young woman, and as he spoke he withdrew a revolver from one of his pockets. "This," he said, "would make them produce."[24] Whether he was talking about future rape victims, or the robbery he was planning, was not clear. But he told everyone within earshot that he was planning on using the gun to rob a mail carrier and a couple of hog producers. He said he needed money, and had every intention of unloading his gun on the men he was intending to rob.

On May 9, Shelley showed up at the home of a friend sometime after 8:00 p.m. and asked if he could stay the night. The next day he took out a revolver, and told his host and his friend's housekeeper that he recently stole the gun and was planning on using it. He said that robbing people was how he earned a living, and suggested that the pair "would hear of a man being shot before the week was out."[25] Just then a couple of farmers hauling hogs went by. They caught Shelley's attention, and he asked if his friend wanted to help him rob the men when they passed on their way home. Before his friend could reply, Shelley told him that "he would just as soon shoot a man as a dog."[26] That settled it; Shelley's buddy said he wanted no part of murder. When Shelley left he started walking towards the farm of Christian Shoup, a local miller who lived some distance away. It was after 4:00 p.m. by the time he reached the home of John Carr, a man he had known all his life. He stayed the night, and late the next morning again set out towards the Shoup farm, now about two miles away.

The miller was picking up roots in a field near his house when his wife passed him around 2:00 p.m. on the way to her garden. As she walked by she noticed a man in the near distance, but thought nothing of it. About five minutes later she thought she heard a shot. Thinking it was just a hunter, she continued gardening. In retrospect, she should have paid more attention. The milling business she and her husband operated was one of the largest in the area, and the couple was known to keep on hand a large amount of money. It was this rumour that attracted the attention of Shelley, and it was he who she saw walking towards Shoup.

A little before 4:00 p.m. Mary Shoup started back to her house, expecting to chat with her husband on the way. She thought it a little odd that he was not in the field, so she walked to the farm nearest theirs and asked her stepson if he knew where his father was. He did not, so she returned home to start preparing the evening meal. She did not think much about her husband's absence until he failed to show up for supper. She was now worried, and when she saw a man stop to water his horse, she rushed out to talk to him. He told her he had not seen her husband, and she walked out to the field where Christian had been working. That was where she found him, a bullet wound just to the right of his mouth.

Almost as soon as the police were informed of the murder they suspected that Shelley was somehow involved. Finding him would not be difficult. With two fingers missing from one hand, and a habit of hanging around cafés and bars, he was seldom far from sight. In Simcoe, the largest town near the Shoup murder scene, the police talked to William Lambert, a friend of Shelley's. What he had to say removed any doubt about the identity of Shoup's killer. Lambert said that a little less than a week earlier he, Shelley, and a few others were standing outside a local hotel when

Shelley asked if anyone wanted to help him out. He told them he was going to shoot and rob the town's mail carrier, and "also mentioned a hog buyer and Mr. Shoup. He said the hog buyer came into a town where there was no bank, and that he always carried six or seven hundred dollars. He would get him first, then the mail driver, and then Mr. Shoup, after which he would beat it for Detroit."[27]

The officers investigating Shoup's murder contacted their counterparts throughout the area, and less than twenty-four hours later a constable in Woodstock noticed a small group of men talking on a street corner. He noticed one of them was missing two fingers on one hand, and he walked over and arrested Shelley for rape. Once Shelley was taken into custody there was little talk about the sexual assault (Shelley admitted right away that he was guilty), but there were a lot of questions about Shelley's whereabouts the afternoon Shoup was murdered. The young killer was arrested on suspicion of rape on May 12, and within forty-eight hours pled guilty and was on his way to begin a two year sentence in Kingston Penitentiary. His absence did nothing to slow the investigation into Shoup's death, however, and when a coroner's jury concluded that the miller almost certainly was killed by Shelley, the career criminal was charged with murder. Three weeks later he was committed to stand trial. The result was foreordained. Seven months after vowing that someone would be dead by the end of the week, it was Shelley's turn to face his destiny.

Although Emerson Shelley spent most of his life in trouble with the law, he seldom accepted responsibility for his actions. His conviction for murdering Christian Shoup meant that the stakes were much higher this time, but Shelley had little doubt he would survive his ordeal. When one of the jail's spiritual advisers showed up the morning after he was sentenced to hang, he dismissed the unfortunate man at once. When a second man of the cloth appeared, he too was sent away. Turning to one of his guards, Shelley asked, "What the hell are these preachers coming around for?"[28] It turned out that the condemned young man had a plan in mind, which he firmly believed would see him released from prison. The plan: I didn't kill Shoup, my buddy James Carr did. For it to work, however, Shelley required Carr's presence. To obtain it Shelley told his jailors that he had something to say by way of a confession, and could they send someone to his cell to hear it.

And so it was that two weeks after being sentenced to hang, Shelley confessed to taking part in the robbery of a general store. His accomplice — John Carr. By the way, Shelley added, it was Carr who actually shot Shoup. Carr was promptly arrested, and just as Shelley hoped, he was put in the cell next to his. The men talked freely, and with a guard within hearing distance, Shelley turned the conversation to Shoup's murder. Speaking in a voice loud enough for there to be no doubt about what was being said, he discussed the killing as if it was planned and carried out by Carr. Shelley's attempt to shift blame for the murder was sufficiently obvious that no one in authority was the least interested in what he had to say. Having lost his audience, Shelley moved on to Plan B. He began to act erratically, displaying what he no doubt thought were signs of mental illness. His efforts persisted, and in time jail officials asked that he be examined by "alienists." The doctors, now referred to as psychiatrists, quickly concluded Shelley was faking, and there was no reason on the ground of insanity to delay his execution. The prisoner's spiritual adviser had been telling him for some time that he would do better to make himself ready to die than play act at being unbalanced, and forty-eight hours before he was scheduled to hang, Shelly finally agreed.

He wanted to make one last confession. This one, he assured his minister, would be the truth. And what a confession it was. He started by blaming his plight on his upbringing. "I was never sent to Sunday School or Church. [I was] taught that there was no God, and that sin did not amount to anything, except among Church people. That I might do what I wished and it was all right so long as I got off with it."[29] Then Shelley turned to his best friend, John Carr, and described in detail the first serious crime he was asked to commit.

> When I was quite young John Carr wanted to kill his wife's parents. He said I could do it with a shot gun, and that as John's wife was the only child, he would get all the money. He offered me a hundred dollars and a black horse for the job. He said, "You go up to the old man's through the night and lay for him at the barn when he comes out to do the chores. When he comes out you shoot him, and if his wife comes out to see what is wrong shoot her.[30]

Reflecting on his past misdeeds seemed to energize Shelley, and he recalled crime after crime, almost all of which he committed with Carr. "The first thing we did together," he said, "was to steal chickens," and with that he launched into considerable detail. Then, he said, they stole a woman's watch and purse. He thought that was one time Carr showed considerable ingenuity. The men were in a local train station when they noticed a woman sitting by herself, reading a book, her purse sitting nearby. Shelley told his listeners that the two sat behind her, and Carr took from his pocket a long copper wire, which he carried for just this kind of opportunity. Carr attached a hook to the end of the wire, and manipulated it through the seat separating the crooks from their target, and snagged the purse. "I got twenty-five dollars out of that steal."[31]

Through his stories Shelley made it clear that he was not someone who took a slight lightly. After a quarrel with a relative of Carr's, he burned down the house of the man's father. "I understood there was no insurance on it, so I burnt it."[32] On another occasion a friend offered him $1 to burn the home of a neighbour, with whom the friend was having a disagreement. Shelley did so.

On a third occasion Shelley decided he did not like a neighbour, and burned his house as well.[33] However, it was not the use of fire that came to characterize the various crimes perpetrated by Shelley, but guns. A case in point was the robbery of an area storekeeper.

> The old man, who lived all alone, was in his house and had locked up for the night, but we saw some sign of light at a back window. I left the rig and Carr turned the horse round, and stood at the front door while I went round the back to the store door. When I rapped the old man asked my name and would not open the door. I told him I was Oran, one of his neighbours, but he would not open the door. Then I told him I wanted his money, and he said he had none. I flourished a revolver in front of his window and threatened to shoot if he did not open up. He ran out the front door and passed Carr who stood so surprised that he let him go. There was nothing left but to take what we could eat, for no money could be found.[34]

Shelley's recollection of his life of crime ended with a retelling of the Shoup murder. The recollection was chillingly brief. "I went up to him where he was picking up some sticks off the ground, and told him I wanted his money. He would not give it to me. I drew my revolver and told him I would shoot if he did not. He just looked at me and then ducked and ran at me, and I shot him as he came."[35]

The night before he was executed Shelley slept for about six hours and then ate a light breakfast. By the time he finished his spiritual adviser arrived. He was one of the men so curtly dismissed the day after Shelley was convicted for murder. The two spent forty-five minutes in prayer, and were still on their knees when the hangman entered. Without delay he pinioned Shelley's hands behind his back, and then led the condemned man into an adjoining cell, where a wooden trap door had been built over a hole cut in the floor. Shelley said nothing as he took his position on the trap, and remained speechless when the executioner slipped a hood over his head and a noose was tightened around his neck. While this was going on

Author's photo.

Larry Hansen was a member of a club numbering less than a dozen Canadians — he was convicted of two separate murders. At the time of the first murder, which occurred in 1976, he was living alone in this house. Following his parole, he moved back in, but sold a parcel of land just south of his residence to a man who was once in the witness protection program. In 1998 he became Hansen's second murder victim.

the condemned man's spiritual adviser was reciting the *Lord's Prayer*. As he came to the end, the trapdoor was released. For the next twenty minutes Shelley's body hung in the cell below, and before he was yet dead a black flag was raised over the jail house, visible evidence that a sentence of death had been carried out. No one outside the prison seemed to notice. "There was," said a reporter who covered the execution for a local newspaper, "very little unusual stir about the square during or immediately after the hour of execution."[36]

A few days before the execution, Shelley's mother received permission to bury the body of her son in Jericho Cemetery, near the grave of his father. In a sad irony, Christian Shoup lay less than a metre away, his grave not yet covered with grass. A little further down on the other side was the last resting place of Michael Hall. The graves are visible evidence of both a killer, and his crimes.

Larry Harold Hansen: Killed by His Best Friend

Larry Hansen was his second victim's closest friend, and even sang at his funeral. Years earlier he sold John McKay the parcel of land on which McKay and his wife settled, about 100 kilometres north of Brandon, Manitoba. The two became neighbours, regularly sharing meals, along with their hopes and aspirations. Yet in the early hours of a spring morning in 1998, Hansen waited in a bush outside his friend's isolated farm house, and as the unsuspecting McKay drove out of his yard, he shot him.

When McKay's wife heard three shots fired in rapid succession she rushed from her house to see what happened. Two hundred metres in front of her she saw her husband's truck, his body lying beside it. A few minutes later a passing motorist noticed a woman half seated on the ground beside a man who even at a distance appeared not to be moving. Beside them was an older model truck, its driver-side window shot out, and beyond it, tacked to a fence post, a NO SHOOTING sign.

Local residents initially thought the killing was payback for McKay's work as an informant in a Royal Canadian Mounted Police sting known as Operation Decode. In exchange for $250,000, he provided information to police that resulted in the arrest and imprisonment of a gang of smugglers who used snowmobiles and all-terrain vehicles to transport contraband liquor and cigarettes into Manitoba from North Dakota. Credence was given that theory because in the weeks preceding his murder, McKay received a number of death threats, one of which came from a man charged as a result of his testimony. So it was natural that many area residents thought the victim's death was an act of revenge.

Certainly news media made that connection. Almost every story about the killing started with reference to McKay's work as "a former police informant." The reports brought an immediate response from the dead man's wife. She was upset by descriptions of her husband as an informer. "An informant is when you get caught and you are getting yourself out of it by snitching on someone else."[37] Her husband, she said, never did that. "Why drag him through the mud when he was only trying to do the right thing? He was excellent. He tried his best. He gave his all with no credit in return."[38] Investigators, however, were never persuaded that the murder of the Mountain Road resident had anything to do with "payback." According to an RCMP spokesperson, "That is the obvious observation about this but at the same time it's not the only or the strongest theory we are pursuing."[39]

Although McKay's background demanded that police look into the possibility that his death was connected to Operation Decode, Hansen's history suggested he was a more likely suspect, and within hours of the murder of his neighbour the police arrived on his doorstep. Hansen admitted that before the shooting he was walking in the bush near the victim's house, but said he was over a kilometre away. When he heard gun shots Hansen said his first thought was that someone was shooting at geese on the small lake that bordered his property. By the time he reached the road, police cars were everywhere.

Hansen was seen by some of those attracted to the McKay yard-site by the sound of shooting, a solitary figure standing a few dozen yards north of where his best friend lay dead. It struck many as odd that Hansen just stood watching, and then casually turned and walked into his farm yard. It was not the reaction expected of a next door neighbour, let alone a friend. The story of the murder, however, actually started twenty-two years earlier, over an argument about a tree.

Much of the land around Erickson, a town about an hour's drive north of Brandon, is owned by the Crown. The right to graze cattle and cut timber is often given to owners of property adjacent to Crown land.

Occasionally the rights are split, so one neighbour has grazing rights, another the right to cut trees. In 1976 Hansen owned grazing rights on land across a municipal road from his farm. Joseph Baraniuk was his neighbour and a twenty-seven-year-old bachelor, and he owned timber rights on the same parcel of land. The day before Baraniuk was killed he and a friend were harvesting trees opposite the farm of Hansen. Their efforts attracted his attention, and Hansen confronted the men. Baraniuk told him that he had the right to cut whatever timber he wanted, including the tree Hansen told the men was special to him. With that Hansen turned and walked away. The next afternoon the timber-cutters returned, and Hansen was waiting. While his friend was skidding logs out of the bush, Baraniuk worked alone. Hansen walked up to him and shot him in the chest with a single blast from his 12-gauge shotgun. He then reloaded, stood over Baraniuk, and shot him in the head.

Six months later Hansen pled guilty to a charge of second degree murder, and was sentenced to life in prison. During his sentencing the statement he gave police was read into the court record. In it he said the land on which his victim had been cutting trees had always been important to his family.

> That land has been the best part of our families' holdings for as long as I can remember and people have always more or less respected it as if it were our property. We left the bush close by because it looked nice. Lots of times the cows would lie under that tree and chew their cud when they came home. When I saw that greedy bastard cut down that tree I just went completely berserk and shot him.[40]

When he was paroled from prison Hansen returned to his farm. One afternoon while having coffee with friends he was asked what it felt like to kill someone. He looked up and, without any trace of emotion, said "It's not as hard as you'd think."[41]

As McKay drove out of his yard the Thursday morning he was murdered he may have been thinking of his son, born a few weeks earlier; or perhaps he was reflecting on how much more comfortable his life was now, compared to the two years he and his wife spent on the road waiting for publicity over his "secret agent" work to die down. It was work he made no attempt to keep secret, certainly not from Hansen. "The first time I met him, that's when he told me the story of being a secret agent. Anybody he'd made friends with, he'd tell them what he did and why he did it."[42] Hansen talked about his victim a lot in the days following McKay's murder. In one interview he said that, "He told me he heard there was a $50,000 award on him dead and $100,000 if he was brought in alive because they wanted to run him through a combine. But I don't think he was scared. He was proud of what he had done."[43]

Although there is no evidence reporters covering the murder investigation noticed discrepancies in the various statements Hansen made to the press, the differences were there. In a comment made the day after the shooting Hansen said when he walked out of the bush he saw six police cars surrounding the victim's truck. Five days later he changed his story.

Author's photo.

This photo is of the area directly beneath the gallows at Manitoba's Headingley jail. The partially covered pit served two purposes. It provided a margin of error for cases when a prisoner was dropped further than intended, avoiding a repeat of one case in which an unconscious killer slowly strangled to death while suspended on his knees. The pit also was the collection point into which urine and other body fluids dripped. The four-step set of stairs beside the pit was used by jail doctors to check the heartbeat of executed prisoners.

Now when he came out of the bush he saw only the victim's truck, and nothing else. Nobody was around, and no vehicles were in the area, which was why he was stunned when the police arrived an hour later and informed him that "his good friend had been killed."[44]

During his funeral McKay's pastor spoke of the close relationship the deceased had with Hansen. The dead man often invited his neighbour over for meals, and Hansen was like a grandfather to McKay's son. The two were so close that McKay's widow asked her neighbour to sing at John's funeral. Ironically, the song Hansen chose was "I have a Friend."

Two months after the shooting Hansen was convicted of dangerous driving and driving while impaired. Because he was still on parole from the murder of his "other" neighbour, he was sent back to Stony Mountain Penitentiary for violating the conditions under which he had been released. In mid-September 1998, Hansen hanged himself in his cell. A police spokesperson said "it would be premature to suggest the case is closed as a result of the suicide."[45] Nonetheless, the RCMP ended its investigation.

A week after Hansen committed suicide he was buried in the same cemetery as his best friend. The man he killed nearly a quarter of a century earlier is buried six miles west.

3

Reprieved to Kill Again

One of the arguments often advanced against giving convicted killers a second chance is that they might use it to murder again. All three stories in this chapter are of individuals who murdered someone, were sent to death row, and at the last minute had their sentence commuted to life imprisonment. Each of them used their second chance to kill again.

Garry Richard Barrett: One Second Chance Too Many

Garry Richard Barrett likely did not deserve all the second chances life gave him. He had two opportunities to be a loyal husband and loving father, but threw them away when he murdered his stepson. Then the federal government commuted his death sentence, and gave him a chance to make something of what remained of his life. That opportunity was also squandered. Instead of being thankful for what he had been given, Barrett grew increasingly resentful and morose and with one swing of an axe assured himself a place in Canadian history, becoming one of few people hanged in a federal penitentiary.

Although Barrett was born in Detroit, Michigan, in 1852, his descent into self-destruction and murder started when he was about to turn fifty. The father of eight got a job on the railway, and deserted his wife and children to start a new life on the American frontier. He eventually settled in Utah, where in due course he met a widowed mother of three.

His Mormon wife-to-be was a practical woman, and accepted the real-
ities of the time, which suggested she was better off with a man she
did not love than with no man at all. So it was that Barrett converted
to Mormonism, and with his new family in tow, headed for northern
Saskatchewan. The Barretts put down roots at Egg Lake, approximately
fifty-eight kilometres north of Prince Albert. While the widow Johnson
and her children were accepted in the tiny community at face value, the
same could not be said of Barrett. He was a gloomy man, given to wild
swings of emotion, and it was apparent to even a casual observer that he
was struggling with inner demons. The birth of a baby boy did little to
calm him, and he grew preoccupied with the idea of killing his family,
and ending his misery. Some nights he sat alone in the kitchen, oblivious
to the sounds of the children and his wife's entreaties to come to bed.
Around 11:00 p.m. on October 13, 1907, he came to some kind of reso-
lution. When he went upstairs his wife was already in bed, but instead of
joining her, he sat in the darkness and began talking.

He told his wife that he felt that he was nothing but a servant.
Everything on the farm belonged to her, including the cows and pigs,
even the chickens. He was going to slaughter them all, thereby removing
the barrier he felt separated her from him. His straight-laced wife had
suffered through similar rants of self-loathing for months, and was fed
up. Go ahead, she said, kill everything, just pay me what the animals are
worth. She told him that she gladly would take the kids and head back
to Utah. Her lack of sympathy for what he was going through incensed
Barrett, and he grabbed a revolver and forced his wife onto her knees. The
widow's two eldest children heard the commotion, and silently edged
into their parent's bedroom. There they saw Barrett walk over to their
mother, put the gun to her head, and pull the trigger. But instead of an
explosion, all they heard was a click. The sound galvanized twelve-year-
old Burnell, and he grabbed his stepfather's arm. Barrett flung the young
man off, pointed the gun at him, and once more pulled the trigger. This
time the pistol worked. The bullet hit Burnell's arm, severing an artery.
The boy's mother struggled to her feet in an attempt to help her son, but
Barrett forced her back to the floor, and for the second time, threatened
to kill her. After what must have seemed an eternity to his wife, Barrett
suddenly turned and left the room.

Burnell's mother bound her son's arm in an effort to stem the flow of blood pouring from the wound, then left him with his sister while she ran to the home of her nearest neighbour, two miles away. Within minutes a group of armed men descended on the Barrett residence. They found Barrett trying to re-bind the bandage now soaked in blood. The posse took control of Burnell and his stepfather, loaded both into a wagon, and headed for Prince Albert. When they arrived the men turned Barrett over to the police and rushed Burnell to the hospital. He was in critical condition, and although he hung on for a week, he was never given much chance of surviving. Barrett was charged with murder, and a little less than eight months later he went to trial. When the authorities were able to prove that the alleged killer was never legally married to his victim's mother, she was allowed to testify. But even without her evidence it was obvious that Barrett killed his stepson. The only real question was whether it was an accident or murder. The trial got underway on June 2, 1908, and lasted two days. Barrett took the stand in his own defence, and testified that all he wanted to do was scare his wife; he never meant to hurt anyone. "It was me that done it," he told jurors, "but it was an accident. It was a self-cocker and it went off."[1] Ethel, the younger of his two stepdaughters, disagreed. "There was no accident about it. I seen him turn and shoot my brother."[2]

Members of his jury did not believe Barrett's version of events, but while they had no doubt that the shooting was murder, they had qualms about whether Barrett should hang. The federal cabinet shared their misgivings, especially after the minister of justice informed it that with proper treatment Burnell Johnson should not have died. Shortly before he was to hang Barrett was informed that his sentence had been commuted to life imprisonment. With that the killer was transferred to the Alberta Penitentiary at Edmonton, and for what remained of his life was known as "Prisoner 135."

Barrett never adjusted to life in jail, and he grew increasingly morose and dejected, obsessed by what he felt was an unjust verdict. He certainly never learned to appreciate what the Edmonton penitentiary had to offer. It was one of the country's newest prisons, with room for thirty-seven male and five female inmates, and featured two kitchens, a library, and several large workrooms. Shortly after entering the facility Barrett was diagnosed with a heart condition. To protect what remained of his health he was

reassigned from heavy duty to the carpentry shop, where he was made a
runner. Six months after entering prison he asked Richard Stedman, the
deputy warden, for permission to see the doctor. Like Stedman, Barrett
was a Mason, and he no doubt expected that his request would be granted.
But Stedman said no. Barrett asked again, several times, and on each occasion Stedman turned him down. There was nothing physically wrong with
Barrett, he said, and after every request the convicted killer was returned
to the carpentry shop, where he and four fellow inmates worked under a
supervisor and a handful of guards.

For the next three months things settled into a routine. Barrett was his
gloomy self, and made it clear to one and all that he hated his surroundings.
In hindsight, the warning signs should have been obvious. As Barrett grew
more despondent, he began complaining that Stedman was using Masonic
symbols to threaten and torment him. His mood darkened, just as it had a
year and a half earlier. Still, on April 15, 1909, no one, least of all Stedman, was
concerned when the deputy warden entered the carpentry shop. Stedman
walked past Barrett to the shop supervisor, who wanted to show him a
chain he just finished repairing. Neither noticed Barrett pick up a hatchet.
As Stedman leaned over to inspect the chain, Barrett moved up behind him
and struck the unsuspecting man on the back of his neck, nearly decapitating
him. Blood spurted everywhere, completely covering the bench and everything on it, including the mortally wounded deputy warden. One of the
inmates working near Stedman rushed over and tried to help. The deputy
was tugging at one of his pockets, and the prisoner asked if he wanted his
watch. Stedman could only manage "time" before collapsing.

Barrett, meanwhile, used his apron to wipe blood off the blade of
the hatchet, and then laid the murder weapon on the floor. After that he
waited for the guards to arrest him, repeating over and over, "I wouldn't
have done it if the deputy warden had let me see the doctor."[3] By the
time the sixty-year-old officer was rushed to a hospital, it was too late.
One month and two days later Barrett was again on trial for murder. This
time no one suggested that the killing was an accident, and it took jurors
only five minutes to reject his defence of insanity and find the two-time
killer guilty of murder. Normally, condemned killers were held in a jail in
the judicial district closest to where the murder took place, and hanged
in that facility. Because Stedman's murder occurred in a federal prison,

however, it was decided to execute his killer there. That was just one of the anomalies associated with the execution of Barrett.

In its history, Canada has had only one official executioner. That man was John Radclive. Barrett was scheduled to be hanged on June 22, 1909, but by that time Radclive had a serious drinking problem, and he often failed to show up at executions. As a result, sheriffs across the country were forced to use the services of other hangmen. On this day no one with experience was available. The man who appeared at Barrett's cell was a novice. Although he wore a mask and a false moustache, he made no effort to hide his prison-issue boots, the footwear assigned to him when he became a guard. It took the known but unnamed executioner just seconds to escort Stedman's killer to the scaffold, which was built in a hallway. Once Barrett was noosed and positioned on the trap, he was given a chance to say a few last words. Most of those present were friends of the murdered man, and had little sympathy for the killer who was about to forfeit his life. That did nothing to prevent Barrett from saying what he had to say. "Gentlemen, I am going to be hanged, but I killed the deputy warden in self-defence. Had I not done so, my flesh would not be food for vultures."[4] When the prison chaplain realized Barrett was going to continue, he began reciting the *Lord's Prayer*. When he did the hangman pulled the lever holding the trap door shut. Ostensibly, Barrett should have been dropped to a quick and certain death. For an inordinately long time it was neither.

The normal procedure in executions by hanging is to position the knot of the noose under the condemned prisoner's left ear, so that when the person falls a carefully prescribed number of feet, the weight of her or his body coming to an abrupt stop snaps the victim's head back, breaking the prisoner's neck. This immediately renders the person unconscious. After that it usually takes someone about eight minutes to die, whether by strangulation or as a result of a broken neck. If the knot is tied properly, there is virtually no movement of the rope. In Barrett's case, things went very, very wrong. The knot moved as he dropped, so that when his neck snapped back it was not broken, and the killer's heart continued to beat. Twice the inexperienced hangman started to cut the rope suspending the two-time murderer, and on both occasions the prison doctor stopped him. Finally, a full fifteen minutes after he plummeted through the trap doors of his makeshift scaffold, Barrett was declared dead.

By tradition an executioner was entitled to keep the rope he used to hang a killer, and as soon as the noose was removed from Barrett's neck, his hangman began cutting the rope into pieces. He quickly began handing them out to the guards who witnessed the execution. A little later the local sheriff sent a one sentence telegram to Ottawa: "The execution of Garry R. Barrett," it said, "has taken place without a hitch."[5] And so ended the life of a gloomy, morose man who once got away with murder.

John Boyko: Marry Me or Die

John Boyko gave Thekla "Tessy" Oliansky two options — marry him, or give him his share of the profits generated by their hot dog business. When she said no to both, her fate was sealed.

On November 28, 1946, Oliansky's seventeen-year-old son came home to discover her badly beaten body. An hour later Boyko walked into a Montreal police station and announced to the officer in charge, "Me in big trouble. I took a hammer and broke her head. That's all."[6] The officer told Boyko to have a seat, and asked the obviously distraught man what the problem was. All he got was the same two sentences, repeated over and over: "Me in great trouble. You want me."[7] That was enough for the sergeant, and he asked a detective to take over the questioning. As the two policemen walked towards the lobby of the station, Detective Sergeant Albert Laroche mentioned in passing that someone had just beaten a woman to death, and his men were looking for her killer. Well, said the desk sergeant, "I think your man is here now."[8]

After talking to Boyko for a few minutes it was apparent to Laroche that the killer thought to be on the loose was at hand, and he immediately turned Boyko over to the two officers in charge of the investigation. Although Boyko spoke only broken English, it was clear that he wanted to confess, and confess he did. "I come give myself to police. I know this is not church and I will be punished. Me too old anyway. Me want no lawyer. I do not want to live long in jail. I want to hang."[9] That was a wish that eventually was to be granted, but not for this murder.

Boyko told his arresting officers that when he met Tessy Oliansky in 1941, she was living with a man. Two weeks later she ended that relationship, and suggested to Boyko that the two of them go into business together. When they saved enough money, she said they would get married. "If you want to work make nice money and buy couple houses, and after me finish that job and make lots of money get married to me."[10] Boyko said he accepted the proposition. The next day he came home for lunch to find on the table a Bible. Oliansky made him swear an oath taken by many of those in Ukraine who plan to marry: "Thekla I take you as my wife. I swear to you before Jesus Christ I will not leave you so help me God." Then, he said, Oliansky swore the same oath.

Over the next five years the couple bought seven houses, and a chip wagon, where they worked together. All in all they saved more than enough to get married. The only thing preventing them from becoming man and wife was the fact that Boyko was already married to a woman still living in Ukraine. That hurdle was removed in June 1946, when Boyko's wife was murdered by Russian soldiers.

A few weeks before their final disagreement, Boyko felt the time was at last right. He told investigating officers that he said, "Tessie come to church and marry. You have lot of property now."[11]

She turned him down flat. "I'm sorry you too old for me."[12] His response was simple: if you don't want to marry me, give me my share of our business profits. He told her that since she had five properties, she could keep three and he should get two, and then he would be out of her life for good. She said all he deserved was $2,000, and that was all she was going to give him. "Me give you money. Me give you $2,000 and you scram."[13] With that he gathered up some of his clothes and moved out of the house they were sharing.

Boyko went on to tell officers that he became angry when he found out that he no sooner moved out of Oliansky's house than she approached a male friend, who had been pursuing a romantic relationship with her, and told him that she would marry him if he could come up with $9,000. The man immediately deposited $2,000 to her credit in a bank. The next day she gave Boyko a cheque in the amount of $2,250, and told him to stay away from her. But Boyko felt he was too old to keep working, and asked a couple of his friends to meet with Oliansky to persuade her to give him more money. When they failed, he dropped by his former residence himself. She would have nothing to do with him. "Me give you nothing. Get out from my house."[14] Boyko pleaded with her, asking what he would do when the money she had given him ran out. "When you make finish money, take a rope and hang you up."[15]

The day before Oliansky was murdered Boyko again showed up at her home, this time with a friend. Boyko heard a rumour that Oliansky was trying to have him arrested, and he wanted to hear directly from her that it was not true. The three talked for a bit, and before the men left they all shook hands. Unfortunately, whatever goodwill may have existed then did not last long. On the day of the murder Boyko approached Oliansky once more, this time when she was working in the couple's chip wagon. He said he wanted his clothes and money. She told him to come by her house at supper time. At his trial Boyko told a slightly different story than the one he related to officers when he turned himself in. Then he said that when he got to the house sometime after six, she took him to the cellar to get his clothes. "In the cellar I'm tell him Tessie please give me more money. She says nothing. I take the hammer, broke her head, that's all."[16] When he finished confessing Boyko threw his bank book down and told the officers to see that the money in his account went to Oliansky's son. One of the detectives suggested he keep the money, and use it to pay for a

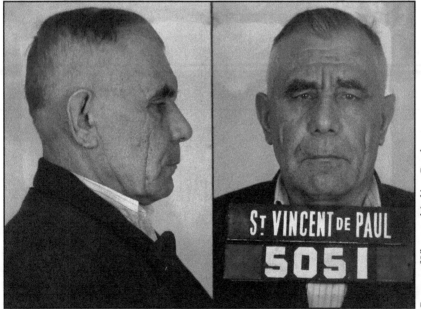

John Boyko was a violent man who murdered the woman he loved, and the man he most disliked. After each killing he quickly confessed to what he had done.

Courtesy of Library and Archives Canada.

lawyer. Boyko was adamant. "Me no want lawyer. Me too old to rot in jail. Me just as soon hang up."[17]

At trial Boyko said that in the cellar he asked Oliansky for more money, and she responded by spitting in his face and calling him names. She then picked up an axe, ordered him out of her house, and for no reason suddenly attacked him. The head of the axe was loose, and when Oliansky swung, it slid down the handle to her hands. As a result, when the blow landed, he was only struck by the wooden handle. He testified that it was at this point he started to fight back. "I picked up the hammer, which was lying there, and struck her on the head three times."[18] In fact, the distraught man hit Olianksy on the head, neck, and shoulders somewhere between sixteen and twenty-six times.

Although Boyko may have forgotten how many times he smashed Oliansky's head, he had a clear recollection of how much money she owed him. He told jurors that he was forty-seven when he met thirty-six-year-old Oliansky in March 1941. He started working at her chip wagon almost immediately, on the understanding that he would receive 20 percent of whatever money came in. Over five years, the business grossed $40,000. According to his calculations, that meant he was owed $8,000. It wasn't fair that she was now "throwing me out with $2,000 because I was too old, and she wanted to get married."[19]

On February 25, 1947, it took jurors just under three hours to find Boyko guilty of murder, rather than manslaughter. The former Austrian army officer was sentenced to hang three and a half months later, but a week before the sentence was to be carried out, it was commuted to life imprisonment. Boyko was promptly transferred from Montreal's Bordeaux Jail to St-Vincent-de-Paul Penitentiary, at nearby Laval. For the next year and a half the heavy-set Ukrainian seemed to be adjusting to prison life, but this period of calm ended when the two things Boyko hated most came together in the persons of Dominic "Nick" Tedesco and former Member of Parliament Fred Rose.

Although Boyko was in jail because he was a murderer, he regarded himself as an honest man, someone morally superior to the "common thieves and robbers" who surrounded him in prison.[20] Few inmates in St-Vincent-de-Paul fit that description more than Tedesco. In 1942, the Montrealer and a partner held up the Tic Toc Café. When the proprietor refused to reveal the combination to his safe, the men removed his shoes and socks and burned the soles of his feet with lighted matches. Before sentencing Tedesco to twenty years in jail and ten lashes, the judge who presided over the twenty-six-year-old's trial made clear how upset he was at the brutality displayed by Tedesco and his partner. "Never in the years that I have been a judge have I sentenced anyone to be whipped, but under the circumstances, and especially in view of the brutality used by the two accused, I am forced to impose not only a lengthy sentence but also the whip."[21]

In prison Tedesco grew close to a man who stood for something Boyko detested — communism. The man was Rose. Born in Poland, Rose immigrated to Canada in 1916, and almost immediately joined the Young Communist League. After that he became a member of the Communist Party, and in 1943 he was elected to the House of Commons as a member of the Labour-Progressive Party of Canada. The organization was the legal arm of the Communist Party, which during the opening years of the Second World War was officially banned. Shortly after the war ended a cipher clerk stationed at the Soviet embassy in Ottawa defected, taking with him evidence that a spy ring was operating in Canada. Rose had the highest profile of the targets pursued by investigators. Charged with violating the *Official Secrets Act*, he refused to testify in his own defence, and was eventually sentenced to six years in prison. In late January 1947, he was officially expelled from Parliament.

Rose and Tedesco hit it off in prison, and they were probably both amused and irritated by Boyko's insistence that he would rather hang than live with communists. To provoke the Ukrainian, they constantly badgered him about his anti-communist beliefs. Boyko's growing irritation reached the boiling point on November 24, 1948, when his daily ration of tobacco suddenly disappeared. The murderer was convinced Tedesco stole it, and when his victim was bent over a machine in the prison carpentry shop, Boyko plunged a chisel into his back, killing him almost instantly. The act made the former army officer the first person in the history of Montreal to face a second murder charge after being sentenced to hang for a previous killing.

As was the case almost exactly two years earlier, Boyko immediately confessed to the murder. He said that:

Many Sundays we walk in prison yard. All the time Tedesco and Fred Rose talk together and one time Tedesco tell me that Fred Rose said to him, me no Communist, me Fascist. Tedesco is rob man [thief] and Communist and for that I hate him and I kill him. Yes, I kill Tedesco and want jury and judge give me sentence, anything I will thank them.[22]

On May 6, 1946, a Montreal jury obliged and three months and three weeks later so did a hangman.

Albert Victor Westgate: Fascination Leads to Murder

Although Albert Victor Westgate was born into money, his English parents were embarrassed by his troublemaking, and in his mid-teens he was shipped to Canada. Like other "remittance men" of the early twentieth century, his family sent him enough money to assure his survival, but not enough to return home.

Westgate arrived in Winnipeg at the start of the First World War, just in time to enlist in the Canadian Expeditionary Force. He was immediately sent to France with the 1st Canadian Division's 5th Battalion, eventually leaving the army with an honourable discharge, and wounds to his head, arms, and stomach. When he returned to Winnipeg he got a job driving a taxi. He was a hard worker, and seldom spoke, earning the nickname "Wordless Westgate."

Early in 1924, Westgate met Lottie Adams, the wife of a store detective. He became infatuated, buying her gifts and paying messengers $1.00 for each of his letters they delivered to her residence. Westgate's overtures became too much for the Adams family, and Lottie asked him to leave her alone. In mid-February 1928, he begged for one last meeting. She agreed, and two days later Westgate picked her up, in full view of her neighbours. During their drive around the city Westgate pleaded with Lottie to run away with him. When she refused, he stopped the car near a golf course, pulled out a .32 calibre revolver, and fired, missing Lottie but sending a bullet through the vehicle's roof. Lottie realized the trouble that she was in and tried to fight Westgate off, badly bruising herself in the process.

Westgate's second shot hit Adams in the left side of her head, splattering blood all over the inside of the car.

For some unknown reason Westgate stabbed the obviously dead woman in the face, dragged her into a ditch, and hit her four times over the head with an axe. He then covered her body with snow and drove away. Unfortunately for him, he was so preoccupied with throwing her clothes out the window he drove into a snow bank. Half a dozen people asked if he needed help before a tow truck finally arrived. Westgate then drove to his rooming house, where he tried to wash off Lottie's blood before returning the car to its owner.

Although Lottie's husband reported her missing, the body of the dead woman was not discovered for almost fourteen days, and then it was found by chance. An unusual mild spell started melting the snow that had fallen the previous two weeks, and a man walking his dog noticed a human hand sticking out of a drift. Before the day was out Westgate was arrested. His trial lasted four days and ended in his conviction. Although Westgate was sentenced to be hanged, his lawyer appealed the verdict, arguing that because a juror suffered from dementia twelve years earlier, he should have been disqualified from serving. The Court of Appeal agreed and ordered a new hearing. It too ended with a guilty verdict.

For a second time Westgate was sentenced to be hanged, but two days before he was to die his sentence was commuted to life in prison. During his fourteen years in Stony Mountain Penitentiary the diminutive killer (he stood only 5'6" and weighed just 136 pounds) was a model prisoner. After he was paroled in June 1943, he took a room in a Winnipeg boarding house and got a job as a mechanic. Two months later a sixteen-year-old girl moved into an adjoining apartment.

Edith Cook left home because of her parents' lectures over her fascination with older men in uniform, and she quickly became infatuated with the forty-two-year-old war veteran. Although Cook worked as a waitress in one of Winnipeg's most popular restaurants, she agreed to give up her job and move to Vancouver with Westgate after he promised to pay her way and get her a job. The pair made plans to leave in early December 1943. But Westgate had no connections in British Columbia, and he was prohibited from leaving Winnipeg because of his parole conditions. Apart from those things, he could not even afford the price of Edith's train ticket.

Notwithstanding his economic circumstances, Westgate suggested that Cook rent a room at the Marlborough Hotel for the time remaining before their departure, and on December 2, she moved into unit 503. For the next day and a half the two were seen several times in the hotel, but sometime in the subsequent twenty-four hours Westgate squeezed Edith by the throat until she stopped breathing.

When Edith's parents did not hear from her by Sunday they became frantic and went to Westgate's rooming house to ask if he had seen her. He said that he had not, but suggested they look for her at the Marlborough, even volunteering to accompany them. Although they received no answer to their knock, they noticed a strong odour coming from room 503, and had a chambermaid open the door. Inside they found Edith, lying in bed with the covers around her head, obviously dead. Westgate was held on a coroner's warrant until the cause of death was established, and then formally arrested. Four months later his third murder trial got underway. It lasted six days, and like his previous hearings, ended with a verdict of guilty. For the only time in Canadian history, a murderer was three times sentenced to hang for committing two separate murders.

Author's photo.

In 1943 Albert Victor Westgate, a decorated veteran of the First World War, was paroled after serving fourteen years in penitentiary for murdering the wife of a Winnipeg store detective. Within a few months of his release he strangled a sixteen-year-old waitress. After his execution he was interred in the military section of Winnipeg's Brookside Cemetery. To satisfy an enraged public, his headstone was removed, leaving him to spend eternity in an unmarked grave.

Albert Victor Westgate was executed just after 1:00 a.m. on July 24, 1944. At that time the *Criminal Code* provided the bodies of those executed were to be buried within the walls of the institution in which they were put to death. Because Westgate was a veteran, however, his body was released, and he was given a military funeral. Later the government re-thought its decision, and although Westgate's remains were left undisturbed, his headstone was removed.

Whether out of anger at their daughter's killer, or in frustration with a legal system that gave him a second chance to murder, the Cooks filed a $100,000 lawsuit against Westgate. The Manitoba Court of Appeal dismissed the claim, but it is the only time in our nation's history that a man on death row was sued by the family of his victim.

Albert Victory Westgate is buried in the military section of Winnipeg's Brookside Cemetery. Edith Cook is also buried in Brookside, a short distance from her killer.

4

Loved Ones Tell All

Canadian law has long protected the communication between spouses. Historically, that meant that a wife and husband could not testify against each other. Children, on the other hand, were free to say whatever they wanted, both in and out of court. So are lovers. The stories in this chapter are about people who were once close to a murderer, but who could not keep a confidence. In each case, the result was that someone had to die.

Oliver Prévost: The Piggery Murders

The two pig farmers were like so many late nineteenth-century Canadian pioneers: they worked hard, kept to themselves, and lived with few luxuries. Still, they were making progress. In the few years he had been in Canada, René D'Aubigné settled comfortably into the farm and pig business he and a partner purchased three kilometres north of Port Arthur, Ontario (now Thunder Bay). The two men built a new residence next to the long, low stable in which they housed their sixty-five pigs, and to give each some semblance of privacy, the house was occupied by D'Aubigné, while Fred Carrier lived in a smaller, older shanty a few dozen yards away. On Thursday, February 11, 1897, whatever dreams of their business future the partners shared came to an abrupt end.

Just after 6:00 a.m. two men on their way to cut cordwood passed the pig farm of D'Aubigné and Carrier, and noticed the smouldering remains of buildings. They also saw a mule, a calf, three dogs, a cat, and a few geese standing near a haystack, about halfway between what were once two small houses and a shed. Their first reaction was that there had been a tragic accident; tragic, because plainly visible in the ruins of one of the buildings were what looked like human remains.

By noon a coroner's inquest was convened, and its members taken to view the accident site. The inquest then adjourned until the next day, when one witness after another swore that the fire was no accident. When the session ended, jurors had reached five conclusions. First, it would have been impossible for a fire to have spread from D'Aubigné's house to the building occupied by his partner without setting fire to the haystack that separated the structures, particularly when the wind had been blowing away from Carrier's shack; second, the night he died the door to the residence of D'Aubigné was fastened shut by a wooden peg shoved through an iron hasp — from the outside; third, footprints in freshly fallen snow led to and from the burned buildings; fourth, it was inconceivable that two men living within a few metres of sixty-five pigs would not have been awoken by the squealing of the animals as they were burned alive; and last, if Carrier's body had fallen through the wooden floor of his shack after it was destroyed in the fire, the debris that covered him would have been beneath his remains, not on top of them. Jurors also thought it odd that the calf, which was habitually tied in a shed during the night, was found outside with a rope around its neck, a rope that had been cut.

Oliver Prévost was among the last witnesses heard by jurors. He testified that he and his wife were living in the Victoria Hotel, long abandoned by the time they moved in, and that the day before D'Aubigné and Carrier died he purchased from them a horse, a hog, and some potatoes. He said that after delivering the potatoes, Carrier declined an invitation to stay for supper, and headed home.

On February 26, the coroner's jury reconvened. Among those heard was a young man who testified that the evening before the fire he saw Carrier driving a sleigh on his way home from town. The witness said a woman in a black dress with a shawl covering her head was walking beside the cutter. Although the route Carrier was taking was not one he usually took on his way from Port Arthur to his piggery, the young man did not think anything was amiss. Asked if the woman appeared to be trying to hide her identity, the witness said no, he did not think so. As it later turned out, he was wrong.

Following the testimony about the sleigh and the mysterious woman, the inquest adjourned until the next afternoon, when jurors met for the final time. Unbeknownst to anyone, among the last witnesses heard was the woman in the shawl. Because she was sick in bed, the evidence of Rosanna Gauthier, who described herself as Mrs. Prévost, was taken from her in the form of a written statement and read to jury members. She had nothing to say that they had not already heard. In fact, the jurors concluded they had heard all the new evidence they were likely to hear, and ended their deliberations by concluding: "That the said R. Dabin [René D'Aubigné] and F. Corrier [Fred Carrier] came to their death on the night of the 10th of February, 1897, through foul play, at the hands of some party or parties unknown to the jury, and that the buildings occupied by the men were set on fire to cover up the crime."[1]

The cover-up worked perfectly, for about ten months. By then the killers had gone their separate ways: Rosanna Gauthier to her husband and home in Valleyfield, Quebec, and Oliver Prévost back to a life of crime. Even then things would have been different had not Oliver harboured a sense of resentment he could not contain, or had the insanity that ran through his family not finally surfaced.

The beginning of the end came in November 1897, when Prévost pled guilty to stealing furs and pork in Renfrew, Ontario. Because of his lengthy criminal record, he was sentenced to seven years in prison. Before he was transferred from Pembroke to the Kingston Penitentiary, he told the attorney prosecuting him that he had something to get off his chest. His story was equal parts fact and fiction, but it certainly captured the attention of his listener. According to Prévost, a little more than a year earlier he met Rosanna Gauthier, who was then in her late teens. The two were travelling from Montreal to Valleyfield, and through her he met her husband. In time the men agreed to become partners in the hotel business in Port Arthur, but when it came time to head west, Gautier changed his mind. Rosanna, however, was still enthused about going, and she, Prévost, and Prévost's three children left without him. Prévost told the Crown Attorney that Rosanna was fascinated by poison, and she carried a small container of it wherever she went. Early the previous February two men stopped by the derelict hotel in which he and Rosanna were living, and they stayed for supper. For no reason he can understand, Gauthier poisoned them. Realizing the trouble they were in, the couple loaded the bodies on to a sleigh, and headed out for the men's farm. There he and Gauthier laid the corpses on their beds, and after stripping them of everything of value, set fire to their houses to cover up their crime. A short while later Prévost and Gauthier separated.

On the strength of Prévost's statement, Gauthier was arrested in Valleyfield and brought to Pembroke, where her preliminary hearing got underway early in December 1897. She seemed not to take the proceedings seriously. At times she appeared amused about what was going on, and the allegation she murdered two men did nothing to keep her attention focussed on the proceedings. Gauthier's features did not change even when Prévost was called to the stand. He spoke as if what transpired in Port Arthur was a fairy tale, and in the words of a spectator, the "awfulness of the crime did not for a minute impress him."[2]

Prévost testified that fifteen minutes after D'Aubigné and Carrier sat down for supper with him and Gauthier, Carrier suddenly got up and walked over to a pail to get a glass of water. Realizing it was empty, he turned and went outside to drink from the pump. D'Aubigné then said that he too was thirsty, and went looking for water in the kitchen. Prévost picked up the water pail, and as he opened the door separating the kitchen from the dining room, he saw D'Aubigné leaning against a shelf. Just as his guest slipped to the floor Prévost turned his head slightly, and noticed through an open door Carrier on his hands and knees near the stable. Prévost said he rushed back to the dining room to get a lamp, and told Gauthier that Carrier was sick. She said not to bother with him, "I have dosed the men with poison."[3] Prévost told the inquiry that Gauthier pleaded with him not to tell anyone what she had done. The couple decided to haul the bodies into the dining room, where they left them while they figured out what to do next. Prévost asked why Gauthier poisoned the men, and told the presiding magistrate that she claimed Carrier had sexually assaulted her, and she was getting even. It was then that she suggested they put the bodies in the sleigh the farmers came to town in, and take them back to their piggery.

But, he said, that was not as easy as they hoped it would be. When the pair went to get the mule and sleigh, they found that the animal somehow had gotten loose and was already on its way home. They pursued it at once, but by the time they caught up to the rig they were at the piggery. Since they were there anyway, they searched the buildings and took whatever valuables they could find, including a gold watch, blankets, clothes, a small chest containing some money, and a pail of lard. On their way home he said they saw a young man in the distance, and Gauthier got off the sleigh and walked a little ways behind, her head covered with a shawl.

Once they got home, Prévost claimed they took a barn door from the yard, hooked one end to the sleigh, and put the bodies on it. Fearing they might be seen with the bodies, they gave the mule its head, and started out a good ways behind. Before they reached their destination it suddenly occurred to Gauthier that the men likely had some money in their pockets. Prévost said he caught up to the mule, stopped the sleigh, took the bodies off the barn door, and stood watch while Gauthier went through the pockets of the dead men. When they reached the pig farm they dragged the bodies into their respective shacks. As they were leaving Carrier's house Gauthier's lamp hit the door and fell. In no time at all the building was in flames. The culprits then started walking home, although Prévost noticed a rifle in the shack and grabbed it before making his exit.

Prévost said the next day Gauthier showed him the bottle in which she kept her poison. He told the magistrate that the powder was whitish, like salt, with dark flecks mixed in. When he said he doubted that the substance was actually deadly, Gauthier put some of the powder on a piece of bread, and gave it to the neighbour's dog. It obviously did not like the taste of what it ate, and started for home. The dog took only a few steps before it fell to the ground and began convulsing. In seconds the animal was dead.

While being cross-examined Prévost admitted that he was not sure everything he said was true, and there were some questions he could not answer. For the most part, however, he thought his recollections were an accurate retelling of what happened. The magistrate presiding over the hearing agreed, and he committed Gauthier to stand trial. Prévost, meanwhile, was sent back to Kingston. The record of what happened next, or when, is not clear, but sometime in 1898 the Crown dropped the murder charges laid against Gauthier and charged Prévost with killing Carrier and D'Aubigné.

His two-day trial started on December 6, 1898, and the only evidence against him was the testimony of Gauthier. What she said had much more the ring of truth to it than did the rambling account of Prévost. According to Gauthier, he went to the piggery by himself on the evening of February 10, killed the two pig farmers, and came back to town. He forced her to return to the farm and help him ransack the homes of his victims, and then made her sit beside him as they hauled their plunder home. Afterwards, Prévost drove the mule and sleigh to the farm, burned the buildings, and walked back to town.

On the stand Gauthier was a much different person than she was a year earlier. This time she was focussed, and much more serious. Still, probably because spectators were aware of her checkered past, she did not impress everyone. A reporter with the *Daily Mail and Empire* noted that:

> Mrs. Gauthier has had quite a career for her age. In a convent from 10 to 15, married then, lived with her husband for two years, then went off with Prevost, and now, at the early age of 20, has returned to the husband. She gave her evidence very clearly, and did not appear to be rattled at all over the crime with which she was, either willingly or unwillingly, so closely connected.[4]

Perhaps the reason Gauthier was given the benefit of the doubt, in terms of credibility, is because listeners could not help but compare what she had to say with the testimony of Prévost. He testified on his own behalf, but his story did nothing to convince jurors that he was telling the truth, or that he was innocent of committing the two murders. In a considerable understatement, an observer noted that, "Altogether it is a very mixed up story, and it is hard to sift out the truth."[5] After sitting through a very long day of testimony the jury had done all the sifting it was going to do, and at 1:30 a.m. it returned a verdict of guilty. Minutes later Prévost learned his fate — he was about to become the first person hanged in Port Arthur, Ontario.

By tradition the condemned were expected to use the time between their sentence and execution to make themselves right with God, and it was the responsibility of newspapers to advise readers that the job was carried out. Both Prévost and local newspapers played their part, and none played it better than the *Daily Journal*.

It is a comfort to those who are blessed with any religious belief to know that he [Prévost] died full of penitence for the rebellious life, which he had lead, and ended his existence in full acceptance of the rites of the church of his youth. To the Rev. Father he made confession. For the public he simply said he was an innocent man, and that though he suffered it was not wrongly for though innocent of this he had been guilty of other crimes. He was thankful for the long time given him to repent.[6]

Prévost slept only an hour the evening before he was to hang, and although his usual breakfast of buttered toast and coffee was brought to him, he ignored it. While his spiritual adviser was administering the Holy Sacrament of Communion the country's official executioner and a black-smith arrived at the jail. They reached the condemned man's cell slightly after 7:30 a.m. on March 17, 1899. As they entered Prévost stood, tears filling his eyes, and he shook hands with his guests. The blacksmith then asked Prévost to sit while he removed the prisoner's leg irons. That was a more difficult task than usual because a week earlier, in an attempt to remove the irons, Prévost jammed a wire into the lock and it broke off.

With the blacksmith busy with his chisel, the executioner made his way to the scaffold erected in the yard of the jail. It was an ugly thing, standing six metres high, with a platform four metres across. When he was satisfied that all was in order, the hangman returned to the cell occupied by Prévost. As he entered the bells of Port Arthur's Catholic Churches began tolling. His victim was ready for his walk to the gallows, and as the executioner approached to bind his arms behind his back, Prévost put his hand on the man's shoulder, and said "You are doing your duty, but you are hanging an innocent man."[7] The hangman ignored the comment, and fastened around the waist of his victim a thick leather belt, with two small straps sewn into the sides near the front. One of these bindings was made fast around each of the prisoner's wrists. Once that was done someone placed a prayer book in Prévost's hand. After a series of brief goodbyes to those who had been tending to his spiritual needs, the death walk began. In his new dark suit, dress shirt, and black necktie, the man about to be executed was very likely the best dressed member of the party. The clothes were bought with funds raised by townspeople.

While more than three hundred people applied for a ticket to witness the execution, only twenty people were admitted. Prévost walked by them with a firm step, but when he reached the steps leading to the platform of the scaffold he seemed to weaken, and was helped up the stairs. On the gallows he was guided to the trap doors, and the hangman slipped a hood over his head with one hand, and a noose with the other. With this Prévost began to pray, and as he did so the executioner looked at the sheriff, who signalled him to proceed. In a flash the lever was pulled back, and Prévost dropped. As soon as those in attendance saw that there was not the slightest movement of the rope, an almost audible sigh of relief could be heard. So sudden was Prévost rendered unconscious, his prayer book remained firmly clutched in one of his hands. Four minutes later the killer was declared dead, his neck broken.

One of the requirements of the law is that immediately following an execution a coroner's jury had to be empanelled to view the remains of the person executed, and to swear that he was well and truly dead. What the six jurors from Port Arthur saw was a man who looked almost asleep, and were it not for a slight discolouration around his neck, someone might have thought he dozed off with not a worry in the world.

John "Cobalt" Ivanchuk: Too Much to Say

John Ivanchuk was, like so many men and women executed in Canada, inclined to talk too much. He also placed too much trust in a fifteen-year-old young woman. His story is of particular interest because we know so little about what motivated him to kill a northern Ontario liquor inspector, and how he escaped detection while continuing to live in the same small town in which he committed the murder.

Ivanchuk was born in Austria in 1887, and served in the armed forces of his country before immigrating to Canada as a twenty-five-year-old. About the same time he earned his nickname "Cobalt" as a miner in northern Ontario, Ivanchuk began a rapid descent into crime and corruption. Harry Constable, on the other hand, was by all accounts a good person. He was a young war hero, worked hard, participated in community events, took the time to get to know his neighbours, and was liked by everyone. In late October 1926, he spent most of the evening with other members of the Cochrane band. The northern town was proud of its musicians, and most band members took their practice seriously. It was not altogether surprising, then, when by 11:30 p.m. he was not yet home. Still, it was late, and Constable's wife was waiting up. When she heard three shots she at first thought someone was celebrating, but quickly realized that even though it was Friday, it was almost midnight, and in a town the size of Cochrane, that was late. Both curious and worried, she decided to investigate. When she stepped out of her house she noticed a neighbour coming out of his. It was pouring in rain, and dark, and neither could see. Before they had a chance to turn back, the Constable's Airedale emerged out of the darkness. Just then a man from down the street walked up and shone his flashlight along the path. That's when they saw Harry lying against a fence. While Mrs. Constable ran towards her husband, one of the neighbours took off in the opposite direction to phone for a doctor. In less than five minutes two arrived. Although the inspector was alive, everyone could see that there was little that could be done. He had been shot three times. One bullet struck his shoulder, and a second hit him in the abdomen, but neither was noticed at the time. The third wound was clearly visible — there was practically nothing left of his throat. Twenty minutes after she heard the first shot ring out, Constable's wife became a widow.

Courtesy of Library and Archives Canada.

John Ivanchuk was a small time bootlegger in northern Ontario, and somewhere along the line he ran afoul of a Cochrane liquor inspector. Ivanchuk got even for whatever slight he suffered by shooting the officer three times. Although the killer continued to live in the same small town in which he committed the murder, it took the police more than a year to catch him.

From the start the Ontario Provincial Police officers investigating Constable's murder were convinced that the assault was an act of revenge, most likely carried out by someone who was prosecuted by the dead liquor inspector for a violation of the *Ontario Temperance Act*. Within days of offering a $2,000 reward for information leading to the arrest of Constable's killer, the provincial government increased their offer to $5,000.

> In view of the fact that very little progress has been made in obtaining information that would lead to the discovery of the slayer of Inspector Constable. The Government feels that every effort that would be conducive to the capture of the murderer should be made. The Crown officers and Government employees must at all odds be protected in the faithful discharge of their duties.[8]

Although the reward brought in a flood of leads, none proved productive.

That was a little ironic, considering that after shooting Constable, Ivanchuk spoke of the murder to almost everyone he met. But before he did, he put his life in the hands of a fifteen-year-old. Sophia Dincorn was about to enter her house after spending an evening with a friend when Ivanchuk ran up. He thrust a gun into her hand and told her to keep it for him. She did, apparently oblivious to the Constable murder, or unconcerned that she was now an accessory after the fact. If she is to be believed, it was two days before she even looked at what she was keeping for a man with whom she later claimed to have had only a passing acquaintance.

Four days after the murder Ivanchuk showed up unannounced at a shack occupied by a local butcher, near the Taschereau, Ontario, train station. Ivanchuk asked for supper and a place to stay the night. The next morning the men killed an animal the butcher was getting ready to slaughter. That evening, as they chatted, Ivanchuk told his host that he felt he had not been dealt with fairly, without explaining by whom, then blurted out: "me shot Constable at Cochrane."[9] Ivanchuk apparently thought long and hard about what he confessed to, and in the middle of the night woke the butcher and warned him not to tell anyone about the inspector. Ivanchuk looked at his puzzled host, and said he had a good mind to shoot him then and there, to remove any chance he would tell. Full of gin, and exhausted

from lack of sleep, Ivanchuk decided to postpone thoughts of further killing, and went back to bed.

Constable's killer left the next day, and met up with another acquaintance. He suggested that they open a brothel in Kapuskasing. When his
would-be partner said he was too nervous of the police to be part of
such a thing, Ivanchuk told him that if the police interfered he would
shoot them just as he had Constable. Asked if he was not afraid of being
caught, Ivanchuk said he was relying on a friend still living in Cochrane
to keep potential witnesses from talking to the police. To be certain his
listener knew what he meant by reference to the way he killed Constable,
Ivanchuk said he shot the inspector in the body and the neck, ensuring
there was no chance he survived the attack.

It was never made clear at what point the police started to focus their
search on Ivanchuk, but the former army officer made no attempt to stay
out of the spotlight. In the two years between the killing and his arrest,
Ivanchuk continued to reside in Cochrane, and made his living gambling
and selling illicit liquor throughout the north. That came to an end on
November 15, 1928, when Ontario Provincial Police officers descended
on a Cochrane drinking establishment. Although Ivanchuk was arrested,
he was not charged with murder for two days, when investigators were
finally able to confirm his identity. Five months later his trial got underway.

A lot happened to Sophia Dincorn in the two and a half years since
Constable was murdered. For one thing, she was no longer fifteen, and for
another, she was now a mother, living in Schumacher, Ontario. Early in her
trial testimony it was revealed that she was likely responsible for Ivanchuk's
arrest, since it was the information she gave officers a few days before he was
apprehended that pointed them in the right direction. Still, what she said at
trial was not consistent with the testimony of other witnesses. For instance,
she told the court that the evening Constable was killed she was with a
friend at the home where her friend worked as a domestic. That was not
true. On the day in question her friend was not even employed there. She
also testified that she and Ivanchuk once attended a wedding together. He
denied that was true, and no one admitted seeing them together.

Ivanchuk took the stand in his own defence, and denied being in the
places he was said to have been, or knowing the people to whom he was
said to have spoken. He testified that not only did he not know Sophia

Dincorn, he had never seen her before going on trial. The night Constable was shot, Ivanchuk said he went to a movie with a friend, had something to eat, and then rented a room in the Queen's Hotel. When the defence finished putting in its evidence, one of the police officers investigating the murder was recalled to the stand. He told the court that within a few hours of the liquor inspector's murder he started searching the town's hotel rooms, making a note of who was where. Nowhere in his search did he encounter Ivanchuk. To members of the all-male jury, there was just too much evidence against the accused, and too little to like about him, and on April 12, 1929, they found him guilty of murder. Ivanchuk was sentenced to hang in late June. But he was not executed then. His lawyer obtained a one month postponement from the federal department of justice so he could file additional material in support of his client's application for clemency. Whatever was submitted did nothing to persuade the cabinet to commute the killer's sentence, and on July 19, Ivanchuk was put to death in the jail at Haileybury. For a while, it did not look like he would go quietly.

The day before he was to hang, Ivanchuk, always moody, became sullen and almost overcome with anger. At times he pounded on the iron bars of his cell with so much force the sound could be heard by pedestrians outside. A few hours later, however, he seemed to become resigned to his fate, and grew quiet. Shortly before his midnight execution he was offered a dose of morphine, to take the edge off. His refusal initially

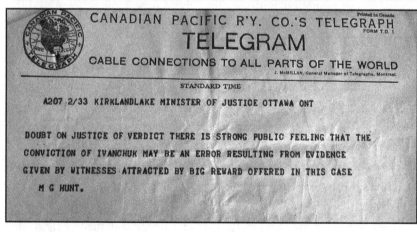

John Ivanchuk made little attempt to keep secret the fact he murdered a Cochrane, Ontario, liquor inspector, and it was only a matter of time before he was turned in. At trial much of the testimony that resulted in his conviction was very likely false.

alarmed members of his death watch, but when Arthur Ellis, the best known of the country's several executioners, arrived at his cell, Ivanchuk gave no trouble. Barefooted and wearing only his striped prison trousers, the condemned man calmly stood to have his arms pinioned behind his back. Perhaps his sense of resignation was the result of the dream he had the night before. In it a black-robed woman told him he would be dead within twenty-four hours.

It was only a few feet from the death cell to the spot in the jail where a makeshift scaffold was constructed, but Ivanchuk asked that he be escorted to the gallows by uniformed police officers. Making the journey with him was an Ontario Provincial Police sergeant, an OPP constable, a member of the Royal Canadian Mounted Police, a chief of police, and a deputy sheriff. Twelve seconds after leaving his cell Ivanchuk was standing on the scaffold. As soon as he arrived his legs were tied, a black hood pulled over his head, and the noose tightened around his neck. Ellis asked if Ivanchuk had any last words. When there was no response, he repeated his question. Ivanchuk responded with a query of his own: "What do you mean — about the murder? My heart is clean."[10] With that the bolt holding the trap door secure was released, and the bound prisoner disappeared from view. Twelve minutes later he was dead. Because no one claimed his body, the remains of John "Cobalt" Ivanchuk were interred in the yard of Haileybury Jail.

Stanley Donald McLaren: A Fatal Mistake

Just after Stanley McLaren's wife turned him in to the police, he told his captors that his three biggest mistakes in life were getting married, beating to death a Calgary fruit merchant, and following his wife's advice to confess to the murder. Before he listened to her, there was absolutely no way McLaren was going to hang.

This sad tale began on a Monday late in September 1945. McLaren was nineteen, and just a month earlier arrived in Calgary. He made the most of his time, and by the end of September was going out regularly with a young woman from Regina. About the only problem he had was a lack of money. McLaren was a plasterer by trade, and while it was only a matter of time before he found a job, he wanted money right away. That may have been why he stole a coat. He was quickly caught, photographed, finger-printed, and fined $10. The conviction did nothing to dissuade McLaren from pursuing a life of crime. When he needed money on September 24, he decided to get it the easy way.

Around 6:00 p.m. he entered the fruit store of Wing Yum Lum, a sixty-five-year merchant who only four years earlier started his business near Calgary's busy Edmonton Trail. When McLaren entered his grocery, Lum barely noticed him and continued serving customers already there. All of them noticed McLaren standing around, but none later identified him as the person they saw. When McLaren was still loitering about an hour and a half later, Lum became anxious. Without saying anything, he left McLaren alone for a few seconds, and slipped into the back to unlock the rear door of the store, in case he had to make a speedy exit. He never got that chance. When Lum returned McLaren told him he wanted a few peaches to take home to his mother. As soon as the fruit grocer bent to pick them out of a case lying on the floor, McLaren pulled a revolver from his coat pocket and demanded the money from the cash register. Whether he was nervous or did not understand what was said, Lum did not move quickly enough, and McLaren began smashing his head with the butt of his pistol.

The cries of the grocer were heard by shopkeepers on either side of his store, and one of them, a baker, rushed out to see what was happening.

> When I heard him scream at first I thought it was kids teasing him and I didn't pay much attention. When the screaming continued I went out and looked through the open door of his shop. Lum was lying on the floor with the man kneeling on his chest, hitting him on the head with a small black gun. Just as I looked in the door and before I could get back to my own shop to call the police, the man ran at me and grabbed me. He looked up and down the street. There wasn't a soul in sight. He ordered me into the Chinese shop. When I refused he stuck a gun in my stomach and said, "You come in here."
>
> Lum had gotten to his feet by this time but I don't think he knew what he was doing. The man ordered me

to empty the cash register. He then attacked the Chinese again, knocking him to the floor and striking him repeatedly after he was down.... He kept glaring at me as I stood by the till, and all the time pounding the old man.... The cash register was a small one with a few bills and some silver in it. I could see a ten and a few ones in the bills. I thought I pushed the ten to the back but it must have been among them when he snatched them from my hand and rushed out the back door.... What I can't understand is why he kept beating the poor old man.[11]

As McLaren was making his getaway through the back door, a young sailor on home leave walked up to the front of the store, where he stood waiting for a friend. All of a sudden two men appeared. Lum was standing beside his would-be rescuer, blood running down his face. The baker told the startled sailor that Lum had been robbed and beaten, and that the culprit escaped through the rear of the store. With that the sailor took off in pursuit. In seconds the young man saw his quarry about two blocks ahead, running up a hill. When the robber noticed that he was being pursued he stopped running, doubled back, and then turned up the hill and disappeared.

For the next three years that was where things stood. Lum died of his head wounds fourteen hours after being admitted to hospital, but not before an interpreter helped the native of Canton, China, give police a description of the man who robbed him. The woman translating for Lum told investigators that she had known the grocer for some time, and like so many immigrants struggling to make a new life in Canada, he was completely devoted to his business. She said Lum spoke very little English, and rarely interacted with anyone besides customers. Even though he was a member of a local Chinese benevolent society, Lum did not mix much with other immigrants. According to the interpreter, he spent every day in his store, either at the front, where he operated his tiny business, or in the rear, where he lived alone.

A year after killing Lum, McLaren married Marie Kayter in Regina, where they resided before moving to Vancouver, and later to northern Ontario. In July 1948, their transient life seemed to be behind them, and the couple settled in Toronto. In the three years between the Calgary

murder and moving east, McLaren made little effort to hide from authorities, probably because no one had any inkling he was involved in Lum's
death. That quickly changed, however, when the hot-tempered killer got
into one argument too many. On August 28, he was involved in a brawl
on a Toronto street corner, and charged with common assault. The police
were barely finished processing him when his wife appeared and asked to
speak to someone in charge. She told the officer that her husband three
years earlier had committed a murder, and was wanted by the authorities
in Calgary. Satisfied she had done her civic duty, or exacted revenge for
whatever wrongs had been done her by McLaren, she went home. After
the police in Toronto heard back from their counterparts in Alberta, they
contacted Marie McLaren by phone. As a result of the additional information she gave them, the officers decided to interrogate McLaren right
away instead of leaving him to be questioned by Calgary police. At this
stage there was nothing except the words of his wife to connect the twen-
ty-three-year-old plasterer to the death of Lum. Had he remained silent,
McLaren would almost certainly have gone free. But he could not keep
his mouth shut.

Detectives Edmund Tong and Roy Perry took McLaren into a small
room as Toronto police headquarters, and began questioning him about the
murder his wife said was committed in 1945. During the first forty minutes
their prisoner denied all knowledge of the crime. Then he suddenly stopped
talking, and asked if he could phone his wife. Tong took McLaren to a
telephone, and dialed her number. When the call was answered McLaren
asked a single question: "Do you still love me, Marie?"[12] The question was
answered, although the detective could not make out what was said. Back in
the interview room, McLaren sat in silence for several minutes. Apparently
satisfied about what he was going to do next, he then looked up, and said,
"I'll tell you the story. I did it."[13] With that, he started talking.

> I had been drinking heavy on the 24th of September,
> 1945, and about 7 p.m. I was going to meet my girlfriend
> Marie Kayter (now McLaren's wife) who worked in the
> Coffee Cabin on 2nd St. E. at 17th Avenue, and I was
> short of money and needed a few dollars to take my girl-
> friend out, and I walked down Fourth St. in Calgary and

I was hungry, so I went into a Chinese fruit store to buy some peaches, and I bought the peaches and eat one in the store and I stayed in the store while eating the peaches, and during this time several customers came in and left. After a while the Chinaman and I were alone in the store, so I pulled out a gun, a revolver of Italian make, from my pocket it was not loaded because it was defective, and I told the Chinaman I wanted his money, and he started to holler and I told him to shut up and then I hit him several times on the head with the butt of the revolver, when the baker from the next store came in and struggled with me and I struck him with my fist and made the baker take the money from the till and give it to me. There was only $13. I run down, through the store and down the lane and through several backyards and two men were chasing me but I got away. I went to my girlfriend's room and she helped clean the blood from my clothing. The next day I read in the paper that the Chinaman had died.[14]

The problem with the statement was that the information it contained was for the most part simply not accurate. For example, in his statement McLaren is alleged to have said that he was on 4th Street when he went into Lum's store. The fruit vendor's shop was actually on 3rd Street. The statement also says that the baker who tried to help Lum came in to the fruit store of his own volition. In fact, he was forced into the store by the man who had been assaulting Lum. An even more glaring error was the assertion that the baker struggled with McLaren, who hit him with his fist. That never happened; there was no struggle, and the baker was not struck by anything. Another mistake of fact was the suggestion that Lum's assailant ran through several backyards. The sailor chasing the man who assaulted Lum denied that the person he was pursuing ran through any backyards, nor were two men in pursuit. Furthermore, the gun that McLaren allegedly confessed to taking out of his pocket was not a revolver, it was an automatic, a distinction with which someone like McLaren would be familiar. Even the language used in the statement is inconsistent with what was normally used by McLaren. The poorly educated labourer, who referred to his victim as a "Chinaman," was unlikely to describe his automatic pistol as a "revolver of Italian make." More likely, he would have said it was "a wop gun."

Ironically, since McLaren's wife could not by law testify against her husband, the alleged killer's statement was the single piece of evidence that implicated him in Lum's murder. The only other comment McLaren is alleged to have made about the crime was something he was supposed to have said to the detective who took his statement when the two men were alone. "I've made three mistakes in my life … First killing the Chinaman. Second, getting married. And third talking to you fellows."[15] When a Calgary trial judge allowed both statements to be admitted into evidence, their prejudicial effect on jurors was incalculable, and McLaren's trip to death row was assured.

Following his return to Calgary, McLaren was held in custody pending the result of a preliminary hearing. When it ended on October 13, 1948, he was committed to stand trial for murder. Before it got underway, however, the *Criminal Code* was amended to give those convicted of a criminal offense an automatic right to appeal their convictions to the Supreme Court of Canada, provided their appeal was based on a question of law. That amendment came into effect fourteen days before McLaren went on trial.

Among the first witnesses called by the Crown were the customers who were in Lum's store between the time McLaren is alleged to have entered, and when Lum was assaulted. They remembered seeing the grocer's killer, but none recognized McLaren as that man. Their failure to identify McLaren was a serious setback to the prosecution's case, and the trial judge seemed determined to set things straight. After one of the customers testified that the man he saw was not one of the men in a police lineup, the Crown Attorney was permitted to ask a follow-up question: was there anyone in the lineup who stood out from the others, for any reason whatsoever? McLaren's lawyer immediately objected to the question. The witness, he said, stated clearly that he did not recognize anyone in the lineup. "If the crown proceeds further it will be cross-examination."[16] The trial judge disagreed and allowed the question. The witness then testified that there was only one person in the lineup with the build of Lum's killer, but he had never seen that person before.

The Crown persisted. "You say there was but one man in the lineup who resembled the man you saw in the store. Can you see him in the courtroom anywhere?"[17] Once again, McLaren's lawyer was on his feet. Addressing the judge, he said "The witness has said he did not recognize anyone. The crown should not have asked the witness that question when there is only one man here [from the lineup] and that man is in the prisoner's box. It is practically coaxing him to say it is the man in the box."[18] The judge allowed the question. He promised that later, presumably after jurors had made their minds up about the guilt of the accused, he would direct the jury as to how much weight they should place on the evidence. When allowed to answer the question, the witness gave the answer the Crown Attorney was looking for: "Yes, he is the man in the prisoner's box."[19]

One question the lawyer for McLaren posed, which was not answered during the trial, was why the police, who had his client's fingerprints on file, did not attempt to match them with fingerprints taken from the rear door through which Lum's killer escaped. He also wondered why investigators did not photograph the bloodstains left on the floor after Lum was beaten. The killer walked through the blood to make his exit — surely from the prints left at the scene the police could make an estimate of the size of the shoe that made the print, and from that the size of the killer's foot.

> Is it possible that there were fingerprints taken that were not produced? It is not my duty to explain that. What are you as a jury to infer from that kind of evidence? It is the right of jury to demand the best type of evidence. They took McLaren's fingerprints in Toronto, but the Calgary police did not hold up its end and take prints from the doorknob so that they could be compared.[20]

The trial judge appeared to be singularly unimpressed with McLaren's lawyer, a leading member of Calgary's defence bar. On one occasion he asked the lawyer to stop yapping at the Crown,[21] and on another told the lawyer that "We are never going to get through this trial if it is going to be a Sunday school debating society."[22] The animosity between the judge and the defendant's counsel spilled over into closing arguments. During his more than two hour charge to the jury, the judge read McLaren's alleged statement, sentence by sentence, ending each with the question: Did the detectives who interviewed the accused make this up? Inconsistencies between what was said in the statement and the facts presented at trial were ignored.[23] The judge concluded with: "A man who makes a confession which a jury accepts as being true, if that confession is in fact a confession of guilt, such a man can be convicted on that confession alone, even though there is no corroboration."[24] When McLaren's lawyer objected to the charge, arguing that the judge failed to advise jurors that they were free to interpret the facts in a way different from what was suggested by the Crown, the judge replied that if counsel did not agree with his charge, he was free to take his objection to the court of appeal.[25] Less than two hours later the jury returned a guilty verdict, with no recommendation for mercy.

McLaren's trial ended late in the afternoon on Saturday, November 20. The next morning he was transferred from Calgary to Lethbridge, where he was to be hanged on the last day of the following March. The case was back in the headlines three weeks before his scheduled date with the hangman, when the Alberta Court of Appeal turned down his request for a new trial. Two and a half weeks later McLaren's lawyer appeared before Mr. Justice Patrick Kerwin of the Supreme Court of Canada to ask that the court hear an appeal from his client's conviction. Technically, the request should have been unnecessary. The amendment to the *Criminal Code*, which gave convicted killers like McLaren an automatic right of appeal, came into effect two weeks before his trial started. That meant that the court had no legal basis for refusing to hear his request for a new trial. Kerwin, however, did not see it that way. He ruled, for a reason he never stated, that McLaren's appeal would not be heard by the Supreme Court.

When Kerwin turned down McLaren's application the condemned man's only remaining hope was that the Governor General, on the advice of the federal cabinet, would commute his death sentence to life imprisonment. That hope was lost on March 29, 1949, less than twenty-four hours before McLaren was to hang. The condemned killer spent his last hours talking to his guards and playing checkers, occasionally standing up and asking "who's afraid of the big bad wolf?"[26] But when the clock struck midnight, McLaren was on his own. He walked to the gallows without assistance, showing no visible sign of emotion. That may have been because

he took advantage of the offer made to those about to be put to death —
would he like a drug, or brandy? Either one made a killer's last walk a little
more bearable.

The trap doors separating Stanley Donald McLaren from eternity
were opened at 12:11 a.m. on March 30. He was pronounced dead fifteen
minutes later. In a sad, almost pathetic postscript to this tragedy, McLaren
was buried in the yard of the Lethbridge jail at almost the same time as
his victim was buried in Calgary. Lum's relatives wanted to bring his body
back to China, and until they could raise the money to do so, the grocer's
remains were kept in a vault at Union Cemetery. The day McLaren was
executed, cemetery officials were told that there was to be no trip home.

Arthur Kendall: Killing in Front of Family

The people and the crimes described in this book share a number of common characteristics. One is that murderers are bullies; a second is that their
crimes are seldom well planned. Arthur Kendall and the murder of his wife
are examples of both.

In the 1940s and 1950s the labourer and part-time farmer lived in
the Walkerton district of southwestern Ontario and was the father of five
children. The eldest was a thirteen-year-old son; the rest were daughters,
aged eleven, nine, seven, and eighteen months. Kendall ruled his brood, and
his wife, with an iron fist. When he spoke of his wife it was always to tear
her down. Once he described her to a neighbour as "just a cow." When
he married her he said, "she was supposed to be a virgin, but [she was] no
more a virgin than a 12 year-old cow."[27] Despite his lack of respect for his
spouse, Kendall enjoyed the company of women. Shortly before Helen
Kendall disappeared her husband and three friends went into the bush
near Wiarton, Ontario, to work at a saw mill. All four lived in the same
cabin, and they soon began dating local women. One of the men knew
the Kendalls well, and had a great deal of respect for Helen. He was a little
surprised, and perhaps disappointed, when Arthur began bragging about
the woman he was seeing. It did not come as total surprise when he later
found out that Kendall's new relationship was not new at all. In July 1952,
he moved his family from their farm into a one-room cabin at Johnson
Harbour, near Tobermory. A few days later Kendall left them on their own

to take his other woman, and her five children, for a weekend trip to the farm that he had just left.

Shortly after this Kendall and his family were alone in their cabin, when his two oldest daughters were wakened. They slept on a bunk directly above the bed of their parents, and had long before learned to follow instructions never to make a noise, or get up before being called. On August 2, 1952, the fight they listened to was worse than normal. Nine-year-old Anne and her older sister Margaret huddled together in absolute silence, not really understanding what was happening. Then they heard the last words their mother was to speak: "Arthur, please don't." As the two girls peeked over the edge of the bed, they saw their father place a knife on the table, and then drag the body of their mother out of the cabin. About thirty minutes later Kendall returned. While Anne and Margaret pretended to be asleep, he began wiping blood off the table and floor with a sheet. When he finished he stuffed the blood-soaked items, together with the knife, into a shopping bag and for a second time left the cabin. When he came back he washed the floor again.[28]

The next morning their father instructed each of his children not to talk about their mother. If anyone asked, they were to tell them that she left home a couple of days earlier. That evening their father told the kids they were coming with him to visit a sick friend, Beatrice Hogue. The children stayed with Hogue and her five children for most of the next week, then everyone, all twelve of them, moved to Kendall's farm seventy-five miles south, in Perth County. This activity did not go unnoticed, and rumours began to spread that something was amiss. When an acquaintance of Kendall's dropped by for a visit, he could not help but notice that things were different. All his friend would say was "My wife has skinned out with another man."[29] Kendall told someone else that his wife had run off to Brantford with her lover. The man suggested he go and bring her back, but Kendall rejected the notion: "let her go to hell."[30]

There was so much whispering about the missing Mrs. Kendall that word eventually reached the authorities. A month after their mother disappeared, the two oldest children were interviewed by an inspector with the Ontario Provincial Police. The children were well rehearsed. Asked where her mother was, Margaret said she left after a fight with her father, during which her mother threw a cup of tea into his face. In fact, the daughter recalled, they were having supper when her mother announced she was leaving: "she said I'll never be back — never — she wasn't crying.... I want her to be found, but I don't care if she comes to live with us. I like my daddy best."[31] The children even remembered the clothing their mother wore when she left the house, and the things she put into the shopping bag she took with her.

Probably the most suspicious evidence that came to the attention of the inspector was a cardboard box found by a neighbour in the woods near the Kendall farm. Inside the box were articles of women's clothing, including two slips and a July edition of the *Farmer's Advocate* with Kendall's mailing address visible on the front cover. When the items were examined in the police lab, two bloodstains were discovered on the front page of the magazine. The problem for investigators was that there was no proof the stains were human; and even though Kendall was seen walking through a freshly worked field in the area where the box was discovered, there was nothing concrete to connect him to it. The police eventually dug up the local garbage dump and the fields around the Kendall home, but nothing was found.

So it was that with little to go on, the investigation into the disappearance of Helen Kendall ground to halt. While life for the missing woman's children went on, times were much tougher than they once had been. For two years the youngsters lived in foster homes, then were returned to the crowded residence of their father and the Hogues. After that Kendall talked openly about what might or might not have happened to their mother. James later recalled that his father seemed almost proud of what everyone suspected he had done. He "always said there was no jail that would hold him. He liked to boast a bit — he discussed it openly in front of us."[32] Anne remembered that when she or one of her siblings accused their father of murdering their mother, he would always reply: "Prove it."[33]

After brooding for nine years, Anne could no longer keep the family secret, and in January 1961, she went to the police. So too did Margaret. Before the month was out Kendall was arrested at the Royal Air Force base at Clinton, Ontario, where he worked as a carpenter. By the time his murder trial got underway on October 24, Anne's brother also gave investigators a statement implicating his father in the disappearance of his mother. With nothing physical connecting Kendall to the crime, the Crown built its case on circumstantial evidence. It was enough. The trial ended after four days of testimony. The presiding judge stressed to jurors that there was nothing in the law that prevented them from bringing in a verdict of guilty in the absence of a body. There was ample evidence, he suggested, for the jury to reach two conclusions: Helen Kendall was dead; and her death was brought about by her husband. In less than three hours the jurors rendered their verdict — guilty.

When Charles Dubin's appeal of Kendall's conviction was heard by the Ontario Court of Appeal on January 23, 1962, his petition made reference to a number of legal points, but apart from arguing that the trial judge misdirected the jury, he really had only one thing to ask the court: if Kendall really did murder his wife, why did the couple's children remain silent for nine years? He argued that when they were out of the control and influence of their father, the children had many opportunities to tell someone — members of the Children's Aid Society, or the people in foster homes, for instance — about what happened. The appellate court deliberated for just eight minutes before dismissing the appeal. Two weeks later the same court granted the killer a stay of execution so that Dubin could try his luck with the Supreme Court of Canada. There he advanced the same argument, suggesting that the trial judge improperly instructed the jury when he failed to warn jurors against convicting Kendall solely on the strength of the distant memories of three of his five children. The Supreme Court, like the Court of Appeal, disagreed, and unanimously dismissed the appeal. Now all that was left for the killer was to ask the federal cabinet for clemency. This time he was more successful.

Kendall made legal history when he was convicted of murdering his wife. A month earlier the *Criminal Code* was amended to divide murder into capital and non-capital charges. Capital murder involved either a pre-meditated killing, or a murder committed during a burglary, indecent assault, rape, escape from custody, piracy, sabotage, arson, treason, or the killing of a police officer. The sentence for a conviction under either category was mandatory. In the case of capital murder, it was death; in the case of non-capital murder, the sentence was life imprisonment. Kendall was the first person convicted of capital murder after the amendments came into effect. On April 10, 1962, the government of John George Diefenbaker commuted his death sentence to life imprisonment. It added to the commutation a condition that he was not to be released without the approval of the federal cabinet. When Walkerton's sheriff advised Kendall that he was not going to hang, the killer did not say a word.

Since at least the 1920s it has been the policy of provincial governments to release to family the body of a loved one who was executed. Occasionally, that meant a killer was buried near the body of his or her victim. The churchyard burial of murderers was most often allowed when a killer was predeceased by a family member. After two of his children died in infancy, Kendall purchased a plot in the Bayfield Cemetery, near Goderich, Ontario. Before his sentence was commuted, members of the cemetery's board of trustees feared that the killer would seek to have his body buried next to those of his sons. To avoid that possibility, the board passed a motion refusing to allow the sheriff where Kendall was to be hanged permission to inter his body in Bayfield. That decision did not go down well with the editor of the *Globe and Mail*.

> By voting to refuse burial in the cemetery to a convicted murderer, Arthur Kendall, the board of trustees of the Bayfield Cemetery of Goderich have in no way protected or enhanced the sanctity of their ground. Kendall's sentence has been commuted to life imprisonment, but it is regrettable that anyone should have wished to extend punishment beyond death.[34]

If Kendall was not welcome in Goderich the same could not be said for Terrance, British Columbia. The killer's relationship with the west coast town began on February 13, 1971, when he failed to return to the Kingston area minimum security jail, where he was serving his life sentence, after being granted a day pass. At some point Kendall made his way to Guelph, where he posted three letters to the warden of Joyceville Penitentiary. Although the contents of the letters were not released, according to an Ontario Provincial Police spokesperson, "They were rambling letters and he said he had no intention of going back to prison. He even mentioned he is going to write a book about his life."[35] Even if he was serious about penning his autobiography, Kendall did not have time. On February 25, he was recaptured at the Terrace home of one of his stepsons. After that he was returned to prison, and like his wife, disappeared from public view.

5

Suspicions Linger

Some of the stories of murder and treachery in this book suggest that the perfect crime is often the one committed most openly. That was the case with Marie Louis Cloutier and Achille Grondin, and Marie Beaulne and Philibert Lefebvre, four early-twentieth-century lovers who made no effort to hide their illicit romances. In fact, the longer the affairs lasted, the more they were accepted by residents of the small Quebec villages in which the two couples lived. Although no one in southwestern Alberta tolerated the murder of John Benson by William Jasper Collins, he, like the Quebec lovers, would almost certainly have escaped the hangman had he only exercised a little discretion after the fact.

William Jasper Collins: Too Much Money

In the opening decade of the twentieth century few lawyers around Braymer, Missouri, prospered more than John Benson. Although over the years he acquired property, considerable wealth, and a young wife and child, he yearned for something more. What he wanted was the experience of homesteading on the Canadian prairies. Before that happened, however, he took on one more client, a teenager charged with sexually assaulting his sister. In the days Benson spent preparing for trial he got to know William Jasper Collins well, and for some reason grew attached to the young man. After he obtained an acquittal, Benson became Collins's benefactor and employer. So it was that when the lawyer filed a homestead claim near the tiny Alberta community of Cereal, he brought Collins with him. Over the next eight months Benson sold his land holdings in Braymer, and on April 4, 1913, he and Collins set off for western Canada. Three weeks later they finished building a barn and a small house, and Benson wrote home, asking his wife to meet him in Saskatoon.

Clara Benson left Missouri on May 3, and when she reached Saskatoon she checked into the King Edward Hotel. Almost immediately she was handed a pair of telegrams, informing her of the death of John Benson. She promptly left for Kindersley, Saskatchewan, to collect the body of her husband. There she saw Collins in a hotel hallway. She rushed to him. "Oh, Jasper, tell me how it all happened."[1] And he did. Not for one moment did it occur to her that he was lying.

Collins told her that he was about a mile from the house watering horses when he heard a loud sound, like a shot. He finished with the animals, and then headed back. He arrived to find the shack on fire, and promptly rushed to the nearest neighbour. By the time he got back to the small dwelling, it was completely destroyed. In the ruins he found what was left of Benson. It was his opinion, said Collins, that Benson must have tried to put gasoline in the oil stove, and thereby caused the explosion.[2]

When she met Collins at Kindersley, Benson asked him if any money was found in the ruins of the burned shack. She thought it a little strange when he told her there was none, since her husband wore a money belt, and when he left Braymer it contained somewhere between $3,500 and $4,000. Thinking perhaps John might have deposited his savings in a bank, she asked Collins if he ever saw her husband put anything under his pillow at night — perhaps a bank book? He said he did not notice anything because Benson always slept with a coat over his head.

After she met Collins, Clara Benson and the young man quickly left for Cereal, where she made inquiries into the circumstances surrounding the fire and death. She was told that both the police and the local coroner were notified in the aftermath of her husband's death, and a wire was sent to Braymer, advising friends of the dead lawyer what happened. Because there was no reason to think anything was amiss, no inquest was held. The widow discovered nothing to make her suspect that what everyone was calling an accident was really a murder, so she and Collins headed back to Saskatoon. There she purchased a ticket home for herself and the body of her husband. When Collins told her he did not have enough money to buy one for himself, she bought his as well. As soon as she arrived home Benson made arrangements to have her husband buried, and did what she could to settle into the life of a single parent. It was not long, however, before she began hearing rumours that Collins was spending a lot of money.

Although he was jobless and professed to have no money, Collins started making a number of unusually large purchases. To hide what he was doing, he made them in towns around Braymer, but he brought what he bought back on the train, and in no time what he tried to keep secret was common knowledge. When Clara heard the talk she contacted the Masons. Her husband had been a member of the local order, and his friends in the organization were alarmed enough at what they were told that they hired a Pinkerton detective to investigate. When they received his report, the Masons arranged to have Benson's body exhumed. There was not a lot of it left. The registrar of deaths for Caldwell County, Missouri conducted the post mortem. He found that one of the dead man's hands and one foot were completely gone, there was some but not much flesh left on his chest, and a large piece of his skull was missing. There was also evidence of a blood clot at the base of the brain and a hole through his heart. He concluded that the cause of death was a blow to the head with a blunt instrument, and that the heart was struck by a bullet fired after the victim was dead.

With the autopsy report in hand the Masons contacted the Braymer police. They took Collins into custody and searched his room. There they found a money belt containing $1,800 in twenty dollar bills, a fortune for a young man with no income. Arrangements were made to place Collins in a cell in the nearest jail, just down the road in Kingston. Before Collins and his minders got there Collins told them he was prepared to make a deal: if he was taken back to Braymer, he would tell them everything. So they turned around, and within the hour Collins confessed to murder.

> My name is William Jasper Collins and I live in Braymer, MO. I left the latter town with John Benson for the Canadian territory to take up a claim with him. Within a week after the completion of the house on the claim

of John Benson, while in the house I struck him on the
left side of the head with my fist, which knocked him
down, and he then pulled a razor and I then drew a gun
of .33-calibre and shot him. I then threw the gun away.
After he had been dead an hour I poured oil about the
house and set it afire. I took his money, which was under
his pillow. There is some of the money in the lot taken by
Constable Burnett that belongs to me which Benson paid
me, but I owed him my expenses to Canada and while
there. This sum is in the amount of about $200. This state-
ment is made of my own free will and accord and without
consideration of promises of any nature.[3]

Once the confession was signed, Collins and his entourage were at once
back on the highway to Kingston, and a few days later, to Calgary, Alberta.
His trial got underway at a special sitting of the province's superior court on
November 27, 1913. Calgarians lined up hours before court opened, hoping
to get a seat in the tiny courtroom. Despite the cool, late fall weather, the
court was "crowded to suffocation."[4] That was especially so when Collins
was sentenced. Although he sat through much of his trial with his head
down, arm hanging over a railing of the prisoner's box, apparently little
interested in what was going on, the accused killer paid rapt attention when
the jury returned with its verdict. After the panel's foreman announced that
Collins was guilty of murdering John Benson, Collins seemed shocked. In
fact, everyone in the courtroom sat in silence. The only outward sign that
Collins understood the significance of what he just heard was a change in
his complexion — his face turned white, and he began licking his lips.

The trial judge was Horace Harvey, a Quaker from Ontario who three
years earlier was appointed chief justice of Alberta. As soon as he heard
the verdict he picked up his pen, and made ready to pass sentence. He
told the jurors that he agreed with their decision, and asked Collins if he
had anything to say before sentence was passed. The youthful murderer
said nothing. Taking his silence as licence to proceed, the judge imposed
the only sentence he could — death. Collins was to be taken back to the
barracks of the Royal North West Mounted Police, and there he was to be
hanged on February 17, 1914.

No one is sure what Collins was thinking, but shortly after he started his two-and-a-half month wait to die he decided not to eat. His jailors grew increasingly anxious, and the *Calgary Herald* equated his conduct to that of early twentieth-century feminists. In refusing to take nourishment, it said, the condemned man was following the example of "militant suffragettes."[5] By January 18, 1914, the condemned prisoner was near death, and jail officials decided to force feed him. That was easier said than done. It took three large guards to subdue the prisoner while a special feeding tube was forced down his throat, and even then there was no guarantee he would gain enough strength to be put to death. Making matters worse, health wise, was that as his execution drew nearer, Collins became more and more nervous, and slept little.

His mood no doubt darkened even more when carpenters began building his scaffold. The sound of hammering and the chatter of workmen could easily be heard in his cell, and even more noise was created by the crowds attracted to the jail when the top of the gallows rose above the fence surrounding the barracks. The throng milling about grew much larger the morning of the execution. Although Collins said he was prepared to die, until the very end he firmly believed his sentence would be commuted.

Because the condemned man was so weak, arrangements were made to carry him to the scaffold. When the hangman arrived at his cell shortly before 8:00 a.m., however, that was not necessary. Although in obvious physical distress, Collins walked unaided, and ascended the steps of the gallows on his own. But the journey took all the energy the twenty-two-year-old

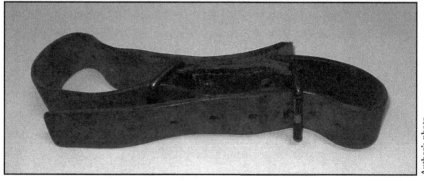

Author's photo.

This photo is of a leather strap used to bind the ankles of a condemned prisoner. It took an executioner about two seconds to complete that process. On the only occasion when a prisoner refused to be bound, the executioner used the strap to beat the prisoner into submission.

possessed, and as soon as he reached the top of the scaffold he walked to an armchair already positioned on the trap, and sat. From the moment he was tied to it things went downhill. Collins was hooded and noosed while sitting, and dropped in that position. If events had been left to take their inevitable course, there might have been a different outcome. But the hangman was anxious, and five minutes after Collins was hanged, he cut the prisoner down; the problem was, the unfortunate man was not yet dead. With an unconscious, but obviously living prisoner lying at their feet, officials debated what to do next. If precedent were a guide, the comatose killer should have been carried back up the scaffold, noosed, held over the open space where the trap doors were once closed, and dropped by guards. The debate raged for nearly twenty minutes before fate intervened and Collins died.

Members of the coroner's jury empanelled to confirm that the sentence of the court was carried out were required to witness the execution, and to a man were indignant. Their report makes evident the revulsion they felt.

> We find that Jasper Collins died in Calgary on February 17, at the barracks of the R.N.W.M.P., as a result of partial dislocation of the neck and suffocation caused by being hanged by the neck following the sentence of death passed upon the said Jasper Collins in the Supreme Court of Alberta.
>
> We further desire to add that in our opinion the sentence of the court was not carried out, owing to the fact that the said Jasper Collins was not hanged by the neck until dead, but was, contrary to the sentence of the court, cut down by the executioner before life was extinct.
>
> We further desire to express our dissatisfaction with the manner in which the execution was carried out by the hangman, and we feel that in the interests of justice, and of the public weal there should be an investigation in order that future executions should be carried out properly.
>
> We further desire to add that we do not in any way censure any other officials.[6]

Canada has had only one official executioner, but between 1912 and 1934 Arthur Ellis was considered by federal and provincial governments, and the general public, to be the country's preeminent hangman. But putting people to death was a competitive business, and Ellis did not always get the work. He was, however, a relentless self-promoter, and determined to keep his name front and centre. Although the federal government has sole responsibility for the administration of criminal law and the commutation of death penalties, the sheriff of the judicial district in which someone was to be hanged was the person who hired and paid the executioner who carried out a death sentence. When Ellis heard that Collins was to be executed, he wrote Calgary's sheriff and offered his services. He was not pleased with the response: "Received yours of February 2. Will not require you, as I have engaged a local man to look after the execution." Ellis may not have been happy that he was denied the Collins contract, but he was downright alarmed when news reports of the botched hanging contained no reference to the name of the man who carried out the execution. A week after the hanging he contacted the press in Toronto, to set the record straight.

> As a man very much in the public eye, I feel that people should know that I was not concerned in the execution at Calgary. I am well known all over Canada and it would hurt my reputation if it were thought that I was responsible. I understand that a man named Holmes, living in Calgary, was hired for the execution. He was a mere novice and I took the matter up with the attorney-general of Alberta before it took place. He would not interfere.[7]

If young William Jasper Collins had only kept his ill-gotten gains hidden from his Braymer neighbours for a few months, he almost certainly would have gotten away with murder.

Marie Beaulne and Philibert Lefebvre:
Poison Does the Trick

Philibert Lefebvre and Zephyr Viau had a lot in common. The men were friends, each cut wood and trapped for a living near Montpellier, in the southwest corner of the province of Quebec. In addition, both were illiterate, not gifted intellectually, and in love with the same woman. The principal difference between them was that in 1929 the sixty-two-year-old Viau was married to Marie Beaulne, the mother of his eight children, and Philibert was not.

For most of his adult life Viau left his family every year to go into the woods, where for several months he lived in a tiny shanty, chopping wood and trapping whatever animals he could find. In late 1928 he left behind not only his wife and kids, but his friend Lefebvre as well. Romance was long gone from the Viau marriage, although until his last trip into the woods there was no suggestion that loyalty had disappeared as well. That changed for some reason, and by the time Zephyr returned, his wife and his friend were in love. Beaulne gave considerable thought to what she was going to do when her husband came home. Leaving her children was not an option and divorce in a staunchly Roman Catholic settlement like the one she lived in was out of the question; in the end she concluded that murder was the only solution. In early twentieth-century Canada, when wives murdered their spouses, they usually resorted to poison, and so it was in this case.

The first time Beaule put strychnine in her husband's soup the poison made him sick, but it certainly did not kill him. Beaulne decided to increase the dosage, and on January 22, 1929, she got it right. When the woodcutter died suddenly his neighbours were a little suspicious. Almost everyone suspected his forty-two-year-old widow was carrying on with his thirty-two-year-old friend behind Viau's back, but that alone was not enough to suggest a murder was committed. The sense that something was not right grew, however, when Marie insisted on burying her husband right away, without waiting for the traditional period of mourning to end. Even with that, Beaulne and Lefebvre would likely have gotten away with murder had not the Reverend Lucien Polydore Major been their parish priest. Major once saw a man die from strychnine poisoning, and what Viau went through triggered a memory. He decided to contact the provincial police. When officers arrived on the scene, just about everyone they talked to told them about Beaulne and Lefebvre, and suggested that the widow's late husband did not die a natural death.

Two weeks after Viau's funeral the body of the woodcutter was exhumed and an autopsy performed to determine what caused his death. It did not take long to learn what happened — in the dead man's stomach the medical examiner found enough strychnine to kill half a dozen people. Beaulne and Lefebvre were promptly taken into custody and charged with murder. Six months after Viau died in excruciating pain, the murder trial of his killers got underway. Neither denied they committed the crime, and after initially blaming each other, accepted responsibility for what they did. Although Beaulne administered the poison that killed her husband, the judge presiding over his trial blamed Lefebvre for the crime. It was he and he alone who provided both the motive and the means to carry out the murder. Worse, Zephyr Viau was given only two or three days between being poisoned and dying, hardly sufficient time to make peace with God. Lefebvre, said the visibly upset jurist, would have two months. And with that the judge told the lovers that they were to be hanged on August 23, 1929.

It soon became apparent to Beaulne's lawyers that although the widow had neighbours, no one was her friend. After their client was sentenced to hang, the two young barristers who defended her started to circulate a petition for clemency. Over the next few weeks not a single person signed it. The lawyers persevered, however, perhaps because they saw in her case the chance to be thought of as something other than the youngest and most inexperienced members of the Hull bar. It is not known why they did not appeal their client's verdict, but what they lacked in experience, they made up for in enthusiasm. Because both Beaulne and Lefebvre confessed to poisoning Viau, there was no point in arguing law when they filed their petition for clemency. Instead, they advanced seventeen social and moral reasons for commuting the death sentences. For one thing, the killers were raised in a community where moral and religious training were almost unheard of, a claim that likely did not go over well with the Reverend Father Major. Their ignorance, it was argued, made it impossible for them to appreciate the enormity of what they had done. The lawyers also suggested that when the trial judge asked if there was any reason why sentence should not be imposed on them, neither Beaulne nor Philibert were intellectually aware of what his words meant, or of the consequence of the sentence imposed.

As a kind of backup plan, the lawyers continued in their efforts to persuade members of the condemned couple's parish to sign a petition in support of clemency. After several attempts, they finally had some success. In the weeks immediately preceding the scheduled execution they obtained five hundred signatures, including those of the priest whose suspicions resulted in the apprehension of Beaulne and Lefebvre, the father of the murdered man, and the father of the victim's wife. Three days before the murderers' date with the hangman the federal cabinet rejected their application for clemency. That same day carpenters began constructing the scaffold on which the two condemned prisoners were to die.

After their verdict was announced, the couple was transported to Montreal. They were held there until the day before their execution, when they were transferred back to Hull. Beaulne spent her time in the Fullum Street Prison for Women. When Lefebvre saw his cell in the infamous Bordeaux Jail, the First World War veteran broke down in tears. Over the next two months, he seemed to have banished from his mind the possibility he might be executed. On August 22, however, he finally realized that the possibility was about to become a reality, and was unable to keep his emotions in check. One thing he was sure about, though: he wanted no part of a last minute visit with Beaulne.

Reporters were denied access to the execution, but one newsman was able to sneak past guards and into the jail proper. He was discovered just before midnight, when the executions were originally scheduled to be carried out, and escorted from the prison. Just about the time he was ejected, Arthur Ellis, the country's unofficial chief executioner, was advised by provincial officials that the executions were to be postponed until dawn the next morning. When the day broke, it was pouring in rain, and the sky was full of lightning, making an execution dangerous even for those who were not going to be hanged. The sheriff decided to put things off until 8:00 a.m.

Neither prisoner knew the order in which they were to be put to death, but officials decided shortly after the couple were sentenced that the honour should go to the tall, lanky woodcutter. Just before Ellis arrived at his cell, Lefebvre composed himself long enough to write a letter to his father, in which he begged forgiveness for the disgrace and heartbreak he brought to his family. But even Lefebvre's spiritual adviser could do little to calm the condemned man, and after his arms were pinioned behind his back, guards had to carry the prostrate poisoner from his cell to the prison yard. Ellis was distraught and fidgety all morning, and with all this carrying-on he had to make a visible effort to calm himself. By the time Lefebvre reached the huge, red scaffold, however, everything was under control. At exactly the appointed hour, the trap doors were released. To ensure that no one outside the jail, or prisoners inside, could catch a glimpse of what was going on, black curtains surrounded the platform on which Ellis and his victim stood, and boards covered the space between the platform and the pit into which the bodies were to drop.

A quarter of an hour later Beaulne began her walk to the gallows, straining for a glimpse of her lover. She was much more composed than Lefebvre had been, and required neither spiritual nor physical assistance from anyone. In the hours preceding her execution she wrote a letter to each of her eight children, and to her mother and assorted other relatives. The effort seemed to calm her, and when her death walk began she showed no emotion, and seemed oblivious to the noise made by the hundreds of people who milled around in front of the jail, awaiting news of the executions.

Although the body of Philibert was claimed by his father an hour after it was removed from the gallows, no one wanted the corpse of Beaulne. That was something not anticipated by the provincial government, as it had made no arrangements for her burial. The longer the woman's body lay in the Hull jail, the more anxious prison officials became, and it was hours before they received word that she was to be buried in an unmarked pauper's grave in Hull's Notre Dame cemetery. The only official told to attend was the sheriff.

Newspapers across Canada reported the double execution, but made little other comment. That was not the case with a paper in Salt Lake City, Utah. The attitude of its editor likely reflected the beliefs of the paper's Mormon readers, but the article seemed a little inappropriate in light of the key role Beaulne played in the murder of her husband:

Both deserved death, except that a woman in "the dangerous age" is often not responsible. But the eight children must live as "the children of a woman hanged for murder." These children had committed no crime. Why not hang the trapper and let the woman work to support her children the rest of her life?[8]

Marie Louise Cloutier and Achille Grondin: Married Too Soon

The story of Marie and Achille started eighteen years after Marie married Vilmond Brochu. The short, stout bride was very much the intellectual superior of her husband, but outwardly appeared content to labour alongside him on their small farm near Ste. Methode, Quebec, south of the St. Lawrence River. By 1934 the couple had achieved a semblance of financial security, and Brochu decided to purchase a taxi. For the next two years he divided his time between farming, peddling the meat he butchered, and driving his cab. Brochu was away a lot, and most of the work done on the farm now became Cloutier's responsibility. She began to feel a little hard done by. So much so that she gave her husband an ultimatum — help out more, or she was leaving. The compromise they worked out was that Brochu would hire someone to help her on the farm. That is when Achille Grondin entered the picture. Within a few months of starting work he and his boss's wife began an affair, although it was never anything exclusive. Marie was a fiercely independent woman, and made little effort to hide her relationship with other men.

One of those others was Adolphe Gilbert, who farmed near the Brochu's. He and Grondin got along well, and through sharing the affections of the same woman, actually became friends. Neither was sophisticated in the ways of the world, and each allowed himself to be manipulated by Cloutier. Their solution when Cloutier spoke to them about getting rid of her husband was to send away for a book of spells and incantations. Using it, they put a hex on Brochu. In the firm belief it would work, the men met to discuss which of them would become the widow-to-be's next husband. Grondin won the honour by default. When it came down to the crunch, Gilbert decided he had too many children from his first marriage to take on any more responsibilities. The problem for Grondin and Cloutier, however, was that the spells did not work, and Brochu continued to drive his cab around southern Quebec, sewing his own wild oats.

By late 1936 Brochu was tired of Grondin's continued presence around Cloutier, and fired him. Not only that, he hired a lawyer to sue his former hired man for alienating the affection of his wife, a lawsuit he felt was worth $500. As soon as Grondin left the farm, so too did Cloutier. She spent about a month at the home of a friend who lived in a town east and a little south of Ste. Methode. From there she kept in touch with her lover, and between the lines of the letters the couple wrote they began planning a future without Brochu. The problem was that Grondin could neither read nor write. As a consequence, he asked a friend to compose his letters, and to tell him what Cloutier wrote in hers. The letter writing became common knowledge in the small community, principally because the postmistress could hardly avoid noticing who was writing whom.

Brochu made a number of trips to Magog, where his wayward wife was staying. Over and over he pleaded with her to return, and he even enlisted the support of the couple's parish priest. Cloutier eventually

Marie Cloutier may not have looked like a femme fatale, but she certainly had considerable influence over several of the men residing in her rural Quebec village. She spent the afternoon before her marriage in the bed of her accomplice's friend. Unlike her new husband, she needed no help walking to the scaffold on which she was put to death.

Courtesy of Library and Archives Canada.

agreed to come back, on three conditions: her husband was to discontinue his law suit against Grondin; they were to live in the village; and Brochu was not to complain about her ongoing relationship with their hired man. Brochu agreed to everything, and in the waning months of 1936 the pair was reunited. That was not a good thing for Brochu. Cloutier wanted to be close to her husband for one reason — to do him in.

It is difficult to know if Cloutier really loved Grondin, keeping in mind her hectic social schedule. He was certainly no catch. Barely intelligent enough to function on his own, he had little sense of the ways of the world. That made it easy for Cloutier to talk him into using something more than a curse to do away with her husband. The method she chose was poison, perhaps because arsenic was something she knew a little about, having used it to grow her vegetables. Cloutier did not want to be seen buying the poison herself, since that would make everyone suspicious if her husband were to die suddenly, so she opted for subtlety — she had her lover purchase it. Subtlety, however, was not part of Grondin's character. When he was told to get a little arsenic, he bought a kilogram of it.

Cloutier began poisoning her husband sometime in November 1936, but it was not until New Year's Day that Brochu first complained of stomach pain. He recovered though, and for the next six months showed no ill effects. That changed on June 21, when his discomfort became so acute that his wife was forced to drive him to a hospital. The diagnosis was indigestion. A month later Brochu ended up in a different hospital, and this time he was kept five days for observation. Denied the poison his wife had been sprinkling on his food, he recovered his health, and was released back into Cloutier's care. It was at this point that the conspirators tired of Brochu's unwillingness to die. Cloutier upped his dosage, and to be on the safe side, Grondin and Gilbert put another curse on their rival. The double-barrelled approach worked, and on August 16, 1937, Brochu became ill for the last time. When a friend dropped by to see how he was feeling, the man suggested that since Brochu would not be farming any time soon, he might consider selling him some uncut hay. Brochu refused; he was going to give it away. Cloutier heard the conversation, and told the friend to come back in two or three days. By then, she said, her husband would be dead, and she would sell him the hay. She was right. Three days later Brochu died.[9]

At this juncture Cloutier and Grondin may have gotten away with murder had they been a little more patient and a lot less greedy. The day after her husband died, Cloutier applied for the proceeds of his life insurance policy. No one said anything, but neighbours thought she was moving a little too quickly. Two or three days later Grondin moved in with the widow. After this the dead man's friends and family grew suspicious about the haste. The community's sense of discomfort gave way to something more than nagging suspicion when villagers learned that less than a week after Brochu's funeral Cloutier and her lover asked their parish priest for permission to marry. Rather than refuse it, he merely put them off, and when they came back a few weeks later, he gave in. Before the ceremony Gilbert showed up at the couple's home, ostensibly to pick up something he bought at an auction. His real purpose was to spend a last afternoon in the bed of the bride-to-be. Neighbours likely noticed his visit, but no one said anything; Cloutier was now Grondin's problem. Less than two months after helping murder the man he once worked for, Grondin had his house, his property, and his wife. That was too much for Brochu's sister.

While her former sister-in-law and her new husband were honeymooning, she took the train to Montreal and spoke to the chief of the Quebec Provincial Police. After she filled him in on all that had transpired over the past several months, he too became suspicious, and he decided to have his force dig into things, including the grave so recently occupied by Vilmond Brochu. Within days his body was exhumed, and a provincial pathologist provided the police with his report: Brochu did not die of indigestion, as his attending physician indicated on the dead man's death certificate.

The wheels of justice in the province of Quebec may sometimes grind slowly, but they move inexorably forward. Cloutier and Grondin were taken into custody pending the results of a coroner's inquest, and on November 29, 1937, it concluded that they were almost certainly responsible for the death of Brochu. Six days later a magistrate agreed, and he bound the couple over for trial. Cloutier went first. From the day her trial began in September 1938, Quebeckers read daily accounts with more than a little morbid interest. The star of the show looked very much like a grieving widow, although by this time she had remarried. Dressed completely in black and wearing a silver crucifix, she was the person everyone

wanted to see. That included prisoners in the jail attached to the courthouse, who spent hours each day peering through the bars of their cells,
trying to catch a glimpse of the accused killer.

The testimony of one of the first witnesses called by the Crown set the
stage for what was to come. The young man was an assistant undertaker,
and he told the court that Cloutier was his mother's friend. While visiting
one day she asked him to explain how the embalming process worked.
He did not think anything about it until Cloutier told his mother about
a recent visit she had with a fortune teller. His mother said that when the
fortune teller informed Cloutier that she would soon be in mourning,
Cloutier replied, "Instead of wearing black I'll put on my red dress."[10]
Only later did the mother and son start wondering why Cloutier was so
preoccupied with death.

It turned out that the accused was also a little obsessed with putting on a red dress. A friend of the prisoner told the court that when
Cloutier was leaving the cemetery following her husband's interment she
was approached by Brochu's sister. Her former sister-in-law told Cloutier
that Brochu was better off in the ground than with her. The widow shot
back: "with people like you about, it's better to wear red for mourning
than black." Asked at her trial if the comment reflected her sentiment
towards her husband, Cloutier thought it might have, since by the time
her husband died she had no feelings for him whatsoever. The prosecutor
wondered whether the witness thought it a bit strange that she used the
same expression twice, both times in the context of the death of her first
husband. Cloutier said she did not think so. "When I used it first I had
been joking. The other times I was angry. They said I hadn't taken good
care of Villemond."[11]

Other statements the barely grieving widow made both before and
after her first husband's funeral came back to haunt her. The Crown
Attorney focussed particularly on what Cloutier had to say when she
heard that the police were thinking about digging up the body of Brochu.
She told friends that if they found poison, they would not find very much.
The prosecutor asked why she mentioned poison before the police even
knew of its presence. "Did you know before the coroner's inquest into
Brochu's death that he had been poisoned?" Her response did not satisfy
the lawyer: "I only knew what the doctors had said that he was poisoned

by his liver and his kidneys." But, he wondered, "how did you know before the inquest then that there was poison in his body — you told Mrs. Joseph Carrier before the inquest and the result of the autopsy was known that "They may find some but they have to see it given." Different versions of the same question were asked over and over, but Cloutier refused to back down. The clearly exasperated prosecutor asked Cloutier to explain why, after her husband's body was exhumed, she told detectives if they found anything in his body they could not have found much. She denied everything. "I didn't say that. I showed them a mortuary card made after my husband died and asked them if the body they dug up looked anything like the picture on the card and they said it didn't."[12]

A subject of considerable interest to all of the participants in Cloutier's trial was Brochu's extended illness. The first doctor to treat the former cab driver said Brochu arrived at his office on July 16, 1937, complaining of a severe burning sensation in his stomach. The doctor testified that Brochu told him he had not eaten any bad food, nor had he been drinking. After examining the patient, the physician admitted that he "wasn't able to determine the cause of his sickness. I decided his illness was inflammation of the stomach and not indigestion as I had first believed. It seemed as though he might have suffered some kind of poisoning through his food."[13] After Brochu left, the doctor said he continued to think about his patient's condition and decided to stop by the Brochu residence to see how the cabbie was feeling. "I didn't stay long at the home because Mrs. Brochu did not receive me very well."[14]

The next medical practitioner to treat the murder victim was a doctor working at the hospital in Thetford Mines. He testified that Cloutier showed up with her husband on July 21. "Brochu was having considerable pain from his stomach. I was unable to find out what was the cause of his trouble and apparently he did not know himself. His illness might have been caused, I thought first, by contaminated water, improperly cooked food or even green vegetables." But, he said, after five days of rest Brochu left, "apparently cured."[15]

Last to treat Brochu was a physician who examined him several times in the days before the patient died. He was convinced Brochu was suffering from some kind of indigestion. "I treated him with ordinary indigestion and the medicine I prescribed for him did not help. In most cases of that

kind, which were common in the district at that time, it would have."[16]
When asked about the circumstances surrounding the making of Brochu's
death certificate, the practitioner said his patient's widow told him that she
needed a death certificate before she could collect on her husband's life
insurance, so he made one out, listing indigestion as the cause of death.
What he did not know was that Cloutier made the same request to two
other doctors. They both refused to provide her with the certificate.

The pathologist who examined Brochu's body following its exhumation felt very strongly that the dead man was not well served by his doctors.
He told the court that after someone consumes arsenic they feel:

> violent pains and burning in the stomach, and vomiting
> follows. The hands and feet swell, the face becomes swollen
> and the eyes are affected. Later the victim feels pain in his
> limbs, which finally become paralyzed. There are eruptions
> on the skin. The victim becomes weaker. The pulse slows
> up, and then death comes.[17]

The pathologist, who sat through the trial making notes, said every symptom he heard described was a symptom associated with arsenic poisoning.

During his address to the jury Cloutier's lawyer dismissed the testimony
about witchcraft as "ridiculous and foolish talk," and then bore down on the
crux of the Crown's case — the evidence that Brochu had been poisoned.
That allegation was simply not something an honest and intelligent person
could accept as true.

> Did Brochu die poisoned? Was it proved he was poisoned?
> Was poison really found? Medicine says yes. But med-
> icine isn't a certain science — it's a theoretical science.
> Was medicine right before Pasteur? Doctors before him
> were sure of their ground just as we are sure of ours today.
> They were wrong though. Doctors giving testimony in
> courts before Pasteur came didn't perjure themselves
> when they said what they thought was truth. They didn't
> perjure themselves but they were still wrong. Dr. Roussel
> insisted the arsenic had been administered to Brochu in

more than one dose. But three other doctors who had treated Brochu during his last illness in the summer of 1937 said his sickness was acute indigestion. Now all four doctors were trained in medicine. They should know what they are talking about. But they don't agree. Brochu was a drinker and evidence during his trial was that liquor often made him sick. Three doctors who treated him said he was poisoning himself through his liver and kidneys. Perhaps he died a natural death. There was no evidence to show Mrs. Grondin ever had arsenic in her hands except for her gardening.[18]

The defence lawyer concluded with his strongest argument. He caught the Crown's medical expert in what he referred to as a monumental "error of analysis." Holding up the container seized from Grondin's home, he reminded jurors that the expert said it contained arsenic. But that was not true. It was not a mixture of paris green and carbonate of lime, as the Crown's witness alleged. The supposed poison was nothing more than ordinary wood ashes. "If the doctor made a simple mistake like that, maybe he was wrong when he said there was arsenic in Brochu's body."[19] The lawyer may have been right, but the jury was not buying his argument. After sitting for a month and hearing testimony from more than one hundred witnesses, it took jurors one hour and fifteen minutes to find Cloutier guilty of murder. Perhaps they came to their decision so quickly because it was divinely inspired. When the jury was told it was to begin its deliberations, the foreman asked the judge for a "special favour." Could they walk a few steps down the street to St. Joseph's old Roman Catholic Church and pray for a bit. That is what they did. After spending twenty minutes on their knees, the jurors rose and returned to the courthouse. Ninety minutes later Cloutier was sentenced to hang.[20]

The trial of his wife ended on October 8, 1938, and Grondin's got underway before the same judge a month later. His hearing lasted almost as long as that of his co-accused, and much of the evidence was the same. One thing that became clear at the very beginning of the trial was that from the day he became Brochu's hired man, Grondin was seldom apart from his lover. The murder victim's fourteen-year-old niece and her brother lived with the Brochus the summer her uncle died. She testified that every day just after lunch Grondin showed up, and as soon as he did the siblings were banished to the second floor of the tiny home. "She [Cloutier] told us she would beat us if we did not leave." Once they got to the second floor, she said, her aunt lowered a trapdoor at the top of the staircase. "We only came down again after Grondin had left."[21]

Although the trial continued for another three weeks, the result for Grondin was the same as it had been for his wife: guilty. His date with the hangman was set for the end of April 1939, by which time his wife should have been dead — except that was not the way things turned out. When Cloutier received permission to appeal her verdict, her death sentence was postponed. After the Quebec Court of Appeal denied her application for a new trial, her sentence was postponed a second time so that she could appeal to the Supreme Court of Canada. That court reserved judgment after hearing arguments, and by the time the various appeals of Grondin and Cloutier were dealt with, the couple spent almost a year and a half on death row.

In early February one last wrinkle had to be ironed out before they could be executed. According to law, condemned persons are to be hanged in the judicial district closest to where the crime was committed. In the case of Cloutier and Grondin, that meant their execution was to take place in the village of St. Joseph de Beauce. No one had ever been hanged there before, and its townspeople had no appetite for such a spectacle. By this time Cloutier did not care where she was put to death, she just wanted to get it over with. As usual, Grondin said nothing. When the provincial government was petitioned to change the location of the hanging, it agreed to do so: the couple was to hang in the courtyard of Montreal's Bordeaux Jail.

Grondin went first. A little over sixteen minutes later his widow began her death walk. She was dropped at 7:10 a.m., and as her body was cut down a black flag was raised to half mast. The tolling bells of the city's Catholic Churches brought to an end the lives of two lovers who, with a little more patience, may have gotten away with murder.

6

The Two Rolands

Love, booze, and one too many suicides are the themes of the two stories in this chapter. Both are set in the province of Quebec. Sadly, four people died, three of whom were women. In the first tale a killer got away with murder until his lover was overcome by guilt and committed suicide. The police thought it unlikely that a man and wife would each take their own lives, and it was their reopened investigation that sent her lover to the gallows. The second story is all about brutality involving a woman who would do anything for her man. That included killing his wife.

Roland Asselin: Fifty-Five Weeks between Murders

Ulric Gauthier was a big man in St. Telesphore, a small Quebec town located just west of Montreal. The large garage-man was one of the community's most prosperous business persons, and drank with gusto. His stentorian voice, steeped in liquor, was often heard echoing down the town's main street. But he died quietly, or at least as quietly as someone who shot himself can die. After Gauthier's death was ruled a suicide, everyone seemed to forget about him — everyone, that is, except his widow. When she hanged herself three months after her husband died, the authorities thought it was one suicide too many, and reopened an investigation into the death of Ulric. That was bad news for Roland Asselin. One year and three weeks after he shot his lover's husband in the side of the head, he was called to account.

If Roland Asselin did not have a lot of close friends, he was at least well known. When not driving his cab he often stopped by local garages to kill time. Asselin was at the business operated by Joseph Babineau so often that no one noticed when he began wandering around the garage, opening drawers and poking about. In retrospect, as soon as it was discovered that a revolver was missing, Asselin should have been considered the likely thief. That was not the case, however, and although Babineau noticed the gun was gone sometime in mid-1946, he neither reported it missing nor made an issue of its disappearance. But Asselin knew where it was. In fact, the taxi man made little attempt to hide it. Perhaps that is why he had it in his jacket pocket on November 9, when he picked Gauthier up for a night of drinking.

No one saw where the men went, but the next morning it was all too apparent where Gauthier ended up. His body was discovered lying on a dirt road a few miles out of town by an area farmer. The man slowed as he passed the corpse, but did not stop until he encountered some friends. The group returned to the remains, and despite the shock of finding the body of a man everyone knew, they could not help think that something was not right with the scene. Babineau's missing revolver was lying on one side of Gauthier, and a bottle of beer on the other. Two things struck the men as odd: the fingers of the garage owner's left hand were hooked into one of the pockets of his vest, as if he died in the middle of a casual conversation. And the men thought it unlikely someone could shoot himself in the left side of his head with his right hand. It was also strange that although it had poured rain the night before, the soles of the shoes of the dead man were dry, and there were no tracks in the mud leading up to or away from the spot where Gauthier lay.

A few days later a coroner's inquest was held in a local restaurant. Jurors were undecided about how Gauthier died. Some believed Asselin when he testified that the evening before Gauthier's body was found the two were out drinking, and he dropped off his passenger near the spot where his body was found. Others were convinced the death was the result of some kind of accident, while a few felt Asselin was not telling the truth. As a result, the inquest was terminated, and a second one convened. This time jurors had no doubt — it was death by suicide. The police promptly closed their files, and life went back to normal.

On the occasions when someone in town spoke of Gauthier, it was likely to relate a story about his drinking. The mayor, for instance, recalled the time he dropped by Gauthier's house. As he walked up to the door, a bullet whizzed by his head. Gauthier quickly admitted to the shooting, but said he was not really trying to hit the mayor, just scare him a bit. The two men had a long relationship, albeit not a particularly pleasant one. The mayor frequently received complaints about Gauthier's rowdiness, and once, when things had gone too far, he ordered local hotels to stop serving the garage-man. But that did not stop Gauthier from drinking and acting rowdy. Typical was an anecdote told by the town secretary, who remembered Gauthier breaking three window panes trying to get into his house one morning at 3:00 a.m. Gauthier said he wanted to pay his property taxes.

If Gauthier's widow had been better able to cope with her husband's death, things would almost certainly not have ended as they did. Although Alice married Ulric in 1937, she was never really committed to making the marriage work. After Alice hanged herself, the police reopened their investigation into the death of Ulric, and most of the people they interviewed were asked the same question: "Did you ever hear that Gauthier's wife ran around with other men?" Almost everyone agreed that he had. The exception was the local veterinarian, who, when asked the question, replied, "No, I never heard she ran around with other men."[1] Well, then what did you hear? "I heard only that she had relations with other men." According to most of those who testified, Roland Asselin was one of those with whom she was most intimate.

These rumours could not be ignored, and for the next ten months Quebec Provincial Police officers looked for some concrete evidence that Asselin, or Asselin and Alice, murdered Ulric Gauthier. Persistence paid off. On December 29, 1947, a little over a year after Gauthier was killed, Asselin confessed, not to murdering the husband of his lover, but to accidently shooting him. According to Asselin, the two men drank beer at several bars just outside St. Telesphore. As they left the last one they got into a heated discussion over Gauthier's insistence that he drive Asselin's cab. The two argued, and Gauthier produced a revolver. They fought, and during the scuffle Asselin wrestled the gun away from Gauthier. He fired a single shot, to scare him, but the bullet struck Gauthier in the side of the head.

After Asselin gave his statement to the police he was taken into custody. A third coroner's inquest was quickly convened to look into the death of Ulric Gauthier. The hearing lasted just two hours, and it took juror's only fifteen minutes to find Asselin criminally responsible for Gauthier's death. A week later the cabbie was arraigned on a charge of murder. His trial got underway during the second week of June 1948, and after six days of testimony he was found guilty. The only real question was whether Gauthier's death was the result of manslaughter or murder. The presiding judge had little doubt about which it was, and shared his conviction with jurors. He told them that they should not believe that Gauthier was shot with his own gun, since it was unthinkable that someone as demonstrative as the dead man could possess a revolver and not wave it around in front of others. On the other hand, they could accept as fact that Asselin had a gun on the evening in question.

Jurors reached a verdict in a little over an hour. Once they made their decision known, court was adjourned for a few minutes to allow the presiding justice to prepare his sentencing remarks. Only one sentence was available to him. Although Asselin showed little emotion throughout his trial, as soon as he was returned to his cell to await the return of the judge, he collapsed. His guards quickly laid him on a bench, and summoned a doctor. After a lengthy delay, Mr. Justice Wilfrid Lazure formally postponed

The deaths cells where condemned prisoners were held were small, utilitarian, and totally lacking in privacy. Twenty-four hours a day a member of the death watch sat outside the cell, keeping a written record of everything the prisoner said or did. The windows shown in this photo were covered when a death cell was occupied so that a prisoner would not know how quickly, or slowly, time passed.

Author's photo.

sentencing until the following morning, when Asselin was informed he was to hang on October 1. But he was not executed then, nor on January 14, 1949, March 25, or March 31. Asselin's luck ran out when the Quebec Court of Appeal ruled there would be no more reprieves; the condemned man was to be executed on June 10. Just after midnight Asselin was hanged, and one half hour later he was declared dead.

Roland Genest:
He Never Murdered a Woman He Didn't Love

They made quite a pair. Both were young, vivacious, and seemed to get fulfillment out a relationship that seemed equal parts love and violence. She was only twenty-one when she met the good looking twenty-five-year-old. By the time she realized he was married, the woman was deeply in love. So much so that when he suggested she kill his wife, she did not hesitate. For almost two years the pair got away with murder, and then he tired of her constant nagging. That's when it all came to an end.

Rita Genest was the first to die. She was just twenty-three, but in the opinion of her husband, she was no fun. A few months before Rita was beaten to death Roland Genest was on his own when he noticed a young woman riding by on a bicycle. They began to talk, and before long were dating. She was already in love when Genest told her that they would have to stop seeing each other — he was a married man. At his trial Genest said he forgot who brought up the subject, but he distinctly remembered that his lover volunteered to murder Rita. That way, she said, Roland would have an alibi, and he would be single again. In a matter of a few hours they decided to do it. Genest bought an iron bar, gave his co-conspirator a key to his apartment, and told her to set fire to the room when Rita was dead; which is exactly what she did.

Rita Genest was murdered on May 21, 1951. The evening she died Rita and her husband went out to supper with her brother. After dropping her off at home, the men spent the rest of the evening drinking and gambling. About 11:00 p.m. neighbours noticed smoke coming from the Genest apartment and called the fire department. By the time fire fighters arrived, the bedroom was completely gutted. All that remained was a smouldering mattress and blood. Lots of it. Firefighters promptly called the police. About an hour after they arrived, Roland Genest drove up. When he was taken to police headquarters twenty minutes later his alibi paid off in spades. He was released after providing investigators with a satisfactory account of his whereabouts when the fire started.

A coroner's inquest was held on May 30, but soon adjourned to give investigators more time to gather evidence. Before it adjourned, however, jurors heard from the two provincial medico-legal experts assigned to the Genest case. They testified that Rita died from two skull fractures, inflicted by a blunt instrument with a narrow edge, and that she was dead when her bedroom was set on fire. Their conclusion was based on both the extent of her head injuries, and the fact there was no trace of carbon dioxide in her blood. The last anyone heard about the investigation was a brief report published a few days after the murder. According to the newspaper article, Montreal homicide detectives had absolutely no clue who murdered Rita. For the next twenty-one months her file lay untouched.

That changed on February 19, 1953, when the nude body of a woman was discovered lying in a farmer's field on Île Bizard, a small island now a suburb of greater Montreal. The woman was found about one hundred feet from a much travelled road, and had been badly beaten about the head. She had also been stabbed numerous times. A near total absence of blood at the scene suggested to investigators that the victim was murdered elsewhere, and her body transported to the field. As one detective noted, "There was hardly any blood around the body, which leads us to believe she was carried there in a blanket after being knifed and hammered to death."[2]

Although the body of the woman lay in their morgue, the police had no clue who she was. They ran her fingerprints through their own database and that of the Royal Canadian Mounted Police, but the searches produced no leads. They decided to publish a photo of the woman's face in local newspapers and invite Montrealers to visit the city morgue. Their appeal attracted an assortment of the morbidly curious, and those desperate to know whether the corpse was that of a missing loved one. For two days and nights hundreds of men, and a few women, slowly walked by the gurney on which the body lay. The detective leading the investigation made no apologies for what his team of investigators did. "Some of these people were just curious" he said. "But they claimed the victim's description fitted that of someone they knew. We can't take chances, because our only chance of learning who the woman is lies with somebody that knew her."[3] Ultimately, that somebody was her mother. Two hours after she and two sisters of the victim identified the missing woman as Marie Paule Langlais, the police took Roland Genest into custody as a material witness. Forty-eight hours later he confessed to the murder, although there is considerable doubt he did so voluntarily.

According to Genest, after the police picked him up on a Montreal street they took him to a police station, where he was put in a cell. The next morning officers read him his rights, and began questioning him about what he knew of the murder of Langlais. All he admitted was that he saw her the day before her body was found, and that the two had a disagreement. Langlais accused him of flirting with another woman. And that was that, at least according to the detectives who interviewed Genest. They said that when they returned to his cell the following day, they again read him his rights, but this time he wanted to get something off his chest, and he began talking. By the time they were done Genest confessed not only to killing Langlais, but to taking part in the murder of his wife as well. At least that was the official version of events. Genest saw it differently.

He said after he was picked up one of the investigating officers came into his cell alone. The detective took off his rings and watch, rolled up his sleeves, and began hitting him. For fifteen minutes the officer punched him in the face and body, and he smashed Genest's head on a table. By the time the policeman tired, Genest said he was ready to confess. The detective then stopped hitting him, took out a statement already written on a piece of paper, and had Genest sign it.

At his trial the lawyer prosecuting the case could not see what the problem was. He asked the accused killer if he had indeed "told the police you hit Marie Paule over the head with a baseball bat? Do you admit that this is true." Genest said yes, he said that. "Do you admit that you told them you hid the body on Île Bizard. Do you admit this is true?" Again the answer was yes. "Do you admit you told them where her clothes were? Do you admit this is true?" Another yes. Then Justice Wilfrid Lazure (the same judge who sentenced Roland Asselin to death) interrupted. Lazure wanted to know why Genest would tell the police these things if they were not true. Because, the accused said, he was told the beating was going to continue until he confessed. He did not even read the statement he signed.[4]

Before his murder trial got underway, however, the inquest adjourned after the body of Langlais was discovered was reconvened. Sitting in the crowded coroner's court were the mother, five sisters, and four brothers of the dead woman. The statement Genest made to the police was not admitted into evidence, but the court heard testimony from a number of the officers who investigated the murder. They said as a result of information given them by Genest, they recovered several items connected with the killing, including the partially burned clothes of the dead woman, found just outside a Montreal area village, a bloodstained knife recovered from the third story roof of an east end apartment building, and engagement and wedding rings were found in a private residence. Also recovered was the baseball bat used to beat Marie, and the bloodstained tarpaulin on which Genest placed Langlais when he transported her body to the spot where it was discovered.

After hearing the evidence the coroner's jury deliberated six minutes before finding Genest criminally responsible for causing the death of Marie Paule Langlais. Moments later the short, dapper accused killer was formally charged with murdering his girlfriend. Everything that followed the confession was a mere formality, and when Genest's trial got underway on May 19, 1953, his guilt was never in question. The only issue was whether he should be convicted of murder or the lesser charge of manslaughter. The first offence involves an element of premeditation and planning, while the second consists of a killing carried out in the heat of passion.

Genest was the first witness to testify. He said he picked up his girlfriend when she got off work at the Saint-Jean-de-Dieu hospital, and the two drove to a garage he rented, where they washed his car. They began to argue over medicine he kept in a trunk.

> The argument got hotter and she called me names. I called her names, and I told her she was crazy. She went to hit me with a baseball bat. I grabbed the bat and began to hit her on the head with it. I don't know why — but I reached for a knife and began to stab her. I don't know how many times I did. I must have gone beserk.[5]

As soon as he stopped beating her he began to realize what he had done. "I got frightened and nervous. I wanted to escape … I took off her clothes and put them in a bag. There was lots of blood and I cleaned up the garage. I left there about six o'clock and I wanted to take the road to Toronto. I was driving around the north end of the island when I came to a wood. The place looked lonely and there were no homes there. I carried the body into the woods and left it there."

Genest said he was barely home when he remembered that his girlfriend wore a ring. He promptly returned to her body, and removed it. "The next day I took her clothes and burned them with gasoline."[6]

Genest's lawyer used his client's confession to try and persuade jurors that the murder of Langlais was not premeditated. It happened, he suggested, only because the victim goaded her killer into hitting her.[7] The prosecutor saw things differently, and suggested to the jury that it should look at what Genest did after the murder for evidence of what was in his mind when he killed Langlais.

> The accused committed the crime knowingly and voluntarily. He did everything humanly possible to hide his crime. He brought the body to a lonely place on Île Bizard. He burned her clothes and he scattered the tarpaulin he carried the body in, the baseball bat and the knife at places miles apart.[8]

This man, he suggested, was not a fool. He was a cold-blooded murderer.

The jury had no difficulty agreeing, and despite a lack of evidence proving that Genest planned the killing, it deliberated only fifteen minutes before it convicted him of murder. Without doubt jurors were significantly influenced by the fact the accused killer had already gotten away with one murder. They were not prepared to see him get away with another. Justice Lazure also had no sympathy for Genest. After adjourning court briefly while he made himself ready to sentence the convicted murderer, Lazure re-entered wearing the traditional three-cornered hat and black gloves. He got right to the point. "It is never easy for me to pronounce the death sentence on an accused." But, he said, "You have only yourself to blame for this predicament."[9]

Three months later Genest paid the price for his crime. The condemned killer was led from his cell in Montreal's Bordeaux Jail shortly before 1:00 a.m. on Friday, August 28, 1953. Five minutes later his arms and legs were pinioned and a cloth hood was slipped over his head. After a noose was tightened around his neck, its knot secured under his left ear, the trap was sprung. Fifteen minutes later, the same length of time it took a jury to find him guilty of murder, Roland Genest was declared dead.

Author's photo.

In this photo, the metal door in the corner separates the cell from the death chamber. In the case of the Headingley jail in Manitoba, it took an executioner about ten seconds to lead a prisoner from the death cell to scaffold, and another four or five seconds to strap, noose, hood, and drop the condemned person. When a doctor standing below the death chamber declared a prisoner dead, a jail guard standing to one side of the scaffold used a long, metal hook to pull the rope by which the dead person was suspended to one side. Other officers then took hold of it and cut the executed killer down. Until relatively late in Canada's experience with capital punishment the rope used to execute a killer became the property of the executioner, along with the clothing of the dead prisoner(s), and pieces of it were sold to souvenir hunters. In some cases, executioners purchased dozens of feet of extra rope, pieces of which were also sold off.

7

Confessions and Presumptions of Guilt

The brutality of murder is occasionally mind-numbing. That there are people in society who care so little that they would take the life of another without qualm is hard for most of us to accept. The five stories in this chapter are all about that kind of person. Poral Stefoff, John Barty, John Kooting, and John Pawluk were all violent men, whose adult lives showed little evidence of concern for others. But that could not be said of James Alfred Kelsey. He was considered a good man by all who knew him, or at least all of those who testified at his murder trial. The thread that runs through these stories is that each got away with murder for quite a long time.

Poral Stefoff:
Last Minute Confession of a Serial Killer
Poral Stefoff was a vicious, brutal man who committed at least four murders. Although he was arrested within minutes of committing the crime for which, in December 1909, he was hanged, Stefoff was actually pretty successful at getting away with killing people.

It is probably never a good thing for a killer to report the death of his victim, and in the case of Poral Stefoff, it was a fatal mistake. Stefoff was a labourer from Macedonia, and lived in a downtown Toronto boarding house with nearly a dozen of his countrymen. He was the only member of the group not to have a regular job, and around 6:00 a.m. on April 22, 1909, he started looking for work. In his absence Evan Simoff, a second-cousin, returned from his night shift as a cleaner for the Grand Trunk Railway. Stefoff expected his cousin to be at home, and when he returned from his job search was a little surprised to find that the door leading to the basement suite occupied by the Macedonians was locked. He walked to the front of the house and started down a narrow staircase connecting a ground floor sitting room to the basement. As he did he noticed Simoff lying at the bottom of the stairs. Stefoff turned around and rushed outside, where he sought help from a Macedonian living across the street. He in turn called the police. Within minutes five officers, closely followed by the city coroner, arrived on the scene. What they found was mind-numbing brutality.

A hatchet was lying a few feet from the body of an adult male, who was lying in a pool of blood. The man's pants were undone at the waist, presumably when the killer went searching for a money belt of the kind often worn by eastern European immigrants. When those first to arrive checked to see if the victim had any valuables on his person, they found blood stains on the inside of his right pocket, likely left when his killer took whatever the pocket once contained. Since nothing in the basement was disturbed, investigators concluded there had been no struggle. That meant the dead man probably knew the person who attacked him. Police thought the assault may have been interrupted, since whoever murdered Simoff left on his body $100 in gold pieces that he had sewn into the lining of his vest. Indeed, if the killer searched all of Simoff's clothing it may have taken some time — the dead man was wearing two of almost everything, including pants and vest.

As soon as they could, detectives rounded up the men who lived with the victim, and through an interpreter began questioning them. Three hours later everyone was allowed to leave, except the person who discovered the dead man's body. Investigators could not help notice that Stefoff's clothes were spotted with what looked like blood. He was asked how the stains got on his clothes. "I got them," he replied, "at the Harris Abattoir, where I worked for twelve days."[1] Stefoff's questioners were not convinced by the answer, and became outright suspicious when they examined his clothes further, and under his jacket found more stains on the sleeve of his shirt. When they found $140 in Stefoff's pocket, a man who admitted he had not worked for some time, the police took him into custody as a material witness. Four days later he was formally charged with murder.

Much of the Crown's case was based on the fact that on the day of Simoff's murder, Stefoff had on him $140 in bills of the same denomination known to have been in the possession of the victim. It was because of this money that Stefoff's trial was delayed for months. In a statement he gave to the police, the accused killer said the money was a loan from an acquaintance, who shortly after the murder returned to Macedonia. It took the Crown a considerable length of time to persuade the alleged money lender to return to Canada to testify. When he did, he testified for only ten minutes, but what he said struck at the heart of Stefoff's defence. Yes, the witness told the court, he was a friend of both the victim and the victim's alleged killer; but no, he never had any financial dealings with Stefoff, and he certainly never loaned him $140.[2]

After that the Macedonians who shared a house with Stefoff and Simoff were called to the stand, and each said the same thing: Stefoff rarely worked, he never had any money, and he was constantly trying to borrow from them. The clincher for the Crown were the results of tests carried out on the stains noticed on Stefoff's clothes the day of the murder. They were found to contain human blood. Those tests were the reason the alleged killer looked almost dapper as he sat in court. Investigators seized so much of his clothing that they had to find him something else to wear; which was why when court opened he was resplendent in his borrowed finery.

In the end there was likely nothing Stefoff could have done or said to persuade jurors not to find him guilty, although his lawyer certainly tried. He argued that when his client spoke to the police the day Simoff was found, he did not understand their questions, nor did he appreciate that he need not have said anything at all. The lawyer's second submission was novel. He said that just because ten of the twelve jurors recently were subjected to considerable criticism for the decisions they made in two earlier murder trials, they should not feel inclined to make up for those verdicts by finding Stefoff guilty of a crime he did not commit. Pointing to his client, who he referred to as "that poor, dumb foreigner," the lawyer said "Gentlemen, don't allow yourselves to be moved by the demand for victims, and take as your victim this unfortunate foreigner, who doesn't understand the language and who can't defend himself against the vices of the detectives."[3]

When it was the turn of the Crown Attorney to sum up, he referred to the submission of Stefoff's lawyer as "moonshine and balderdash." He told jurors that if the statements made by his learned opponent were true, "it is an awful state of affairs. But it isn't; you know it, and he knows it isn't. So once more let us try to get rid of this truck and rubbish and let us get at the truth, no matter where it leads."[4] Two of the members of the jury were initially not quite sure where that was, and an hour after they started their deliberations the entire panel asked to speak with the judge. The pair not yet convinced of Stefoff's guilt wanted the statement he gave to the police read to them one more time. That done, all twelve jurors left the courtroom to resume their deliberations. Forty minutes later they were back, and the next day Stefoff was sentenced to hang.

Two days later it was learned that the Macedonian labourer had not left the entirety of his defence in the hands of his counsel. When the killer arrived at the Don Jail to await his December 23 execution, he complained that his lawyer and his spiritual adviser conspired against him during his trial. He said the men knew of the existence of a witness who, if called, would testify that Stefoff had in his possession the money he was alleged to have stolen more than two months before Simoff was murdered. When word of the allegation reached the condemned prisoner's minister, the reverend was hurt, and the more he thought about it, the more determined he was to prove the allegation false. The minister hired a cab, and beginning at 6:00 p.m. began making stops at every establishment in the city where Macedonian immigrants were likely to be found. At 2:00 a.m. the next morning he struck pay dirt. The man he was looking for was Elia Petroff, and Petroff was prepared to talk to the police. The Macedonian said he met Stefoff when he, Petroff, was arrested for vagrancy and placed in a cell next to the accused killer. The two talked, and before long Stefoff made his neighbour a proposition: if Petroff agreed to give false testimony on Stefoff's behalf, Stefoff would pay him $150. But when the murderer told his legal counsel about the potential witness, the lawyer refused to call him. He knew whatever Petroff was going to say would be a lie. As for the spiritual adviser, he apparently refused to intercede with the lawyer on Stefoff's behalf.

After Stefoff was arrested, Toronto police officers contacted other forces throughout Canada and the northern United States, and little by little became convinced that the man they had in custody very likely was a serial killer. They learned that a few years earlier an Englishman living in a boarding house in Bedford, Indiana, was murdered by a man matching Stefoff's description. The Macedonians who witnessed the murder refused to help police, however, and the investigation went nowhere. Out of an abundance of caution, Stefoff retreated to Macedonia. When he learned that he was wanted for crimes committed there, he returned to the United States. This time he settled near Buffalo, New York, where he worked in a quarry. Before long he was again on the move, leaving behind the bodies of two of his countrymen. Once more Stefoff opted for caution and returned to Europe. Although he avoided the country of his birth, his reputation followed him wherever he went. After learning that he was about to be extradited to the United States, he decided to leave Europe for Toronto. Six months later Simoff became victim number four.

Stefoff was never considered a talkative man, but that changed the evening before he was to hang. Shortly after 10:00 p.m. he told his guards that he had something to say; and he got right to the point. "I am guilty," he said. "I am the murderer of the man." Stefoff refused to give any details of Simoff's killing, but said his motive was partly greed, and partly revenge for what was a perceived slight. He also admitted to killing an Englishman near Terre Haute, Indiana, but all he would say was that it had nothing to do with a disagreement; he got away with the killing because none of the Macedonians who saw him do it cooperated with the police.

A little after breakfast was served at Toronto's Don Jail on December 23, 1909, Poral Stefoff was executed.

John Barty: The Cold-Set Killer

A cold-set hammer is an ugly tool, used by blacksmiths and metal workers to cut rivets. It is square on one end, wedge-shaped on the other, with a sharpened edge like that of an axe or hatchet. Weighing a little over a kilogram, it makes a deadly weapon, and it was John Barty's favourite implement of death. The Hamilton labourer worked for the Steel Company of Canada (now Stelco), and after his wife died and left him to raise the couple's three children, he spent his leisure hours drinking. But money was tight, and as his family grew older, it became tighter. That was why he was not able to pay his bills, and in 1925 he was sued by one of the people to whom he owed money. None of this, however, excuses what Barty did during the lunch hour on June 10, 1926.

Nancy Cook usually worked in Needle's Shoe Store with someone else, but between noon and 1:00 p.m. things were slow, so she was alone. When Barty walked in to the store, he told Cook he wanted to buy shoes for his son. Cook went to get him a pair, and as she did, he walked over to the cash register. Before he was able to take any money from the till, Cook saw what Barty was doing and rushed over. The diminutive twenty-nine-year-old grabbed the much bigger steel worker, but her struggles seemed only to infuriate Barty. He drew from a pocket a cold-set hammer, and hit her twice on the head. Before he had a chance to strike her a third time his victim's screams were heard by a woman pedestrian. She stopped and peered into the store, witnessing Barty put one arm around Cook and swing the hammer. When the weapon hit its mark the clerk collapsed onto the floor. No longer hindered by anyone, Barty jumped over the prostrate woman and rushed back to the cash register. As he emptied it the pedestrian raised the alarm.

Cook's husband also worked for Sam Needle, and on this Thursday he was just two stores away. When he heard the commotion he and his boss ran to the shoe store, where he saw his wife on the floor, and her apparent assailant standing at the till. Percy Cook was not much larger than Nancy, but he was every bit as brave. He went straight at Barty, who immediately swung his hammer at his slightly-built protagonist. He missed, and Cook grabbed him. In the fight that followed Barty bit down on Cook's hands and nose, and while the two men were struggling, Needle started hitting the would-be thief with a piece of wood. When it broke he turned and ran to get help. Unimpeded by anyone else, Barty focussed on Cook, and was finally able to hit him with the hammer. The shoe salesman fell to his knees, and then rolled onto the floor, unconscious. He no sooner collapsed when two men, attracted by all the shouting, entered the store. One grabbed a small ladder, the other a broom, and both swung at the same time. Neither weapon made any impression on Barty, and when he raised his hammer they backed away, giving the enraged thief a chance to make his getaway. Before he could, a Hamilton police inspector joined the fray. He managed to get an arm around the neck of the larger man, and with his free hand began hitting him. After what no doubt seemed an eternity he got his handcuffs out and slapped one around his opponent's wrist. And that was that. When Barty was searched he had just under $20 in his pocket, including a number of blood-stained bills.

Nancy Cook was rushed to the Hamilton General Hospital. Although she suffered a skull fracture and was badly beaten on the head, she initially seemed to be improving by the hour. That changed around noon two days later. Her condition worsened, and doctors decided to operate, but nothing helped. Almost exactly forty-eight hours after she put up such a brave fight with her assailant, she died. Barty was being held on charges of assault and attempted robbery. To those the police now added one count of murder.

Shortly after Cook's killer was arrested he gave a statement to the police. In it he said that after he paid for his son's shoes he turned to go out the front door of the shoe store, but Cook told him not to leave by that exit. She said he had to leave by the back door. That upset him, and the two got into an argument. When Cook struck him, he hit her back with the shoes he was carrying, in self-defence. That was all he could remember, other than the fact that before he went into the store he consumed a lot of bootleg wine.

During his preliminary hearing Barty denied that he was responsible for Cook's death. He testified that he was informed by a friend that when the police were carrying the unconscious woman from the store to an ambulance, they dropped her on the sidewalk, and she struck her head on the cement. That was what killed her, he claimed, not his attack. No one believed him, not then, nor in October, when he went on trial for murder. Although the trial lasted parts of three days, the outcome was never in doubt. After deliberating a little more than an hour, a jury returned a verdict of guilty. All that was left was the sentence.

In cases of capital murder, a judge had no option but to impose a death sentence; but Mr. Justice H.M. Mowatt had never done it before. After the jury announced its verdict, he asked Barty if there was any reason why sentence should not be passed. When the killer stood in silence, Mowatt said he was ready to do what the law said he must. He paused, struggled with his emotions for a moment, and then resumed talking. After a few seconds he paused a second time, and before he was finished, stopped again. The second and third pauses were so extended court officials were not sure he would be able to continue. Mowatt, however, struggled on. John Barty, he said, you "shall be taken to the place from whence you came, and there confined in solitary confinement until ..." This time when he stopped speaking it was not because of emotion, but because he could not find his calendar. He asked a court clerk for one, and after staring at it for a minute or two, looked up and continued: "the twenty-third day of December next, then he paused, "and then taken to a place of execution," a longer pause this time, "and hanged by the neck until you are dead." Mowatt stiffened slightly, and with considerable effort concluded: "May God have mercy on your soul." Barty, meanwhile, seemed indifferent to everything that was going on.[5]

In the days following his conviction Barty was questioned repeatedly about a triple murder that occurred in Hamilton on June 25, 1925. Sometime that afternoon someone carrying a cold-set hammer climbed a back stairway to a seedy apartment occupied by a bootlegger and his wife. That particular day they had a guest, although it hardly mattered. All three victims were both drunk and asleep. Their killer struck each in turn with

Author's photo.

The trap doors on which a condemned prisoner stood before being dropped were huge, heavy affairs, capable of holding at least two prisoners. When the executioner pulled a lever to which the doors were attached, the noise made by the two halves separating could be heard clearly by prisoners celled near the execution chamber. When several prisoners were to be hanged one after another, the sound must have been terrifying to those awaiting their turn on the gallows. John Pawluk stood on these very doors on August 21, 1936.

the sharpened blade of his weapon, apparently with sufficient force that none of his victims had time to raise an alarm. In fact, there was not a single sign of a struggle. That initially confused investigators because when they walked in it seemed everywhere they looked there was a body. The head and neck of all three people were struck repeatedly, and each body bore evidence that the killer used both ends of his weapon on their faces. No one connected to the investigation had any doubt who committed the murders. A week or so before the slaughter, the bootlegger obtained a judgment against Barty for what he said were groceries, although that was no doubt a euphemism for bootleg wine.

On December 22, the day before Barty was to hang, his lawyer applied for a stay of execution to the Ontario Court of Appeal. The court dismissed his application, and then in a legal oddity, the lawyer walked from the courtroom to the office of one of the justices who just said no, and persuaded him to grant a temporary reprieve. In the end Barty's fate was the same, except that instead of being hanged two days before Christmas, he was executed in the Hamilton jail on January 12, 1927.   .

John Kooting and John Pawluk:
Confessions on the Prairies

According to Saint Augustine, the confession of evil works is the beginning of good works. In the case of two Manitoba men, it was the first step on the way to the gallows.

Shoal Lake farmer John Kooting always got along with his neighbour Dymtro Czayka, and when Czayka left his job at the local creamery it did not seem out of place that he boarded for a time with Kooting and his family. What did seem unusual was that in the first week of November 1921, Czayka would leave the community to return to his native Austria without telling anyone of his plans.

Two months after the former creamery worker was last seen, police questioned Kooting about his absence. Kooting's suggestion that his lodger was staying temporarily with a friend was quickly proven to be a lie, and the farmer was arrested and charged with murdering the missing man. After a short preliminary hearing he was committed to stand trial. When a grand jury heard his case in the spring of 1923, its members were convinced

Kooting was likely guilty, and it brought in a true bill. But there was no evidence that Czayka had been murdered, and instead of prosecuting his alleged killer, the Crown was forced to stay his charge and allow the accused killer to return home a free man.

For the next two years everything returned to normal, at least for the Kootings. Then in early 1925 Kooting became bedridden. Convinced he was going to die, the farmer got in touch with the Royal Canadian Mounted Police and asked if a couple officers might come by to hear what he had to say about the disappearance of Czayka. In his written statement, Kooting said he killed his former neighbour because he needed the man's money to feed his family. After hitting Czayka over the head with an axe and taking his cash, he buried the dead man under a manure pile in his yard. Some months later he built a pig pen over the grave. He told the officers that when asked by neighbours about his friend's disappearance, he told them Czayka had gone missing in a blizzard and likely perished.

Although all that remained of Czayka was bones, a four-inch hole in his skull corroborated Kooting's statement. At trial further corroboration was offered by his son, who testified that on the night of the murder he was sitting on the stairs of his parents' home when his father came in and informed his mother that he had just killed their neighbour. The young man told the court he later found blood-soaked clothing hanging in a shed and bloodstains on the hay rack his father used on the evening of the murder. The only issue at trial was whether Kooting's confession should be admitted into evidence. A Shoal Lake doctor testified that although Kooting was sick when he confessed to murdering Czayka, he was both physically and mentally fit to make "an intelligent statement."[6] The jury was convinced. In less than an hour it returned a guilty verdict.

Shortly before 8:00 a.m. on the third Friday in February 1926, Kooting was led from his death cell in the provincial jail at Portage la Prairie to a scaffold erected in the prison yard. The priest who spent the evening with the condemned man recited prayers for the dying as the procession made its way to the foot of the gallows, with Kooting responding in a clear, emotionless voice.

The trap was sprung moments after the group reached the scaffold. Although witnesses later said the execution was carried out without a hitch, the coroner presiding over the inquest that followed noted that

Kooting died from strangulation, rather than a broken neck. The dead man was buried in an unmarked grave in the yard of Portage jail.

The other Manitoba murder that resulted in the death of a "confessor" bore striking similarities to the crime committed by Kooting, although this time suspicion was aroused when the illiterate man the killer suspected of having an affair with his wife left behind a suicide note.

By 1935 John Pawluk had farmed north of Winnipeg for years. His relationship with his wife was not good, and had not been for years. On at least two occasions Julia disappeared for days before returning to her husband and their three young children. That was why the police were neither surprised nor alarmed when Pawluk reported his wife missing four months before her alleged lover was found shot to death.

Genio Bulega lived near the Pawluks. The day he died a neighbour arrived at the home of the retired farmer to ask for help loading hay. He found the yard strangely quiet, and decided to enter the residence to investigate. He found Bulega sitting in a chair, the top of his head blown off. A shotgun lay beside his body. One end of a piece of binder twine was tied to its trigger, and the other end was wrapped around one of the feet of the dead man. On a table across the room investigators found an unusual, unpunctuated, blood-stained letter, held in place by a carving knife. Officers immediately became suspicious when they opened the suicide note. It was dated more than a month before its author allegedly shot himself, and urged police not to suspect Pawluk of killing his wife.

> Please don't bother anybody about [Julia Pawluk] she was at my place on Monday ... she want me to go away with her and I told her I couldnt go with her she had been bothering me all summer I couldnt go with her and I cant stand her now wherever she went ... don't bother him [John Pawluk] any because he is not to blame for anything this all I have to say goodby everybody please dont bother about his wife.[7]

Any doubt investigators might have harboured that Bulgea was a murder rather than suicide victim was dispelled when they found blood on the inside of the letter. Not only was it impossible for Bulgea to have shot himself and then fold the note, it was unlikely he could have handled the shotgun without leaving evidence that he had done so. The gun had been wiped completely clean of fingerprints. But notwithstanding evidence pointing to his involvement in the death of Bulgea, Pawluk may still have avoided a murder conviction had he not on two separate occasions confessed to killing his wife.

The first time he unburdened himself occurred before Bulega died. A neighbour dropped by for a visit following Julia's disappearance. Without prompting, Pawluk told his startled guest that he no longer had a wife. Asked what he had done to her, he said he shot her with a .22 rifle and buried her body under a manure pile.[8] Pawluk's second confession came after Bulega's murder, while he was being held in the Headingley jail awaiting trial for killing his wife. A friend serving a six-month sentence for obtaining goods by false pretences shared a cell with Pawluk. Again, without prompting, Pawluk confessed to killing his wife. "I hope, now that they have me, they will hang me right away. I don't want to be continually pulled around in the courts."[9]

Author's photo.

Manitoba's cemetery of the executed, where the unclaimed bodies of men hanged in the province between 1932 and 1952 were reinterred after a flooding Red River destroyed the area in which they were first buried. The body of John Pawluk and a handful of other men were moved about a mile west of the jail. There they were interred in a small cemetery located in the middle of a field.

Pawluk need not have worried. Despite taking the stand to deny making either confession, a jury took less than an hour to return a verdict of guilty. Pawluk did not react when he was sentenced to death, and after his judge left the courtroom he calmly relit a half burned cigarette and walked back to his cell with a smile on his face. There were no smiles two months later when the forty-nine-year-old was led out of the death cell that connects to the gallows at the Headingley jail. Less than sixty seconds after Pawluk started his walk the trap was sprung. The *Winnipeg Free Press* summed up the feeling of those who witnessed the execution. "Had he been less talkative it might have been difficult to connect him definitely with the killing."[10]

John Pawluk was hanged on August 21, 1936, and buried near the Assiniboine River on the grounds of the Headingley jail. Thirty-eight years later his and fifteen other bodies were disinterred and reburied in a small enclosure a mile west.

James Alfred Kelsey: A Tendency to Talk Too Much

James Kelsey was a good person who did a terrible thing, but were it not for his tendency to talk too much, he would almost certainly have gotten away with the perfect murder, despite the fact that the person he and his brother beat to death was a close family friend.

In December 1959, Kelsey and his brother Lloyd Cross lived in Welland, Ontario. Although he had no record and was never involved in crime, Kelsey listened when his sibling talked of a way the pair could make some easy money. They were drinking at the Reeta Hotel when Lloyd said all they had to do was hire Sam Delibasich, a family friend and local cabbie, to drive them out of town. Then they would knock him out, take his cab to Toronto, and sell it to a used car dealer. On December 9, that is what they did. They asked Delibasich to drive them to St. Catharines. When they were only a few miles out of Welland the brothers asked the taxi driver to turn down a deserted side road, and then told him to stop. The three men smoked cigarettes for a bit before Kelsey quietly drew from his clothes a hammer and hit Dalibasich over the head. Cross then grabbed the weapon and hit their friend a second time. The badly injured driver managed to get out of the taxi and he started running across a field, closely pursued by Cross. When the elder brother caught up, he knocked Dalibasich to the ground. The winded and frightened cabbie held up his wallet, and as Cross took it Kelsey arrived on the scene. He told his brother that they had to kill Dalibasich, because if they did not, he would go straight to the authorities. "To make sure, I stuck an ice pick into Sam's back."[11] In fact, it turned out that Kelsey stuck it in three times while Dalibasich was alive, and another three after he died.

The brothers left their victim lying in the field and drove to Toronto, stopping once to throw into Lake Ontario some of his belongings, together with the hammer and the ice-pick. When they reached Toronto, the killers made several attempts to sell the cab, but there were no buyers, so they abandoned it on a downtown street. Kelsey and Cross then checked into a hotel, and the next day made their way back to Welland. A resident of the apartment building in front of which Dalibasich's vehicle was left noticed it, and after three or four days contacted the police. They promptly had the cab towed away. The body of Dalibasich, meanwhile, lay unnoticed until December 17, when it was discovered by a rabbit hunter. Although the police quickly connected the body with the cab abandoned in Toronto, they had nothing else to work on, and their investigation ground to a halt. That is the way things would likely have remained were it not for a radio program.

Sometime in the two years following the murder Kelsey moved to Niagara Falls, New York, and a group of his childhood buddies began driving across the border for regular visits. In September 1951, the guys decided to take a trip to Buffalo, and on the way they listened to the radio program *Gang Busters*. When it ended Kelsey asked if anyone remembered the Dalibasich murder. Without waiting for a response, he started to talk. Aubrey Merritt was likely Kelsey's best friend, and for the next several months brooded over what he heard. In January 1952, he got in touch with the Welland police. When they interviewed Kelsey's girlfriend, she said she too was told about his involvement in the murder. With that investigators decided they had enough to lay charges against the brothers, and they were charged with murder. Kelsey made it easy for investigators — he confessed to everything. He even agreed to accompany the police to Toronto. Along the way he pointed out the various stops he and his brother made more than two years earlier. Kelsey showed investigators the road leading to the field where the murder occurred, and where he and his brother threw the murder weapons into Toronto Bay. In Toronto Kelsey took officers to one of the used car lots where they tried to sell the cab, and to the spot on Bloor Street where it was abandoned.

The Crown decided to proceed against Kelsey first, and on March 10, 1952, his preliminary hearing got underway in Welland. Even at this stage if the young killer kept his mouth shut, he may have gotten off. But when he was asked if he had anything to say, he held nothing back. Kelsey's two confessions were the only direct evidence the police had linking him to the murder of Dalibasich, so it did not come as much of a surprise when during his September trial he repudiated everything. He also refused to testify on his own behalf. That meant that all his lawyer could do was to introduce evidence of his previously good character, and argue that there was nothing in his past to suggest he would have allowed himself to become involved in such a brutal murder. His former girlfriend said the same thing. Asked if she believed what her boyfriend told her about his involvement with the Dalibasich murder, she said no, she did not. "I didn't believe him because he was always a good guy."[12]

But by then it was too late. Since Kelsey did not challenge the evidence heard by jurors, and no evidence was led to suggest he had a reason to incriminate himself in a murder, the jury was free to accept as truthful everything they heard. On September 18, it returned a verdict of guilty. To make matters even worse for Kelsey, jurors refused to append to their decision a recommendation for mercy. The convicted killer was sentenced to hang early in the new year. Before then, however, his lawyer appealed the verdict to the Ontario Court of Appeal. Although it dismissed the request, it did grant a stay of execution until March 10, 1953, so Kelsey could take his request for a new trial to the Supreme Court of Canada. That meant he would be alive to give evidence at the trial of his brother, which got underway in mid-January. Kelsey again refused to testify. Since he was already on death row, there was nothing the Crown could do to force him to change his mind. For his part, Cross denied any involvement in the murder. According to his legal counsel, Kelsey acted alone when he murdered Dalibasich, and the lawyer told jury members they should not believe anything Cross's brother told the police. After all, Kelsey was not only a deserter from the Canadian army; he was "a low character."[13] The jury seemed to agree, and on January 13, 1953, it found the accused not guilty.

A month and a week later the Supreme Court heard Kelsey's appeal, and reserved judgment. Kelsey's death sentence was postponed pending their decision. On March 16, Kelsey was once again advised that he was to hang. Before that could happen, however, the federal cabinet commuted his sentence to life imprisonment. With that, the man who talked too much was transferred from his death cell to Kingston Penitentiary.

8

Killers on the Run

Walter Pavlukoff and Henry Séguin had a lot in common. Both were carpenters, both spent much of their adult life in prison, and both escaped after committing murder. Pavlukoff was a native of British Columbia and fled a massive manhunt to live for years in Ontario. Séguin did the opposite: he murdered in Ontario and hid out on Canada's west coast. They had more than one thing in common, but the most memorable is that just before they were to be hanged, each committed suicide virtually in front of their death watch.

Henry Séguin: From Ontario to British Columbia

The execution was to have taken place at midnight. Everything was ready. A grave was dug the day before, hacked out of the frozen ground in a section of the jail courtyard near the outdoor scaffold. The executioner arrived from Montreal about forty-eight hours earlier, and after supervising construction of the gallows was killing time in the office of the prison warden. Nearby, police officials from Ontario and British Columbia were chatting in small groups. Just before the condemned prisoner was to begin his death walk he asked for privacy while he used his night pail. When his priest entered his cell a few minutes later, everything started to go sideways. Within minutes the killer lay dead. How it came to this is the stuff of fiction.

The story started in either Cornwall or Maxville, depending on whether you begin with the killer or his victim. Henry Séguin was born

in Cornwall, a city in eastern Ontario approximately four hundred kilometres east of Toronto. Maxville, the hometown of his victim, is thirty-two
kilometres north. To suggest that Séguin had a troubled childhood is a
gross understatement. He was only nine when he was convicted of break,
enter, and theft and sentenced to an indefinite term in an industrial school
run by a Roman Catholic order known as the Christian Brothers. He was
released four years later.

Six months after leaving St. Joseph's Industrial School Séguin was back,
again convicted of theft. Within days of re-entering the facility he escaped,
albeit for only a day. Shortly after his sixteenth birthday he was sent home,
where his criminal career began in earnest. With only a grade two education and no occupational skills, he took to crime as naturally as a Labrador
retriever to water. Less than a year after being paroled from St. Joseph's he
was sentenced to a seven month term in a provincial jail, and no sooner

Henry Séguin killed three people, two for no other reason than they might sometime in the future be able to identify him. With the official death party waiting outside his cell to escort him to the gallows, he somehow managed to kill himself. In his suicide note he wrote that he was the real victim, not those whom he wronged during a life of crime.

WANTED in Ontario on murder charge, Henry Seguin, 27, was committed for trial at Williams Lake, B.C., Tuesday on wounding and robbery charges.

Courtesy of Vancouver Sun.

had he been released than he received a suspended sentence for another theft. Within weeks he was arrested yet again, re-entering the Guelph jail as a seasoned criminal. It could have been worse. A more serious charge of robbery with violence was dismissed on a technicality.

Shortly after beginning to serve his sentence Séguin escaped. He immediately went on a crime spree, earning himself a term of two years less a day in the institution from which he had just broken out. A year into that term he escaped again. After committing a series of break-ins, he sought refuge in the Canadian army. A routine background check quickly determined that he was an escapee, and he was promptly discharged by the armed forces and arrested by the police. Séguin had finally reached the big leagues — he was about to do his time in a federal penitentiary.

If there was any doubt about Séguin's career path it was put to rest when shortly after being released he returned to Kingston Penitentiary, again convicted of break, enter, and theft. It was following this sentence that the connection between Séguin and Maxville was established. In late February 1952, Séguin left Kingston for the last time, and the now twenty-six-year-old moved home to live with his parents in the dance hall they operated in Cornwall. In a lot adjacent to their business an acquaintance of the Séguins stored a small house trailer. A few weeks after returning to reside with his parents, Henry broke into the unit and stole a Leatherneck Model 150 .22 calibre rifle and a small, three-compartment change purse.

In June, Séguin left Cornwall following a fight with his parents, and he and a man he identified as his uncle rented a cabin a few miles outside his hometown. Weeks later, and now alone, he began sleeping in his car near an unused church on the outskirts of Maxville.

Early in August Séguin was walking down the town's main street when he ran into Douglas McKibben, whom he met while both men were imprisoned in Kingston. Over coffee the two reminisced about their days in prison, then McKibben made the mistake of telling Séguin that he was working as a bookkeeper in a garage owned by one of the town's wealthiest citizens. He compounded his mistake by admitting that when he took the job he did not disclose that he was an ex-con. Séguin immediately realized what that meant, and told McKibben that if he did not supply him with money and food, he would share the bookkeeper's secret with Leonard Hurd, McKibben's boss.

With the cash he was extorting Séguin rented a cabin on a farm near Maxville and began planning his next crime. On August 16, 1952, he carried it out. His target was Hurd, a man widely known to carry on his person large sums of money, often well in excess of $1000. The plan was simple — Séguin would park his beat-up 1934 Chevrolet coup on the side of a road just outside Maxville, then when it got dark walk into town and ask the garage-man for gas and a ride back to his car. Once the two were beyond prying eyes, Séguin would take Hurd's money.

It worked, sort of. Séguin did indeed leave his car outside Maxville, and he had no difficulty locating Hurd. The problem was the wealthy businessman was busy for most of the evening, and did not stop by his garage until 11:30 p.m., by which time several area residents had driven past Séguin's Chevrolet and remembered both it and the stranger walking to town. Nonetheless, Séguin persuaded Hurd to give him a ride back to his car. When they arrived at their destination Séguin exited the rear passenger seat, pulled out his stolen rifle, opened the front passenger door of the vehicle, and shot Hurd five times, three times in the head. He then took the mortally wounded man's wallet and cash, pushed Hurd's car into the ditch, and took off in his coup.

Séguin had no sooner driven away than a car passed the disabled vehicle. It was followed shortly thereafter by several more. The driver of one recognized the car angled into the ditch, and drove into Maxville to report the accident to Hurd. The Good Samaritan happened onto one of Hurd's employees almost as soon as he reached town and the two immediately drove back to what they thought was the scene of an accident. As soon as they looked more closely, however, they realized they were wrong.

Hurd was sprawled across the front seat, his legs on the passenger side of the car, his head under the steering wheel. Even without opening the driver-side door it was obvious Hurd had been shot. The men headed back to town, one to locate the local doctor, the other to report the crime to Maxville's single-member police force.

News of the incident spread like wildfire, and within an hour the murder scene was crowded with spectators. As soon as he realized there was nothing that could be done for Hurd, the town doctor returned home to contact the coroner, and report the robbery-murder to the nearest detachment of the Ontario Provincial Police force. By 2:00 a.m.

the first O.P.P. officer arrived, and he noticed a brown leather bag lying on the floor in the rear of the Hurd vehicle. It was removed when the car, its owner still lying across the front seat, was towed to a Cornwall funeral home, where a post mortem was to be carried out the following day.

On Sunday a senior inspector from the Toronto headquarters of the O.P.P. arrived to take over the investigation. One of his first actions was to inspect the brown satchel. Under a wash cloth and bath towel he found a number of comic books, a shaving kit, clothing, and three articles that tied Séguin directly to the murder. The first was a pay book issued by the Canadian army to Joseph Henry Laurier Séguin. Inside it the inspector discovered a certificate indicating that Séguin had been dishonourably discharged from the armed forces in January 1945. The last item was an Unemployment Insurance Card, also in Séguin's name.

Now that they knew who they were looking for, the police began a very public search for the killer and his unusual looking car. The coup had been modified by a previous owner, and a large wooden box was built into the space normally occupied by the trunk. For the next week the authorities found no trace of either Séguin or his car. But that did not mean that the investigation had not been fruitful. A key piece of evidence tying Séguin to the murder was turned up at the cabin rented by the fugitive. The killer befriended a teenage nephew of the cabin's owner, and the two discussed guns at length. Séguin bragged about how good a shot he was, and told the young man he made it a habit to print his name under the metal butt plate of his guns, ensuring that there was never any doubt about to whom they belonged. In addition, Séguin gave the youth a handful of what he said were unique bullets; bullets which, it turned out, were identical to those that killed Leonard Hurd.

Six days after the murder of the Maxville businessman a member of a highway maintenance crew cutting grass near the scene of the murder discovered the stock of a .22 calibre Leatherneck Model 150 rifle. As soon as the find was reported to the police an organized search of both sides of the road was begun, and it quickly turned up the barrel and trigger mechanism that fit the butt, together with a pouch containing ammunition similar to the bullets used in the murder. Printed in ink under the metal butt plate of the gun was "H. Beaudy," the name used by Séguin when he checked into the cabin he rented shortly before the murder. Ballistic tests later revealed that the bullet recovered from Hurd's body was fired from the rifle discovered by the maintenance crew.

By day's end the O.P.P. were satisfied they had sufficient evidence, and a warrant for the arrest of Séguin was issued. For the next two months the search for Séguin and his car produced no leads, but on October 25, 1952, a hunter walking along the bank of the Ottawa River near the Ontario-Quebec border discovered an unusual looking vehicle at the bottom of a steep embankment. By the next day there was no doubt it was the car seen parked on the side of the road near the spot where Hurd was murdered. The coup's owner, however, was long gone.

In fact, a week and a half after he robbed and murdered Hurd, Séguin began working for a lumber company ten kilometres north of Williams Lake, in the interior of British Columbia. The fugitive gave his name as Henry Godin, and for a month kept much to himself. That changed in early October, with the arrival of Frederick and Jean Labrie. Shortly after Fred began working with the same company as Séguin, the Labries struck up a friendship with the fugitive. Over the course of the next few weeks it grew sufficiently intimate that when Séguin quit his lumber job, he was able to persuade Fred to join him three hundred kilometres away in Kamloops. Jean was already in the city, working as a waitress at the Royal Cafe. The three rented one half of a duplex, and furnished their new home with items the Labries left in storage when they moved to Williams Lake. On November 14, the furniture, the three friends, and the Labries' brown and white dog became a household. Three days later the young couple were dead.

Investigators were never able to determine the precise sequence of events that led to the murder of Fred and Jean Labrie, but they suspect that something happened to make Séguin fear that his past was about to catch up with him. To prevent that from happening he shot Fred twice in the head, and then stabbed Jean to death before dumping their bodies in a streambed sixteen kilometres southwest of Kamloops.

Twenty-four hours after disposing of the Labries, their killer began selling the couple's household effects. A few days later Séguin used Fred's truck as part payment on a used mobile home. Although he moved his purchase into a local trailer park, for the next month he continued to reside in the duplex. The fugitive had enough of Kamloops, and in mid-December caught a westbound bus for Williams Lake. On the fifteenth he was noticed hanging around the Canadian Bank of Commerce, apparently indifferent to the falling snow.

At 11:00 p.m. the manager of the bank finally finished work, and no sooner started his car when Séguin opened the passenger door and slipped in beside him. The Maxville murderer stuck a .32 calibre handgun into the banker's side, and told him to drive out of town. They no sooner reached the countryside when the fugitive said to stop the car. The two sat in silence for a few moments, and then Séguin told the manager to drive back. As they neared the bank they saw two men standing on the sidewalk and Séguin instructed the banker to keep going. Seconds later he told the manager to make a U-turn. The men on the sidewalk were still chatting, and the killer again forced his hostage to head out of town. This time they stopped for a few moments near the town's garbage dump before returning.

At last the sidewalk was empty. Séguin ordered the banker to pull over, park the car, and let him into the bank. The men walked directly to the vault, leaving the front door slightly ajar. One of the individuals who had been visiting on the sidewalk happened to be an employee of the Bank of Commerce, and when he and his friend finished their coffee and started for their respective homes he noticed the open door. Almost as soon as the pair stepped into the bank to see what was wrong they were told to put their hands up, and to stay where they were. With the manager in front of him and the two newcomers behind, Séguin was outflanked. The killer ordered the banker to step away from the vault and join the men by the door, but instead of walking around the counter the hostage started towards Séguin. He no sooner took his first step when a shot rang out and Séguin bolted.

Within minutes all five members of the Williams Lake detachment of the Royal Canadian Mounted Police arrived on the scene, greeted by two badly shaken bystanders and a bank manager with a wound to his leg. Figuring out where the bad guy went was not difficult. Séguin's footsteps were clearly visible in the fresh snow, and officers easily followed them to the highway leading out of town. For a while the robber walked in a relatively straight line down the road, but over the next two miles Séguin periodically left the highway to walk through the ditch on one or the other side of the roadway, as if he were trying to avoid being detected by drivers of passing vehicles. When the fugitive's trail turned down a densely wooded back road, pursuing officers opted for caution and returned to Williams Lake to organize a search party.

Early the next morning trackers followed the footprints of the bank robber to a creek bed just inside the Sugar Cane Indian reserve, and their pursuit slowed to a crawl. Around 9:00 a.m. a constable suddenly shouted that he saw the fugitive. As soon as he did Séguin stepped from behind a tree, gun in hand, and demanded that his pursuers put down their weapons. Instead, all but one of the officers dropped to the ground. As Séguin began shooting at the downed posse members the only policeman with a clear view of him fired, hitting the escaped killer in the chest.

Someone was immediately dispatched to arrange for a doctor to be brought to the scene, and when he arrived the badly wounded criminal was stabilized, and then transported to the Williams Lake hospital. From that point onwards things quickly began to unravel for the Cornwall killer. Six days after he was shot, while still recuperating in hospital from his chest wound, Séguin's fingerprints identified him as the man wanted for the murder of Leonard Hurd. On January 13, 1953, the killer was committed to stand trial, and five days later pled guilty to wounding with intent to kill, shooting with intent to do bodily harm, and robbery while armed. The result was a five year term of imprisonment on each count, the sentences to run concurrently.

In March the provincial Court of Appeal increased Séguin's sentence to twenty years, and dismissed his application for a new trial. With that, British Columbia washed its hands of the killer, and a month and a half later he was returned to Ontario to stand trial for killing Hurd. It's around this time that Séguin began preparing for the worst. Somehow, presumably while he was waiting to be transferred to Ontario, he obtained a small aluminum tube containing enough potassium cyanide to kill four adults. Where he kept the vial for the next nine months is not known, but the fact that he insisted on using a night pail during his imprisonment, rather than a jail washroom, is suggestive.

When Séguin's murder trial got underway in Cornwall on October 26, there was no doubt about its outcome. After a four-day hearing the twenty-eight-year-old was sentenced to be hanged. Between his sentencing and his January date with the executioner Séguin was kept in solitary confinement.

Visits were strictly monitored, and guards checked his food to ensure that it did not contain contraband.

Séguin was scheduled to be hanged just after midnight on January 19, 1954. Although he professed to be an atheist, shortly before his execution he asked to see a priest. When his spiritual adviser arrived, Séguin told him to wait for a few minutes, during which time the priest heard an unusual noise coming from the cell. The sound was later identified. While his priest, a guard, and the jail warden stood in the corridor, the condemned prisoner retrieved the aluminum tube from where it had been inserted, took out its glass vial of poison, and shoved the vial inside an orange. Séguin then bit down on the fruit several times, breaking the glass and releasing its contents. As his spiritual adviser entered his cell, the condemned prisoner finished consuming the poison.

The Catholic father vividly remembered what happened next.

> When I went in, the guards pulled up a chair in front of the cell door. Séguin was pale and upset, a different man than he was the day before. He was sitting down puffing a cigaret. I had a letter from his brother-in-law. He started to read it. I gave him a little Christmas card from his niece. It told him to have a happy death. He began to cry. He said he wanted to make his peace with God. He said he was sorry for his sins. He seemed to get more and more upset. He threw himself on the cot. He pulled a towel over his face. He seemed to get into a convulsion. His hands were shaking, he was turned on his side, breathing heavily. The guards called the governor. The governor went in and took the towel away. He was trying to go to confession when he fell. That is why I gave him conditional absolution from his sins. He had sorrow for his sins, but did not have time to tell them to me before he took his convulsions. He was very concerned about his sins and said he was sorry if he had done anything wrong in his life. He wanted to die a happy death. That was the only thing he could tell me. The he started to sob and cry and threw himself on the cot.[1]

According to the priest, Séguin's last words were: "I am sorry for what I have done. I have paid my debts to society for all the sins I have committed."[2]

By the time the jail doctor arrived, Séguin was dead. An examination of the poison found in his stomach determined that the potassium cyanide was substantially degraded, and had the vial not contained four times the dosage normally considered lethal, the killer would not have died.

In their quest to determine how Séguin acquired the poison, jail officials seized a thirty-two page letter which the condemned man asked to be delivered to his sister following his death. In it Séguin said nothing of the poison, but made clear that even after killing three people he viewed himself as a victim of injustice. "Justice has condemned me as a dog. They will try and hang me like one, but I will try my best not to. I will cheat them to the very last and, if I do succeed to cheat them in the end, I will only be too glad to do so. If I don't cheat them, it will not be because I did not try to do so."[3]

A sad postscript to the saga of Henry Séguin began on September 18, 1955, when a hunter stumbled onto the remains of the Labries. In the three years the bodies of the couple lay exposed to the elements their bones were scattered over an area one hundred metres wide. Near them were the remains of their dog, shot once through the head. In the middle of February 1956, a coroner's jury ruled that the bodies were indeed those of Jean and Frederick Labrie, and that evidence "points to a motive for the killing as being to obtain the victims' personal belongings and furniture."[4]

Walter Pavlukoff:
From British Columbia to Ontario

Vera and Jack Pavlukoff emigrated from Russia in 1913, settling almost immediately in Vancouver. Jack got a job with the city as a labourer, and the security of his employment encouraged the Russian Orthodox couple to begin raising a family. Walter was the second oldest of five children. Following Jack's death in 1929 the family's fortunes, and Walter's life, began a precipitous decline. With their meal ticket gone, the Pavlukoffs moved from home-to-home in east end Vancouver, and Walter was in jail when his two youngest siblings died of tuberculosis.

Pavlukoff was nineteen when he turned to crime. He was caught after committing a series of robberies in Chicago, and spent almost five years in an American prison before being deported to Canada. Three weeks after his return he was arrested for armed assault and sent to the British Columbia Penitentiary. After serving two years he was released, but within months was sentenced to three years in the same institution for committing a robbery with violence. When Pavlukoff was apprehended he was wearing a homemade gun holster and mask around his neck, and in his pocket carried what he referred to as "a sucker list." The names on it included two former provincial lieutenant-governors, the chief justice of British Columbia, and a number of prominent lawyers and businessmen. Pavlukoff told the officers who arrested him that the group was his wish list for the future. "They all have good jobs, nice homes, big cars and smoke good cigars."[5]

Two minutes before closing time on August 25, 1947, a man with a sallow complexion and a .9 millimetre Luger automatic pistol in his pocket walked past a police constable sitting in a parked cruiser and into a fruit shop next door to a west end Vancouver branch of the Canadian Bank of Commerce. He bought a shopping bag, and as he left the store he took the pistol from his pocket and slipped the bag over his hand and gun.

Six customers were standing in line waiting to be served when Pavlukoff stepped into the bank. He quickly raised a newspaper, shielding one side of his face, and dropped the shopping bag. Pavlukoff walked up behind a man standing in front of one of the tellers, and told him to move to the wall, warning "no funny work or I'll let you have it." As terrified customers cringed in fear, Pavlukoff walked to the rear of the bank, pushing past two people. When he stopped, only the bank's accountant and manager remained in front of him. After warning the accountant not to move, he walked towards fifty-five-year-old Sydney Petrie.[6]

The manager was sitting behind an oak desk, typing. Ordered to get up, he exploded from his chair, put his shoulder under the front of the desk, and pushed it over onto Pavlukoff. The startled robber instinctively stepped back, pulling the trigger of the Luger as he did. A copper-jacketed bullet hit the banker under his left arm, travelled through his body before exiting near his hip, then ricocheted off an office chair, over the heads of the cowering customers, and through a plate glass window.

As the mortally wounded Petrie staggered towards the vault, Pavlukoff turned and, without stopping to pick up any money, tore out of the building.

A woman pushing a baby carriage was passing in front of the bank as he emerged, and as Pavlukoff stuffed the gun into his coat pocket he stumbled against her buggy. Sitting in his patrol car a few feet away was the police officer the robber had walked by on his way into the bank. Despite the sound of the gunshot, which attracted the attention of everyone else on the street, the officer remained oblivious to what was going on.

Pavlukoff ran through an alley near the bank and reached an adjoining street before pursuers could see in which direction he turned. The bank robber then walked unnoticed out of the commercial district into a nearby residential area. For the next hour he worked his way north towards Kitsilano Beach, walking through backyards and vaulted fences. Once he almost collided with a woman relaxing in her yard. Six years later she still vividly remembered what happened. "I was next door talking to Betty Hopkins when I heard the gate open. I looked up and saw this fellow coming through. His face was dead white. He unlocked the back gate and side gate. I came around and stood at the side of the house but he never looked back."[7]

Pavlukoff twice more encountered area residents before he finally disappeared from sight. On the first occasion he walked past the window of a basement suite in which a woman was preserving peaches. She watched as he jumped over a railing beside her house, and noticed an ammunition clip slip from his pocket. Her dog was in the back yard and it also saw the intruder. The animal immediately gave chase, almost but not quite catching up to the fleeing bandit.

The killer had a second close call when an eighteen-year-old saw him climb over a fence into the yard of the young man's home. The youth immediately ran out of the house and approached the stranger. The curious teenager said hello, and when Pavlukoff ignored him and kept walking, the teenager followed. "He was dog-trotting and seemed to be forcing himself to keep going. I followed him across the street into the park and he ducked me."[8]

The young man no sooner returned home when he received a telephone call from a friend, who told him of the bank robbery. He immediately realized that the man he met passing through his yard was likely Pavlukoff, and the two friends met to take up the chase. Despite their best efforts, the trail was cold. We "couldn't see him anywhere. We kept searching until the cops picked us up. I think he hid in the park until I'd gone to the beach and then followed me down."[9]

As it later turned out, that is precisely what happened. Pavlukoff waited in the park until he could no longer see any of his pursuers, then took off his suit coat and vest. With them in hand he walked across the road bordering the park and along the side of an apartment building. He quickly made his way to a staircase at the rear of the property, which provided access to the beach. There he almost ran into one of the building's tenants. Before the day was out the startled woman learned just how close she had come to meeting a killer. She said he arrived at the gate leading to the beach slightly before she did. "He said 'pardon me, madam' and opened the gate. He was wearing a shirt and carrying an air force jacket. He was going very quickly, and turned east on the beach."[10]

A few yards from where the tenant and the bank robber met the police recovered the suit jacket and vest Pavlukoff took off in the park. Now coatless, the killer walked parallel to the beach along a clay cliff. Ten feet above him, a stonemason was building a retaining wall, and he noticed Pavlukoff. "He wasn't running but he was going real fast. His black hair was mussed and he didn't look like he was going to the beach. He looked like he had somewhere to go."[11] Within minutes of the two sightings more than fifty police officers descended on the beach, but the quarry apparently left the area.

A day after the attempted robbery the tailor who made the coat Pavlukoff abandoned identified his workmanship, and the police issued a warrant charging Pavlukoff with murder. The search grew in intensity over the next forty-eight hours, when two quite dramatic, and very different, events occurred. The first involved the escaped killer and an elderly hermit.

Adam Tootell was sitting down for supper when Pavlukoff appeared at the door of his shack, offering to split wood in exchange for a meal. The stout, seventy-three-year-old Englishman lived alone near an isolated Canadian Pacific Railway right-of-way and welcomed the company. "I am isolated out there. And I had just got my food in. He looked kind of decent to me so I gave him a meal. He had lots of cigarettes so we sat around and smoked. He seemed like a nice fellow to me."[12]

While the two talked, Tootell noticed the heel of one of Pavlukoff's shoes was missing, and the other was loose. "Well, I had a pair of rubbers in there with a nail that I had stepped on and hurt my foot. They was only size eights though. So I gave him these rubbers and I knocked the nail down a little bit."[13]

Pavlukoff's visit with Tootell ended shortly after Pavlukoff traded his new shirt for one of his host's old ones. The exchange was no sooner completed when an oil delivery truck drove up. Tootell greeted the driver before returning to his shack to find his guest gone. Two days later the British immigrant saw a picture of his guest in a Vancouver newspaper, and notified the city police. Soon after, officers seized the shirt and shoes left in Tootell's shack.

While Tootell and Pavlukoff were getting acquainted west of Vancouver, a former prison guard, who claimed to have once guarded the killer, contacted the authorities to advise that the convict raided a chicken coop outside his acreage just south of the city. The toll collector said he was awakened mid-morning when his dog began barking. Looking out, he noticed Pavlukoff running from his property into an adjoining tract of timber.

> About 10 o'clock I heard Laddie raising hell outside. He sounded desperate. I put on a bathrobe and looked out the kitchen window and saw a man crossing the road. Laddie is a good watchdog and I thought at first that he was just barking at some local guy. I yelled 'Hey' and the man jumped the ditch and started running for the trees. Then it struck me. I said to myself: "It's that so-and-so who shot the bank manager. "Laddie wanted to go after him again but I called the dog back. I called Jim Stokes [a police officer] at Cloverdale and he came right up. We began looking around. I found that so-and-so had been in my henhouse. Then we found the two eggs he dropped as he jumped the ditch and three or four footprints.[14]

Within minutes the police set up roadblocks and temporary headquarters at a local community hall, and a search for the bank robber began in earnest. As night was falling Red, a bloodhound owned by the Monroe State Reformatory and used by Washington State police, arrived to aid in the search. The dog and its two handlers no sooner started out when word was received that a woman spotted a man wearing a tan shirt and dark pants duck into bushes near her home south of the former guard's residence, about ten kilometres from the Canada–United States border. Darkness and dense brush made a night search difficult, so the pursuit was called off until the next morning, when Red and a posse of trackers quickly picked up a scent in a strawberry field. Armed with a machine gun, sawed-off shotguns, rifles, and service revolvers, officers pushed through the field to a gravel road, where Red lost the trail.

The hunt for Pavlukoff throughout the fields and forests of Surrey was the largest in the province's history and the cause of considerable subsequent embarrassment when it was learned that the elusive bank robber was never in the area. At times the search seemed more farce than serious police work.

The Friday following the robbery was typical of the frantic nature of the search. At 6:30 p.m. police were informed that a man matching Pavlukoff's description was sighted crossing a field near a Surrey residential area. Officers promptly rushed to the location of the sighting, and combed the area without finding any evidence of Pavlukoff's presence. Before their search was completed a second call came in, advising that a suspicious character was seen near a railway bridge. Searchers immediately stopped in their tracks, and then took off in a run for their vehicles. Minutes later they reached the bridge. They were just starting to form up to begin their second search of the evening when another call came in. Cars wheeled around, and in a scene more reminiscent of a stockcar race than a police manhunt, tore along gravel roads to yet another bogus sighting.

At 11:00 p.m. a fourth report was received, and minutes later a fifth, when two young women told officers they saw a man in dirty brown clothes peering out at them from a bush. A squad of searchers barely arrived to check out their report when two young males said that they saw Pavlukoff get out of a car. According to the teenagers, the killer asked if there were any police officers in the area.

So many calls were coming in that exhausted officers no sooner arrived at one location when they were called to another. The most exciting report came in around 3:00 a.m. Saturday morning, when the police were advised that a family roused by the barking of their dog believed that they saw

Pavlukoff near their acreage. Hilda Hall told officers that as soon as she heard the noise she woke her oldest son, and the two went to the back door of their home. They decided not to go out when they saw their dog backing away from something, or someone, outside their line of sight.

Everett Hall found the revolver the family kept for protection, and finally opened the door. About seventy-five metres away he saw a man standing in the middle of the gravel road. "When he saw me coming towards him he pulled down his head and ducked into the bush. I fired three shots from my revolver into the air because I didn't want to hit people in the houses behind him."[15]

Almost as soon as the Halls sounded the alarm a flood of police cars swept into their yard. Officers under the command of "Machine Gun" Thompson walked and crawled across nearly a mile of fields in pouring rain and near total darkness. On one occasion, a searcher, startled by a sound behind him, swung around to shoot when he found himself face to face with three cows.

Just before noon Saturday yet another sighting sent a posse on a mad scramble. A fifteen-year-old bicyclist was riding along a road bordered on either side by bush. Although the young man never actually saw anyone, he convinced the police that he at least heard the man everyone was after. "I was riding along on my bike following a police car. Suddenly I heard two steps in the bushes and someone fell down. There was a sound of him getting up and then I heard three more steps."[16]

The number of leads that yielded nothing was a source of frustration to Vancouver police officials, and six days after the murder of Petrie it was becoming apparent that Pavlukoff was not in Surrey, and likely never had been. The search was called off, but by the time Vancouver detectives advised police forces across western Canada to be on the lookout for the fugitive, the killer was already in Ontario. Although investigators could not find Pavlukoff, they at least located the room he occupied during the four days between his release from prison and the bank robbery. While sifting through the sand along Kitsliano Beach near the spot where Pavlukoff dumped his suit coat and vest, investigators found a key. Within hours they were searching his room.

Pavlukoff spent slightly more than five years on the run, and during the last four he lived in Toronto. The fugitive never stayed in one rooming house for long, and invariably wore every article of clothing he owned, prepared to flee at a moment's notice. When apprehended he was wearing so many clothes that arresting officers had difficulty determining whether he had a tattoo on his arm. Although Pavlukoff changed rooms frequently, he stayed most often in the area of Toronto where many of the city's immigrant day labourers resided. According to his last land-lady, the killer avoided contact with others as much as possible and kept his blinds drawn day and night. "He never spoke to anyone and nobody spoke to him."[17]

After living hand-to-mouth for a year, working on construction whenever he could get a job, Pavlukoff was hired on a semi-regular basis by an oil heating company. His boss said the killer called himself Ralph McRae, and when they first met, Pavlukoff was dressed in rags. But "he was well spoken, and I took a liking to him. He was hired on a job-to-job basis. We all knew he had something terrible on his mind all the time we worked with him. But he never said anything."[18]

Although Pavlukoff was offered lots of work, he turned down most jobs, preferring the anonymity of a part-time labourer. The trade-off meant the bank robber often went hungry. A year before he was caught, he called the owner of the heating company and told him he was sick, and asked for help. The man was worried about Pavlukoff, and after taking him to see a doctor, dropped him off at a city hospital. "When he was recovering from his sickness he worked here alone at nights building an office for me. There was often money left around but there was never a cent stolen." Only once did the secretive killer talk to his boss about his background, and "then I knew something bad was on his mind. He said he came from the West, but he couldn't go back."[19]

In the five years between his crime and his capture Pavlukoff was never far from the minds of Vancouver detectives, and every year they arranged to have the fugitive's photograph published in newspapers across the country. A picture of Pavlukoff appeared in Toronto area papers on May 23, 1952. A little over a week later the police received their first solid lead in years. An anonymous caller told police he saw pictures of Canada's most wanted fugitives in a weekend magazine, and recognized Pavlukoff as the man who periodically window shopped in front of his north Toronto store. The caller even directed police to the street corner in North York where the fugitive often loitered. By the time detectives arrived Pavlukoff was nowhere in sight, but investigators continued to monitor the street corner for months. In early January 1953, the tipster called a second time. "The man you are looking for is standing outside my store right now." This time the Good Samaritan kept the escaped killer in sight until police showed up.[20]

Sergeant Arthur Varley was one of two officers sent to find Pavlukoff. Although the killer put on a lot of weight since the bank robbery:

> There was no mistaking Pavlukoff. He looks just like the picture of him that was sent all over the continent following the murder. He seemed relieved that it was all over. He looked drawn — I guess being hunted all over the continent for five years would make anyone look that way. From the few remarks he made I could see he had been leading a lonely, secluded life. His clothes were rather poor. He told us he had been living in Toronto and

After nearly six years on the run and a long trial, Walter Pavlukoff was finally convicted of murdering a Vancouver bank manager during a botched robbery attempt. He spent his last days on death row in British Columbia's Oakalla Prison.

CONDEMNED to hang June 23 for murder of bank manager five and a half years ago, Walter Pavlukoff, flanked by two Mounties, was moved to Oakalla's death row Tuesday night.

Courtesy of *Vancouver Sun.*

doing odd carpenter jobs around Willowdale. Apparently he never stayed in one place long. He was always on the move, in the uneasy way of a hunted man.[21]

Before arresting officers took him to the North York station, Pavlukoff insisted he was Ralph McRae, and that he had done nothing wrong. When he was formally taken into custody the fugitive was searched several times. The police seized a seven inch knife, six hacksaw blades, and two letters. One was addressed "To Whom It May Concern," and the other to his mother.

In his letter to his mother, Pavlukoff made it clear that he viewed himself as a victim, despite spending the greater part of his life victimizing others.

> I was doomed when I was still in my cradle. And it is as certain that I shall be killed. They want to hang me. I expect them to do so. I do not wish to hide my mind from reality. When they go to hang someone the victim sees it so that his becomes a terror-stricken hysterical life. Sometimes they see it so that they go to the gallows quietly. I dread it. To me it is an agony beyond all experience. Death and destruction has overwhelmed our family. Not because of what we did but because of what others did. We looked upon fellow human beings and all we saw in them was our own goodness. But they were evil and cruel and selfish and greedy.[22]

Pavlukoff described thirty years of what he referred to as a life of hunger, taunts, and beatings. I have, he said, been deprived, frustrated, and abused:

"Explain. How can I explain. It is like asking a dead man to explain what it is like being dead." He noted that when he was fourteen he

> was supposed to have the second highest IQ of all the schools in Vancouver. But even then I could feel that I was not as fast mentally as I should have been. And then they began to starve me.

My father worked at pick and shovel in a ditch. In all my life I have never seen anyone with the callouses as he had on his hands. I remember how deep and raw the cracks in his hands were and how he would put Vaseline on them to try and stop them from hurting.... I remember him being tired and how his sweat had stained his undershirt red from the dye in his sweater. I remember how he put wooden boards under the mattress of the old bed that had sagging springs in an effort to help his aching back and to try and sleep.... He died. He tried. He suffered. Now he is dead. I can remember the look in your eyes from starvation and strain.

There is nothing in the future for me. I have lived better in the past four or five years than I have since I was a child. But I have been hungry and cold and wet and done without a good sleep many times ... three years ago I had pneumonia and pleurisy.

I will be carrying a note with me saying I want to be cremated when I am dead. I want to die alone. If you want me cremated in Vancouver it is of no difference to me.... If money cannot be obtained to do this then burn me in a garbage incinerator if necessary. But burn me so that there is nothing left of me as quickly as possible.

My life has been so miserable I wish I had never been born. There just doesn't seem to be any point in having lived it. I have tried to do what was right and decent but I seem to have suffered in the same proportion. I would rather be dead than rot in jail.

From the time they were hunting me to kill me I gave myself five years. Five years in which I would try to live my life as my life wanted to in an effort to get back to my normal self and gain a control. And to prepare so that I could give people some of their own back before I was killed. And to arrange so that when I died I was blown up by explosives into nothing. It has been four years now. People have laughed at me and drove me so hard that I feared for my life … and so I wanted to wait one more year. Now I don't care. Do not worry about me. I am sorry I could not help you. I wish you all well. Goodbye. Your son. Walter Pavlukoff.[23]

As soon as Pavlukoff was officially identified, a detective from Vancouver flew to Toronto to escort the killer home. When the officer advised Pavlukoff that he was being charged with murder, the distraught escapee broke down in tears. When he regained his composure he told the detective: "I don't know what to say. I want to get back and get it all over with. I want to see my mother once more. I have nothing to hope for and there is nothing that I can say that will help me."[24]

A little over a day after being charged with the murder of Sydney Petrie, Pavlukoff was flown back to Vancouver. Though his arrival was greeted with considerable anticipation by some British Columbia residents, his presence on the flight went unnoticed by fellow travellers. When reporters asked passengers what it was like sitting with Pavlukoff, most responded with "Who's he?"[25]

The same could not be said for those waiting on the ground. Even though the authorities tried to keep the timing of Pavlukoff's return a secret, a large group of reporters waited in the airport administration building for a glimpse of the elusive bank robber. A Criminal Investigation Bureau superintendent warned photographers that if they attempted to take any pictures their cameras would be confiscated. The officer said that he planned to put Pavlukoff in a police lineup, and he did not want to give defence counsel possible grounds for calling the identification into question. He need not have worried. After other passengers disembarked the Trans-Canada Airlines North Star Pavlukoff stepped out of the aircraft directly into a police car waiting on the tarmac.

Shortly after the killer arrived at the police station where he was to be held pending his preliminary hearing and trial, his mother walked in. Dressed in an inexpensive, well-worn smock with a large bandana tied around her head, the distraught woman fought back tears as she was taken upstairs to speak with her son. Nearly an hour later she descended, her face buried in a handkerchief and her body wracked with emotion. She said that during her son's flight from the law she seldom ventured from her home, and was nearly paralyzed with worry. "I am sorry I am so nervous," she said, "but every time there is a knock on the door it is a blow against my heart. I may seem alive but inside I am only a shell."[26]

The first bit of good news Pavlukoff had heard for some time was that Thomas Francis Hurley, one of Vancouver's most experienced criminal lawyers, was going to represent him. The day following his return to British Columbia the criminal and his counsel appeared before a police magistrate. Hurley made clear what his defence strategy would be. "I would judge that the question of identification might be one of the vital points in this case. For that reason I would ask for the exclusion of any person ... who is a possible Crown witness."[27]

After two brief appearances in city police court Pavlukoff was remanded for a preliminary hearing, where the Crown was required to show that it had sufficient evidence against the accused to proceed to trial. The preliminary got off to a rough start, at least for Pavlukoff. Instead of leaving the courtroom when the fugitive entered, witnesses were told by the Crown to remain seated. As soon as Hurley realized what happened, he objected.

The Crown was unapologetic. "I wanted these witnesses here to get a look at the accused and I told them to remain in court until he was called." In an admission that seemed to undermine the identification strategy of the defendant, the prosecutor admitted that "It was the only way of identifying the accused. The accused was offered a lineup to avoid this situation and he refused." Over the protests of Hurley, the magistrate allowed the tainted identification in. "Don't lecture me, Mr. Hurley. I want to get to the facts."[28]

One of the first pieces of evidence that went directly to the issue of identification was a moth-eaten hat found near the clothes thrown away by Pavlukoff during his escape. The dark blue fedora, bearing the initials "W.P.", was identified by lead detective Arthur Stewart. Shortly after receiving it the detective testified that he was also given a man's suit jacket and vest. From the markings on the clothing he discovered where the suit was made, and a day after the robbery officers interviewed the tailor who made the garments. In one of his measurement books they found Pavlukoff's name, and attached to his fitting information was a piece of cloth matching that of the suit jacket.

According to the detective, a week after he talked to the tailor he received from Adam Tootell a pair of black shoes and a blue shirt. The officer noted that there were no heels on either shoe, and that one was broken near the heel, while the other looked as though it had been worn without a heel for some time. However poorly he might have been dressed on August 25, 1947, Pavlukoff was a different man during his two-day preliminary hearing. The thirty-nine-year-old wore a new grey, double-breasted suit, rust-coloured sport shirt, and a brightly coloured tie. Evident on each of his new brown shoes was a heel.

Nine people were in the bank when it was robbed, not counting the murdered manager. Of those who testified during the preliminary, four said Pavlukoff did not look like the bank robber, two said he resembled the killer, and two, one of whom was the wife of a Vancouver police detective, were certain he was the man who committed the murder. That was good enough for Magistrate Mackenzie Matheson, and Pavlukoff was committed for trial. It got underway two months later, presided over by a former provincial attorney-general.

In and out of court Mr. Justice Alexander Malcolm Manson was an outspoken, opinionated, abrasive individual, accused by contemporaries of making up his own law as he went along. In the quarter of a century he sat on the bench, more of his judgments were overturned on appeal than those of any other British Columbia judge. A few years after the Pavlukoff trial, Manson spoke as if he was proud of his less than sterling reputation. "As a judge I broke all the rules. Some think it is the sole duty of the court to protect the accused. But it is also its duty to see that society is protected."[29] He seemed almost whimsical when he lamented that "The rock pile has gone and the preachers have done away with hell"[30]

It did not take long for Pavlukoff to complain about Manson's conduct on the bench. After one particularly heated exchange between his lawyer and the judge, Pavlukoff became infuriated. Perhaps sensing his fate, the bank robber jumped to his feet. "Your lordship, I found your behavior very disgusting and you seemed to have formed an opinion already as to my guilt. Not only is my life at stake, but my mother is at home sick, and before you kill her you will have to chain me to this box to keep me here."[31] Justice Manson's response gave some credence to Pavlukoff's complaint about bias. "Fortunately for you, the matter is in the hands of the jury — in the hands of the jury and not in my hands."[32]

After a week-long trial, and a difference of opinion between several Crown witnesses over whether Pavlukoff was the bank robber, it took a jury just one hour to find the career criminal guilty of Petrie's murder, and even less time for Manson to sentence him to be hanged. Until he was, Pavlukoff should have been confined in one of the Oakalla Prison Farm's death row cells. But because his lawyers filed an appeal on his behalf, the bank robber was not regarded as a condemned prisoner. Until that proceeding was finished, he was kept in a section of the prison reserved for those awaiting trial. As a result, he had more privacy than he would have had on death row. He also had access to other prisoners, and contraband.

The beginning of the end for the convicted killer started mid-afternoon on Wednesday, July 8, 1953. After a five-day hearing the provincial Court of Appeal refused his request for a new trial, and one of Pavlukoff's lawyers drove from the courthouse directly to Oakalla. According to the lawyer, his client took the news that he was to be hanged three weeks later without emotion, but seemed pleased Hurley was going to try to take his appeal to the Supreme Court of Canada.

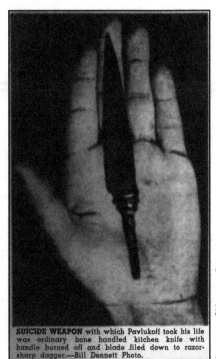

Rules for those about to be executed at Oakalla were relatively relaxed, and Pavlukoff somehow managed to obtain a small knife. Within minutes of learning that the British Columbia Court of Appeal had denied his application for a new trial, the life-long criminal plunged the knife directly into his heart.

SUICIDE WEAPON with which Pavlukoff took his life was ordinary bone handled kitchen knife with handle burned off and blade filed down to razor-sharp dagger.—Bill Dennett Photo.

Courtesy of *Vancouver Sun.*

In an ironic twist of fate, the bank robber was the only person in the prison who knew that his appeal had been rejected. Because of that, instead of being taken directly from his meeting to death row, Pavlukoff was returned to his holding cell. In anticipation of his appeal failing, Pavlukoff somehow obtained a small knife, and removed its handle and sharpened its blade. Where he hid the dagger was never determined, but ten minutes after learning that he was to be executed, the killer placed the point of the knife directly over his heart, then plunged the blade into his chest. Twenty-nine minutes later he was dead.

Hugh Christie, Oakalla's warden, an outspoken opponent of capital punishment, was deeply distressed by the suicide. But as he said later, there was likely no way his officers could have prevented it.

> Manual searches of prisoners are conducted as frequently as once a day. But this was a weapon so small that it could be concealed easily. Pavlukoff may well have concealed it in his mattress. We should have found the knife, but unfortunately we didn't. When a man makes up his mind to kill himself, it's pretty hard to stop him. In any event, it is primarily our fault, because we are supposed to be on the lookout for such things.[33]

Christie said he could not help but to feel that Pavlukoff pondered how to kill himself for a long time before he actually committed the deed. "The precision with which he plunged the blade between two ribs and directly into the heart would indicate that he had spent some time in study. Or else he is just lucky."[34]

9

Pictures on the Dash

Owen "Mickey" Feener

Mickey Feener may have been a high-functioning moron in life, but in death he is the poster child of serial killers. Abandoned as a young man by parents who showed him neither love nor guidance, he married a fifteen-year-old from a similar background, murdered three women infatuated with his good looks and way with words, and did just about everything he could to be caught, short of actually turning himself in to the authorities. He killed on impulse, left his victims where they died, and in each murder was identified as the last person seen with the person he beat to death. Yet despite all this, it took police a year and a half to catch him, and even then they succeeded only because he was driving the flashy red sports car of one of his victims, his name prominently written across its hood with masking tape.

Owen Maxwell Feener was born in Bridgewater, Nova Scotia, in 1937, and from the beginning to the end of the eight years he lived with his parents he was unloved and unwanted. His father was an alcoholic, and Feener was mentally challenged. Add epilepsy to that and you have a child with more than a few problems. Things got worse when Feener was shot in the head and spent three months in hospital. Handed off by his parents to social services, he took his problems with him into foster care. Over the next three years he proved too much to handle, and after being classified as "mentally retarded," he was committed to the Nova Scotia Training School. Feener entered the Truro facility when he was eleven, and left five years later. He could have left earlier, but his mother advised the local Children's Aid Society that she was not prepared to take him back. When he turned sixteen Feener left the school, lonesome, frightened, and absolutely on his own. Not surprisingly, he turned to crime. He was first sentenced to three months in jail for stealing a rifle and hunting knife, and then to a year in reformatory for a couple of auto thefts. As soon as he was released Feener bought himself a car, and for the next three years drove without a licence, worried he was not smart enough to pass a driving test.

Feener was twenty when he married a girl five years his junior. She too came from a troubled background, and before meeting Feener was in and out of trouble with the law. Two years after they married the couple became parents to a daughter, and moved from Kirkland Lake, where Feener was working, back to Nova Scotia. There the relationship came to an abrupt end, in no small part because Feener started an affair with his wife's sister.

> My wife accused me of shacking up with her sister. I tried
> to explain, but no good. That's when our marriage broke
> up. I then accepted her sister.... Well, that didn't last either

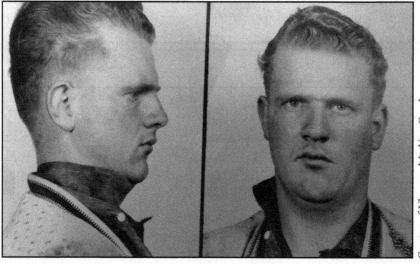

Courtesy of Library and Archives Canada.

Mickey Feener may not look it in this photo, but in the 1950s he was quite the lady's man. He was hanged for murdering two women, and confessed to killing a third. He taped photos of his victims to the dash of his car, along with the pictures of five other women. Although investigators were fairly certainly he killed the unidentified women, Feener kept his mouth shut right to the end.

— well, my wife wanted me back but from then on she got herself in one mess after another. Yes — other men. I then left her for good.[1]

Feener later summed up the relationship he had with his wife as "just cats and dogs — one of us just as bad as the other."[2]

No one knows how Dolly Woods, a seventeen-year-old Kirkland Lake waitress, met Feener, or whether they dated more than once. What is known is that the last time they went out Feener's wife had just given birth, and she was spending the night in the hospital. Woods no doubt found the tall, good-looking, hard rock miner fun to be with, but she kept her last rendezvous with the smooth-talking Feener a secret, at least from her sister, Gloria. The two were living together at a local rooming house, and all her sister knew was that Dolly was there one day, and gone the next. According to Gloria, "she just vanished, leaving all her clothes in my room."

According to Feener, on his date with Woods the couple were driving towards the Ontario-Quebec border with no particular destination in mind. He said they "left Kirkland Lake at midnight and went down the highway to the Quebec border.... It happened at daybreak and I got mad and choked her. I covered the body with brush."[3] He later told investigators that he could not remember where he murdered Woods, or even the exact date, but recalled that he could see the lights of a village fifteen minutes walk away.[4]

In fact, Woods was murdered just after midnight on April 15, 1959, on a lonely stretch of Provincial Highway 48 between Notre-Dame-du-Nord and Rouyn, in the province of Quebec. Ontario investigators reached that conclusion after Feener confessed to beating Woods to death, and they decided to ask their Quebec counterparts if any unidentified bodies had been discovered near the border. Sure enough, berry pickers stumbled onto what was left of Dolly sometime in May or June 1960. A spokesperson for the Ontario Provincial Police said OPP officers had been searching for the body of the missing waitress since she disappeared in April 1959. That may have been true, but one call to Quebec would have saved them a lot of effort. Because the authorities on either side of the border were not talking to each other, Wood's skeleton remained unidentified until Feener told the police where it could be found.

When Feener's second murder victim emigrated to Canada from Belgium she settled in New Glasgow, Nova Scotia, where the thirty-two-year-old opened a dress shop. Sometime over the next two years Cathy Essers met Feener at the Acadia Hotel, a Halifax drinking spot. The two hit it off, and when Essers moved to Toronto in mid-August 1960, she and Feener renewed their relationship. The precise nature of that relationship remains a mystery, at least to Esser's fiancé, Conrad Walther. Walther farmed just north of Toronto, and as far he knew, when Essers disappeared she was on her way home to put her affairs in order before the two were married.

If Essers was truly committed to marrying Walther she certainly had a funny way of showing it. Shortly after arriving in Toronto in her cherry red Austin Healey sports car she and Feener left for Cleveland, then Detroit, with frequent stops along the way for drinks and dancing. On the homeward part of their journey the two got as far as Windsor when they fought and Feener rented a car to return the rest of the way alone. But instead of stopping in Toronto, he drove to Montreal, where he abandoned the rental car on a city street, and took a train home. Within a month Essers and Feener resolved their differences, and when she headed for Nova Scotia in late September 1960, Essers took Feener along. In Fredericton they checked into a hotel as man and wife. According to Feener, at this point everything was fine. He said that when he got back from paying their bill Essers had a drink ready for him. After that one, and a few more, they made love. It was at that point, he recalled, that she started to act funny.

The next day they began arguing about who should drive Esser's car. Esser insisted she should, but Feener said no. She became angry, and hit him over the head with a bottle of beer. Although dazed by the blow, Feener managed to stop the car, then turned on his passenger. "I stopped the car and grabbed her by the throat and almost before I realized it, she was dead."[5] Feener threw his victim's body into the ditch, took her cash, and from her suitcase removed an electric iron. Then he continued on to Nova Scotia. On an impulse, Feener wrote "Mickey" on the hood of Esser's car, in adhesive tape, before returning to Kirkland Lake.

On October 1, Walther reported his fiancée missing, and on the same day someone, presumably Feener, attempted to cash a forged cheque drawn on her bank account. Four days later a badly decomposed body was found in a ditch near Fredericton. It could not be identified; investigators in Nova

Scotia seemed not to have received a copy of the missing person's report filed by Walther.

Feener's third victim grew up resentful. Kathleen Chouinor's father died in 1945, leaving his wife to care for the couple's six sons and three daughters. The widow could not cope with the pressure, and abandoned her children. The eldest daughter, eleven-year-old Kathleen, dropped out of school, and despite her best efforts to care for her siblings, witnessed one after another being placed in a foster home or being forced to take whatever work was available to young men barely in their teens. She never got over the experience, and despite a commitment to family that survived the separation, she grew to resent the life she had been given. By her twenties she was withdrawn, intensely religious, and perhaps out of a sense of failure, obsessed with her reputation. As far as anyone could remember, she rarely socialized. In fact, she went out with a man on only a handful of occasions. Sadly, her last date was with Mickey Feener.

Feener murdered Cathy Essers sometime during the last week of September 1960. On October 4, he showed up unannounced at the residence of a Timmins doctor in whose home Chouinor worked as a domestic. Chouinor had her own room in the large house, and spent most of her evenings alone, listening to country and western or religious music, or reading magazines. On the day she went missing she left on her nightstand *Your Horoscope*, and on her dresser, *Your Dreams*. Chouinor was a complex and secretive person. The attractive twenty-six-year-old spent most of what she earned on her brothers and twin sisters, and was never known to party, yet her closet was full of cocktail dresses. Hanging prominent among them was a fur coat.

When Feener showed up to see Chouinor the two talked in the hallway of Chouinor's employer. The doctor's wife listened to their conversation, just out of eyesight. She heard Feener ask if Chouinor would drive with him to Winnipeg. She refused, and he suggested they could at least go out later that evening. To this she agreed, and Feener left. That Chouinor would agree to the date surprised her employers. Years earlier she went out with Feener, and he made sexual advances, so she refused to see him again. In fact, according to her boss's wife, "Kay grew up with an aversion to men. Apparently she distrusted them and their motives. She was sensitive about her reputation and never considered doing anything that would damage [it] even slightly."[6]

After Feener left, Chouinor told her employer that she thought she may have just made a mistake. Her employer agreed, and tried to talk the young woman out of keeping her appointment, but when Feener showed up at 8:30 p.m., she left in his bright red sports car. No one knows what the couple did for the next three hours, but just before midnight they drove into a service station, and Feener asked the attendant to adjust his car's carburetor. The two then parked somewhere in or near Timmins, and Feener talked about Cathie Essers. At some point Chouinor realized that her companion was confessing to murder. She urged him to go to the police and turn himself in. He refused, she became frightened, and when she tried to get out of the car, Feener grabbed her. "I hit her three times on the back of the head with my flashlight and she passed out. We were still sitting in the car."[7] When Chouinor regained consciousness, she told Feener that she was not afraid to die, and then almost plaintively asked him, "Why, Mickey?" Her attacker said he "then took a hunting knife and struck her on the back of the neck. I don't know how many times."[8]

Although Feener thought Chouinor was dead, she was not, and after driving about twenty miles out of Timmins he realized she was very much alive. He hauled the terrified young woman from the car and carried her to the side of a step bank just off the road. There he threw her to the ground, over and over again, breaking her hip and causing a gush of blood to cover his suit. He ripped from Chouinor the young woman's watch and ring, and killed her with a stab to the throat. Feener then got back in the car and tried to leave. He recalled it was an awful sight. In his panic to get away he got stuck, and his emotions began bubbling over with the realization of what he had just done. He eventually calmed himself, pushed the small car to the roadway, and drove to Kirkland Lake. There he undressed and burned his blood-soaked clothes.

The day he was arrested Feener was later asked by the police to explain what motivated him to brutalize and murder Chouinor. His response was brief. "Not for her money, or sex, but because of the other thing. My nerves were shot. I didn't plan it."[9]

If the failure of the police in Ontario and Quebec to communicate about Dolly Woods is an example of a less-than-stellar investigation, the arrest of Feener speaks volumes about good policing.

When Chouinor failed to return from her date, her employer became concerned, and filed a missing person's report with the Timmins police. While he was doing that, in Kirkland Lake, seventy-five miles south, Detective Ozzie Wright happened to notice Feener walking toward a cherry red sports car. The one-time resident was hard to miss. He stood more than six feet tall in his fancy cowboy boots, weighed every bit of two hundred pounds, and beneath his thick blond hair sprouted the beginnings of a beard. Wright remembered that when Feener left town a year earlier he failed to pay a $33 careless driving fine, and was curious how a deadbeat like Feener could be driving such an expensive-looking sports car. When the detective got closer he could see eight photographs taped to the dashboard, all of women. Wright took Feener and the sports car into custody.

Feener was a smooth talker, but the more he talked, the less Wright believed him. Asked why he was driving a car registered to a woman living in Nova Scotia, Feener told the officer that he and the car's owner met a year earlier in Halifax and renewed acquaintances when she moved to Toronto. She wanted to return to Nova Scotia for some reason, and asked Feener to come with her. Somewhere along the way she gave him her picture. Then she decided that she was not going to Nova Scotia after all. Instead, she was heading for California, and she asked him if he would look after her car. Wright did not believe a word of the story, and contacted the Royal Canadian Mounted Police in New Glasgow. They told him the car belonged to Cathy Essers, a woman reported missing by her boyfriend a week earlier. Wright was also informed that the badly decomposed body of an unidentified woman recently found in a ditch outside Fredericton was almost certainly that of Essers. The RCMP officer had one request: could Wright keep Feener in custody until someone from his detachment arrived with a warrant charging Feener with offering an indignity to a body? That charge would be good enough to hold him until the body was officially identified.

The day after Feener was taken into custody in Kirkland Lake, Timmins police chief Gordon Beacock read a newspaper report of his arrest, and instinctively knew that Feener was somehow involved in the disappearance of Chouinor. Within hours Beacock and two of his detectives were sitting down with the suspect. Feener admitted going out with Chouinor, but claimed he dropped the missing woman off at a bus stop. They got along fine, Feener said, and his date even gave him her picture. Although Feener had an answer for every question, he could not explain why Chouiner would ask to be dropped off at a stop where there had been no bus service for three months. "I didn't know that," he responded. "There used to be when I lived in Timmins. I guess she had to walk then. A long way."[10]

Feener also could not explain why a woman he barely knew would give him her watch and ring, or why he kept talking about her in the past tense, as if she were dead. As soon as Feener realized that no one believed his story, he asked Beacock if he thought that he, Feener, killed Chouinor. The police chief said yes, he guessed he did. Then just like that, Feener confessed. The detectives were back in Timmins by midnight, Feener firmly in hand, and at 2:30 a.m. they discovered Chouinor's badly beaten body lying thirty feet off the road ten miles northwest of town. Her clothing was dishevelled, her underwear was missing, and lying near her coat and scarf was a man's shirt. The murder weapon was found less than a kilometre away. An autopsy conducted the next day revealed that the young woman died fighting for her life. Not only was she slashed multiple times across the chest and back, her hands were badly cut, presumably as she tried to grab the knife with which Feener was stabbing her.

The next day was a Saturday, but it was no day of rest for the RCMP sergeant who arrived in Timmins from Fredericton. He told the officers in charge of the Feener investigation that while the body of Cathy Essers was still not officially identified, there was no doubt it was her. The prisoner, set to be arraigned Sunday for Chouinor's murder, refused to say anything about Essers. Nor would he tell Wright, who the day after Feener was arraigned made the trip from Kirkland Lake to Timmins, anything about the disappearance of Dolly Woods. All he admitted was that he once knew Woods, and that she gave him her picture, which he taped to the dashboard of his car. Asked about the other women whose pictures were alongside those of Essers, Chouinor, and Woods, he said nothing.

At his arraignment on October 12, 1960, Feener was committed to the custody of the Timmins police, pending the outcome of a preliminary hearing to be held two weeks later. None of the fifteen members of the Porcupine Law Society were prepared to represent the accused killer. As a result, during his arraignment he sat alone, occasionally laughing quietly, one hand covering his head. Feener looked every bit the rebel. He walked into the courtroom with his grey pants tucked into his cowboy shoes, his striped shirt open nearly to his waist, his sleeves rolled up to his elbows, and a gold cross hanging from his neck. When Feener's preliminary hearing eventually got underway he was still unrepresented, and made no attempt to cross-examine Crown witnesses. The accused killer was quickly committed to stand trial for the murder of Kay Chouinor.

Before the year was out Toronto lawyer Hugh Latimer agreed to defend Feener against a murder his client freely admitted committing. Latimer quickly launched a motion for a new preliminary hearing, arguing that because his client was not represented at his first hearing, he was effectively denied the right to cross-examine his accusers. A superior court judge agreed, and another preliminary was convened. For the second time Feener was committed to stand trial. It started on March 6, and lasted three days. Key for the defence was the testimony of two psychiatrists from the North Bay Mental Hospital, whose reports were actually prepared at the request of the Crown. The first of the two doctors said that in his opinion Feener "was in an epileptic twilight state at the time of his crime. An epileptic twilight state is a temporary insanity that clears up after some time but has a tendency to recur.… Mr. Feener has been an epileptic for many years."[11] As evidence, the doctor pointed to his dreamlike state of mind, "the explosive outburst of blind destructive aggressiveness, the loss of consciousness, and the consequent well circumscribed amnesia for a considerable part of the event."[12] The second psychiatrist said that after drinking a large quantity of alcohol, Feener had a seizure, and during it he killed Chouinor. There was, he said, no evidence of premeditation.

Latimer did not call Feener as a witness, but in his summation spoke at length of his client's troubled background.

> My one concern in this matter is that an injustice should not be done to a young man, who through an accident of birth was not equipped, mentally and emotionally, to properly look after himself. My client had no motive when he killed this girl of high moral standards. Not sex. Not money. I say the hand that struck the blow was not ruled by the brain.[13]

The Crown Attorney prosecuting Feener acknowledged that the accused had a troubled background, but argued that he was still criminally responsible for his actions. Referring to Feener, he said. "He had a bad upbringing, an abnormal personality and undeveloped mentality, but he is not an imbecile and not an idiot."[14] Members of the all male jury agreed with the prosecutor, and it took them just fifteen minutes to return with a verdict of guilty. The triple killer was sentenced to hang three months and one week later. Before that happened, however, Latimer asked the Ontario Court of Appeal to throw out his client's conviction. They were not prepared to do that, and one month before he was to hang, Feener's remaining hope was an application for clemency.

The federal cabinet met on June 8, to discuss whether to grant a commutation. Some members pointed to evidence that Feener acted like an insane man during his assault on Chouinor, and they suggested that he should be kept in custody for the rest of his life. They felt the murder he was convicted of committing was neither planned nor deliberate, and the method used to kill Chouinor was far from rational.[15] These cabinet members might also have pointed to an amendment to the law dealing with capital murder, which was about to come into effect. It would change

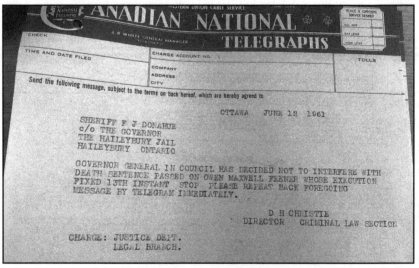

Courtesy of Library and Archives Canada.

To ensure that condemned prisoners did not act up or become violent, the federal government refused to inform death row inmates if they were going to be executed, or have their sentence commuted to life imprisonment. Telegrams like the one received by Mickey Feener typically arrived just hours before a prisoner was scheduled to be hanged.

the definition of the crime, so that in the future capital murder had to be planned and deliberate, two things Feener's was not.

A majority in the cabinet of Conservative Prime Minister John Diefenbaker, however, believed that if Feener was clever enough to try and cover up his crime, and was able to attract women all over eastern Canada, he was sane enough to hang. The majority even rejected the arguments in favour of clemency advanced by Georges Vanier, the country's governor-general. Vanier pointed out that under the *Criminal Code* amendments about to be passed in Parliament, Feener could not be hanged; and, he added, because Feener was by everyone's admission a moron, he should not be hanged.[16] But hanged he was. No doubt members of the federal cabinet, like the jurors who found him guilty at trial, were influenced by a vision of the photos taped to the dash of the killer's car. The three women identified were all murder victims; the fate of the other five remains unknown.

Owen Maxwell Feener was hanged in the courtyard of the Hailey-bury Jail in northeastern Ontario. He died at 1:03 a.m. on June 13, 1961. Whatever concern he may have had for what was to come did not affect his appetite, and he ate with gusto a last meal of steak and French fries. The only thing that seemed to bother him was a sense of guilt over what he had done to Dolly Woods. Two hours before he was to be executed, Feener asked if the sheriff could be summoned to his cell. When the sheriff arrived Feener handed him a scrap of paper, on which he had scribbled a confession. "I'm going to roast in hell," he said. "I'd just as soon do it with a clear conscience."[17] Wherever Feener ended up, it was without his eyes. Just before he began his death walk he decided to make a last gesture: he asked that his eyes be given to an eye bank. His hope, he told those standing around him, was that "the poor devil who gets them trains himself to look at something besides skirts."[18]

The sad and pathetic story of Mickey Feener did not end with his execution in 1961. When her father was put to death, Feener's daughter was a little over two years old. Life was tough for her and her mother, and it got tougher. The daughter was eleven when her only parent gave her away, her mother more committed to a new husband and three new children than she was to the child of a killer. The young girl remembers standing in a phone booth, asking why she was being abandoned.

I felt I was not meant to have any family. And so that is what happened. The mother, the husband and the three other children went on to live their lives and not even take a second to wonder if the little girl that was given away was even alive. It is amazing how the life of my mother [who died during surgery in 2010] and my father may have influenced the choices and the things that occurred in my life. Choosing a wrong partner, going the wrong way and making bad decisions. Having bad things thrust upon me.[19]

Was this, she wondered, her destiny. "I would never understand why."

10

Skeletons Resurface

It is sometimes said that the secrets of our past are sooner or later bound to haunt us. That was certainly the case for the men whose stories are told in this chapter. All three murdered and escaped detection for a considerable time, until the bodies of their victims resurfaced. Strictly speaking, only in one case did a skeleton actually return to the surface; two of the killers simply left their victims where they were killed.

John Munroe:
Nobody Asked About Mother and Daughter

The young architect was anything but subtle. He met his lover at a public event, he courted her in full view of the community, he showed up at her home every Sunday, she gave their baby girl his surname, and virtually everyone who knew him regularly saw the couple out and around Saint John, New Brunswick. When the married father of two (now three) decided to murder the mother of his illegitimate child, he hired a coach and coachman, and twice drove her to the spot where what remained of the mother and child eventually were found. And despite making absolutely no effort to hide his cruel deed, he very nearly got away with the murders.

John Munroe was born in Ireland in 1839, one of three children of a well-to-do carpenter. When the family immigrated to Canada in the 1840s, they settled in Saint John. John worked in his father's lumberyard after school, and it seemed almost inevitable that he would go into the building business. Munroe was ten when his future lover was born. Her father was also a carpenter, but unlike John, Sarah Margaret Vail had anything but an easy life. Her mother died a few months after she was born, and she and her sister made do with whatever was at hand.

Munroe was twenty-three when he married Annie Potts, and before a year passed the couple became the parents of their first child. Three years later the young married man met Sarah at a community event in Caledon, on the outskirts of Saint John. By the time Munroe and his wife had their second boy, Munroe and Vail were lovers. On February 4, 1868, Sarah gave birth to Munroe's baby, a girl she named Ella May Munroe. The affair was public knowledge, except perhaps to Annie.

In 1867 Vail's father died, leaving her the family home. Sarah sold it the following year for $500, a small fortune in nineteenth-century New Brunswick. It seemed only natural that she would turn to her lover for advice about how to invest the money. That was a mistake. Munroe later said he first thought of murdering Sarah and their daughter two days before he committed the crime. With the benefit of hindsight, it is almost certain that he had murder on his mind from the day she sold her home; which perhaps explains why it was then that he purchased a .22 calibre revolver. It was also about this time that he left a letter with a friend in Boston. The letter was addressed to Vail's sister, and was ostensibly written by Sarah. In it Sarah wrote that she had run off with a man she was about to marry, and asked that no one worry about her. The letter was the first step in an ill-conceived plot to murder its alleged author.

Once Vail sold her residence, her life-clock rapidly began winding down. Two weeks before she was murdered, Munroe told Vail that he and a few associates from Saint John were going on a junket to Boston, where they intended to mix a little pleasure with business. When Sarah insisted that she accompany her lover, Munroe obliged her. The pair returned on Friday, October 23, and Vail checked into the Brunswick Hotel as Mrs. Clarke. She informed the proprietor that her husband would soon be joining her and their young girl, and the following day her trunks arrived from the boat. On Monday Munroe showed up in a hired coach. He, Sarah, and Ella May then went for a drive into the countryside north of Saint John. When they returned, Vail checked into the Union Hotel, again as Mrs. Clarke, and Munroe made arrangements for her trunk to be brought from the Brunswick.

Three days later Vail and her daughter were to have left Saint John for Boston, but the day was wet and stormy, and Munroe persuaded Sarah to postpone her trip for a few days. Munroe, on the other hand, did not change his own plans. He and his wife spent the next day and a half on a return trip to Fredericton, New Brunswick. He later said that it was on this trip that he began thinking about murdering Vail and his baby. He kept thinking about how desolate the road was when they drove into the countryside, and became convinced that it would be the perfect place to put an end to the complications his lover brought into his life. With murder in mind, Munroe hired the same coach and driver he retained earlier in the week, and on Saturday he picked up his lover. He also told a number of people that Mrs. Clarke would be leaving for Boston on the following Tuesday, and made arrangements for her trunk to be taken to the steamer *New England*.

When the Munroe party of three reached that part of the road where they stopped the previous Monday, he told the coachman that Mrs. Clarke and her baby would walk from there to the home of friends. He was going to accompany them part way, and would catch up with the driver at a hotel they just passed. With that Munroe and his travelling companions got out and began walking down the deserted road. About an hour later a clearly excited Munroe hurried into the hotel where his driver was eating, and said they were to leave at once for Saint John. Once he got back to the city Munroe put Vail's trunks on the steamer, and for the next year they sat unclaimed in a Boston warehouse.

Despite conducting his affair in full view of almost everyone who knew him, no one seemed to notice that Munroe's lover and her baby were missing. Vail's sister certainly did not care. She and Sarah had a falling out over their father's estate, and there was no one else who might have worried even if they knew the mother and daughter were missing. And indeed, for ten months and twelve days it appeared that John Munroe had committed the perfect murder. Then, on September 12, 1869, a group of berry pickers stumbled across two skeletons, one apparently that of an adult, the other of an infant.

For the next two days dozens of local residents made their way through a hundred feet of bush to see the remains. One of them, William Douglas, was part of a group whose members picked and probed the skeletons to see what they could find. He later recalled that a woman standing near him "took a stick and pulled up a bunch of hair, all braided, then she stuck the stick down again in the same place and turned up a part of a bonnet. I turned over the skull, and out of it ran brains and stuff, making a great smell. There was a little shoe there too, and a stocking in it; there was some kind of corruption in it, which, when the shoe was turned over, ran out, making a bad smell."[1] A considerable amount of braided hair was attached to the skull, a sizeable curl on one side, styled in what then was referred to as a waterfall. Lying near the skull were pieces of a child's smock and a tiny shoe. To even the uneducated eye it was obvious that the remains had been eaten by animals.

When the authorities arrived they were not quite sure what they were dealing with. So little remained of the bodies that were it not for Vail's skull, they might have thought they were looking at the bones of an animal. It did not take long, however, for suspicion to point in the direction of Munroe. Once it became public knowledge that the skeletons were those of a woman and infant, witness after witness recalled seeing Munroe with two such people, and when Vail's trunks were returned from Boston unclaimed on September 29, Munroe's luck ran out. The luggage was quickly indentified as belonging to Vail, and when the authorities opened the trunks, inside one they found a picture of Munroe. He was arrested, and despite several cautions not to say anything, began talking. With him following his arrest were Francis Jones, Chief of Police for the Parish of Portland, and Humphrey Gilbert, a local barrister who doubled as a Saint John police magistrate. Gilbert advised Munroe that because of all the talk about his relationship with a missing woman and child, it was thought appropriate to have him arrested. Gilbert told the prisoner that it was his duty to warn him to keep his own counsel. Gilbert then took Munroe to an office on the second floor of the courthouse, where John Marshall, the Chief of Police for Saint John, was waiting. As soon as Gilbert, Marshall, and Munroe sat down, Munroe started telling his story. Gilbert immediately stopped him: "I then said to the prisoner not to tell anything about it, as we might be brought on the stand. He said he did not care; if he was brought on the stand himself, he would tell the same as he would tell them."[2]

According to Gilbert, Munroe informed them that:

he was introduced to this girl first in Carleton; that he had went to see the girl many a time, said she had a child.... He said last fall he was going away on a little tour to Boston with some gentlemen from the city, partly on business and partly on pleasure; that the day before he left, I think he said Sunday, he went to see her, and she insisted on going with him. [On the return trip] When near Saint John, she asked him to get a coach for her; he did so, and on the way to the American Hotel, she asked him how far it was to Collins', as she wanted to go out there. He told her it was from twelve to fifteen miles, and he promised to drive her out. He said he did drive her out. After they drove out a piece on the road past Bunker's, he took her and the child out of the coach, and they walked on, and sent the coach back to Bunker's. After they got on a piece she went on ahead, and after awhile came back again and said the parties were not at home she expected to see. He said they then walked back to Bunker's, and took the coach and came home; that the understanding between him and her was that they would go out again; they did go out a second time. He said that in going out she complained of being at Mrs. Lordly's; that she did not like Mrs. Lordly. He named some other hotels, and the coachman took them to the Union Hotel, in Union Street. He left her there. The second time they went out he turned the coach back at the same place he did the first time. She walked on ahead again. She came back and told him the parties were home that she wanted to see, and for him to see her trunks for Monday's boat; that on Monday morning he was at the boat and put her trunks on board.[3]

Gilbert and Marshall did not for a moment believe Munroe's story, and after a short preliminary hearing the architect was committed to trial. It got underway on December 7, 1869, before Mr. Justice John Campbell Allan. The attorney-general of New Brunswick was Crown Prosecutor, and he was assisted by a local barrister. Both men were later appointed judges of the Supreme Court of New Brunswick. Munroe was defended by W.H. Tuck, one of the most prominent lawyers in Saint John.

Robert Worden, the driver of the coach in which Munroe and Vail made their two journeys into the countryside, was among the first witnesses called to the stand. His testimony was the strongest evidence against Munroe presented by the Crown.

> He [Munroe] employed me on King Street, in this city, in 1868, in the fall, just before the Commercial Bank failed: it was the first of the week he asked me what I would charge to drive a lady and child to Collins'. I told him I did not care about going. He said it did not matter what the charge was, as it did not come out of him. I then told him it would be worth five dollars. He said for me to drive to the Brunswick House, there was a lady there — a friend's wife — who he had to see out to Collins. He told me to go there and inquire for a lady by the name of Mrs. Clark. I did so, and she said she would be ready soon. Munroe was in the coach. In about five minutes she came down. She had a child with her. I took the child to be about a year old. She carried it down in her arms and got in the coach with it.[4]

According to Worden, after Munroe and the woman were driven a short way into the countryside Munroe told him to stop, and Munroe and the woman got out.

> He took the child and the lady and he got out. He said Collins' was nearby, and they would as leave walk.... He said he would walk back to Bunker's, and for me to go there and feed. He said Collins' were friends of hers.... I went back to Bunker's, put up my horses, and ordered dinner. I think I drove at the rate of five or six miles an hour; it did not take me over ten minutes to come. I had been there about an hour and a half, and had my dinner, when Munroe came back. He asked me if I was ready to

return to town; I said yes. He said the folks were not at home whom Mrs. Clarke wished to see, and they would have to come back another day. He paid me $5.... It was about two o'clock. On the way in he said to me that I need not drive to the Brunswick House again, as Mrs. Clarke and Lordly did not agree. I said I would take her to the Union Hotel. He said that would be handy for me to take her to the boat on Thursday morning. I drove her to Mrs. Lake's, Union Hotel.... [then Munroe] told me to go to Lordly's and get her trunks.

I did not see Munroe again until Saturday.... When I saw Munroe on Saturday following, it was on King street about 9 o'clock in the morning. He said he wanted to go on the same trip again. I told him I would be ready.... I was at Lake's about 11 o'clock in the morning.... The lady came down dressed much as on the former occasion; she had no luggage with her, that I saw, only the child. Munroe was in the coach. She and the child got into the coach again with Munroe. I do not recall of him speaking to me from the place we started until we got to the same place on the Black River road where we had stopped before. He said for me to stop, and they would walk down as before. I stopped and let them out. He told me to go back and feed, and he would soon be back again. I went back to Bunker's. I turned, looked back, and saw them walking along the road — she was carrying the child. They were on opposite sides of the road from each other.

It was before one o'clock when I got there [Bunker's]. He came about half-past one.... He asked me if I were ready to go. I told him that I had ordered my dinner. He said he would rather pay for my dinner than have me wait.... Munroe was sweating, said it was a hard walk, he was wiping his forehead; did not observe anything else wrong.... he told me to take Mrs. Clarke's trunks from Lake's to the American boat, on Monday morning, and he would be there to receive them.... Saw him on Monday morning at the American boat about 7 1/4 in the morning.[5]

Aside from Worden, the Crown called to the stand everyone who resided anywhere near the spot where the skeletons were found. None had ever heard of a Mrs. Clarke, or Sarah Margaret Vail for that matter, and no one was expecting a visit from either woman on the day the murder was believed to have been committed. Among the dozens of other witnesses to testify were a score of experts, including three doctors and a land surveyor. All Munroe's lawyer could offer was a handful of character witnesses and in the trial's closing moments, an alibi. A local farmer told the packed courtroom that a year earlier he was:

> coming to St. John to market with my son ... She came into Mr. Crawford's soon after I got there.... She said she was waiting to come in on the mail. The mail did not come along. She had with her a small child, from nine to twelve months old — a very small child. She told me she would pay me to bring her in; I said all right; I would not allow the lady to walk in at any rate.... My impression is she called herself Mrs. Clark. I am a poor hand at describing. She was a lowish sized woman, dressed in dark clothes, a black straw hat with dark ribbon, I think, crossed over the top of it. I brought her into town to where the old hay scales were, near the Golden Ball. She got off there; she said she would be in the market, in the afternoon or morning and pay me, but I never saw her after.[6]

In the second half of the nineteenth century it was settled law that an accused murderer could not testify on her or his own behalf. By 1869, however, the lawyer for someone on trial for murder could at least make a closing argument to the jury. Munroe's lawyer made just such a statement. He started with what amounted to an extended rant against the state of the law, beginning with an attack on capital punishment.

I have already spoken to you of the unsatisfactory state of our criminal law. I raise my voice once more against it. I would raise my voice in my dying hour did the thought then flash across my mind, against its monstrous cruelty and injustice. It is not my duty now to argue the question of capital punishment. Respecting that, and the right of any state or court to inflict it, we probably all hold different opinions, but it is an awful thing for any court, or any set of men in cold blood, by any machinery of law, to take the life of a fellow being. If you, gentlemen, find a verdict of "guilty" in this case not one of you can escape the responsibility of so taking the life of a human being, and when the scaffold is erected, and the bell is tolling, and the rope is placed on the neck of the victim, in that dread hour not one of you can escape responsibility for what is done.[7]

The lawyer then mounted a vigorous attack on what he alleged was an improperly received confession.

The law of England does not favour such confessions as these. It is harsh enough, severe enough, cruel enough, without authorising its officers to cross-question and torture the prisoners in their custody into making confessions, to be used as evidence against them.... what can the public think of John R. Marshall, whose duty it is to protect the prisoner when in his custody — he who had met this prisoner in the family circle, had known him from boyhood, had worshipped before the same altar with him, and under the guise of friendship entered his cell and said, "Now John, if there is any one in whom you should have confidence, it is in me: I have known you and your family, and your friends, and whatever you say to me shall be in strict confidence," and then, when he had thus betrayed his victim into confession, immediately repeats what he had been told to the authorities.

This is what John R. Marshall did. In the guise of a ser-
pent he obtained a confession, and then betrayed the
confidence of a man he called his friend. No conduct
could be more despicable, mean and contemptible than
this — nothing more horrible in a Christian.... Based
on this statement is the whole or nearly the whole of
the evidence. I do not envy the feelings John R. Marshall
must experience if his miserable, contemptible, sneaking
conduct succeed in making a case.[8]

Before closing his address with a discussion of reasonable doubt,
Munroe's lawyer fired two last salvos at those he suggested were out to
get his client — the Crown and local newspaper editors. He told jurors
that the prosecutors virtually ransacked every corner of the country for
people prepared to say something about the case, however insignificant
it may be.

While I admit that the greatest courtesy has been shown
to myself personally, I must protest most solemnly against
the manner in which the case has been conducted, which
falls little short of being positively blood-thirsty.... Even
the hunted hare is not run to earth without a fair start;
but the law officers of the crown seem determined to
fasten their bloody fangs at once on the prisoner, and at
all hazards send him to the gallows.[9]

If the barrister's criticism of the Crown was strong, his comments
about the local press virtually dripped with venom.

It was bad enough that statements at variance with the
laws of evidence, admitted at the preliminary investigations by gentlemen not very well acquainted with that
law, should have been published; but some of the papers
went even farther than this, and ... some of the religious
papers undertook to sum up the evidence, hold the scales
of justice, weigh the evidence, and decide adversely to

the prisoner. Good God! are we in a Christian country? Did not these writers know that this man would have to undergo a trial on this charge? Was it right, was it fair, was it Christian, to labor thus to create prejudice against him? Do they forget that the same God who gave the commandment "Thou shalt not kill," also commanded "Though shalt not bear false evidence against thy neighbor?"[10]

The defence counsel was at his eloquent best when he again and again returned to the argument that there simply was not enough direct evidence for jurors to be persuaded of his client's guilt.

It is said that Sarah Margaret Vail was taken out by the prisoner to the neighborhood of the Lake and there foully murdered. There is no positive evidence of this.... Is there any testimony to show that this girl whom the prisoner drove out was Sarah Margaret Vail? There is no such testimony. The only evidence on that point is his own admissions. Where is the proof that the Miss Vail he spoke of is Sarah Margaret Vail? No witness proved that. It remains unestablished. Inferences won't do in a case like this. The fact must be incontestably proved.

Then consider that the man who intends to commit murder chooses secrecy, silence, darkness. What secrecy was there in the conduct of the prisoner? In broad daylight, in one of the principal streets of the most populous city of the Province he takes a coachman off the stand, drives to a hotel, there takes up this woman, then drives out in the Lake in view of the whole country. If this was a preparation for murder the annals of the world present no parallels to this act, nor could any one present, in his wildest day dreams, have imagined anything so preposterous as that he should thus, in broad day, have gone to commit such a crime in the light of that sun which at the instant should have been darkened. Good God! it is incredible.

If he wished to commit this murder why did he not do it when they were together in the States. In a large city like Boston there were many opportunities. They were strangers in a strange land. No one knew him or her. Completely under his control, as she was said to be, what was there to prevent his dragging her into a place suited for such a deed, and then committing it under cover of darkness. If her body were afterwards found no one would know her.... why at least did he not make some attempt at concealment? Why did he not get a buggy as he might have done and take her up at some street corner and drive her to the place where he meant to perpetrate this deed? But he did not do this. Did you ever hear anything like this?[11]

Ultimately, the emotional appeal of Munroe's lawyer fell on deaf ears, and after deliberating less than two hours jurors returned a verdict of guilty. There was only one option available to Justice Allan, and he told Munroe that he would have until February 15, 1870, to prepare himself to die. That is precisely what the convicted killer did. In the days immediately preceding his execution he came to accept the inevitability of what was to come, and spent his daylight hours either in prayer, or in conversation with his spiritual advisers. The night before he was to hang, no doubt at their request, he confessed to the two murders.

The first time I went out with Miss Vail it was only for a ride. We had no quarrel and our going was at her wish. We got out of the coach, at or near the place described on the trial, she had a satchel, and we walked along the road, I cannot say how far, sat down, and had a bite to eat. We both fired at a mark, she using a pistol I had given her — one of a pair — a breech loader, same as my own. The mate I gave to a friend. I had learned her to use it. There was no intention on my part to harm her at that time. We came back and I left her at Lake's. She was to have gone to Boston on the Thursday after our first going out, but it was too stormy, and I went with my wife to Fredericton on that day, and came down again on Friday night. It was during that trip to Fredericton I first thought that the spot I had visited with Miss Vail on the Monday previous was a suitable spot to commit a bad act. I went out again with Miss Vail the Saturday following. We went the same road as before and to about the same place. The morning was frosty, the moss crisp and hard. There was no wet on the barren. The road was a little muddy. We went off the road a little way together and sat down. I went into the bushes, the child cried, I came out again, was angry, and strangled the child. I do not know if it was actually dead. As she was rising up, I shot [Miss Vail] in the head — I do not think on the same side as shown in the court. I threw a bush over her face and some over her hands. I found the pistol in her pocket, or just fallen out of it, a common handkerchief and a wallet with only a few dollars in it. I threw the handkerchief and wallet away and left at once and have never been back since. I had previously had some of her money — cannot say how much — perhaps half or a little more. I cannot say that money was not one of the reasons of the motives for the act committed. I do not say it was in self defence I killed Miss Vail. It was the money, my anger with her at the time and my bad thoughts on and after the trip to Fredericton working together, caused me to do the bad act. The letter written to Mrs. Crear [Maggie's sister] was written by me, and mailed in Boston by a friend of mine living in or near Boston. I never killed any other person or child.[12]

The day of Munroe's execution a local paper spoke of the deep sadness enveloping the city. "Today a funeral pall hangs over our city; this a morning of sorrow — deep ineffimable sorrow. The crime of murder — murder the most cold-blooded, brutal and abhorrent — has been expiated by the life of the perpetrator.... Oh! May Munroe's ignominious death, act as a warning to seekers of illicit pleasure, and other degrading vices, turning them back into paths of uprightness and honor."[13]

Munroe woke on the fifteenth about 4:00 a.m., and dressed himself in dark pants, a white shirt, and boots. Never well-off, all he had to leave his wife was a gold watch and chain, and he asked his jailors to ensure that his widow received them. At 7:45 a.m. three things happened almost simultaneously. The executioner who was to hang Munroe entered the condemned man's cell and pinioned his arms to his side; a bell began tolling a notice of the impending execution; and a black flag was raised over the jail. Before Munroe left his cell his hangman placed a white cloth hood over his head, and pulled it down until it rested on the architect's nose. When all was in readiness, the procession of sheriff's officers, spiritual advisers, hangman, and killer started out. As they walked to the gallows everyone, including the guards who lined the corridor, joined in singing *Rock of Ages*.

The scaffold Munroe saw as he stepped from the jail into the court-yard was quite unlike the structure most closely associated with official hangings. This one consisted of a single tall post, to which a long beam

Courtesy of Peel Art Gallery, Museum and Archives.

Typical execution carried out in the courtyard of a Canadian jail. When executions were carried out in jail, courtyard scaffolds were usually constructed as close to the jail as possible, so that a condemned prisoner would have little time to panic after seeing for the first time the instrument of death that was about to take her or his life.

was fastened with a swivel. The noose, which was to be placed around Munroe's neck, was attached to one end of the beam, and the other end of the rope ran along it and through the back door of the jail, where it suspended a weight of several hundred pounds a few feet off the ground. As soon as he was told to proceed, the hangman cut the rope holding the weight. When it dropped, the end of the beam to which Munroe was attached swung up, jerking the condemned man into the air. The force of gravity eventually caused his body to fall back towards the ground, and Munroe's neck received a second jerk before he was left dangling two feet over the platform. It was not a pretty sight, and things soon got worse. "For a moment there was no motion save the swaying of the body, then the hands began to work, the fingers clutching and then closing with a grip. The legs were not drawn up, but by muscular contraction were turned over across the other somewhat. The neck was evidently not broken, death resulting from strangulation."[14] Twenty minutes later the man who very nearly got away with two murders was dead.

Maurice Ryan: Bones of a Brother

It seemed that no matter how hard Maurice Ryan tried, he was always his own worst enemy. Nothing he did turned out right, and certainly not the murder of his brother. In the waning years of the first decade of the twentieth century the Ryans were notorious in the North Bay area of northern Ontario. Francis Joseph was the more high profile of the brothers, and the brothel he operated was one of the region's better known pleasure palaces. Maurice, on the other hand, was a regular in the town's bars and gambling dens. Neither was the type of man who could be trusted. And that was what cost Francis his life.

In many frontier communities like North Bay houses of ill repute were a fact of life. Although not formally part of the established order, they were nonetheless tolerated, provided those who ran them kept a low profile. That was something Francis simply could not do. On November 5, 1907, the authorities finally decided to bring him to account, and charged him with keeping what locals referred to as "a house of ill-fame." But for Francis, going to jail was not an option, and rather than stay around to answer to the charge, he decided he leave town. With his brother in tow, he closed his account at the Ottawa Bank and withdrew his substantial savings, rented a horse and buggy for the trip to the train station, then headed home to pack his bags. While he was there he told the attractive young woman who managed his business that he was leaving for the United States, and after settling his affairs in North Bay he would be back to pay her what she was owed. Around 9:00 p.m. he did just that, and in the process displayed a huge wad of money.

The last anyone saw of Francis, he was sitting beside his brother as the two drove from town towards the train station at nearby Callander. The next morning Maurice returned the rented buggy and claimed he had no idea where the blood came from that was plainly visible all over the wagon and on the suitcase, which Francis apparently forgot to take with him when he got on the train.

For the next few days Maurice was seen everywhere. First he showed up at his brother's former place of business, claiming to have purchased the contents of the house, which he promptly sold to the brothel's new operator. He then headed to his favourite bar, where he paid his tab with bills peeled from a roll of cash surprisingly large for a man previously dependent on the goodwill of others. Asked where the money came from, Maurice said he won it playing poker. Next came a trip back to the livery stable, where Ryan repaid money borrowed from the owner. Apparently worried that he was getting a little low on funds, Maurice showed up at the Traders Bank, and cashed a cheque drawn on an account of his brother's New York bank.

Over the next few weeks Maurice spent time just about everywhere people drank, and when asked about his brother, always responded that Francis was well, and the two were in regular contact. That response may have satisfied strangers, but it did nothing but raise a suspicion in the mind of James, a third Ryan sibling. When he last saw his absent brother, Francis was looking forward to getting out of town and promised to get in touch once he settled somewhere in the United States. Of course, James did not actually expect Francis to write, since he knew his brother was illiterate. You can imagine his surprise, then, when he received not one, but two letters, the first mailed from Vermont, and the second from Ottawa. Although in each the writer claimed to be Francis, James recognized the handwriting. The letters were written by his sister.

Almost exactly a year after Francis was last seen alive a homesteader clearing land eight miles from North Bay literally stumbled across a skeleton lying in bush, about sixty feet off a road. The remains were under two trees, which fell when the area was burned over some months earlier. Although the fire destroyed what was left of the corpse, when investigators removed the bones, they found beneath them a bullet, a watch, and a tag bearing the name "Francis Joseph Ryan."

As soon as Ontario Provincial Police officers knew the identity of the dead man, they were convinced that Maurice killed his brother, and he was promptly arrested. Making matters worse for the black sheep of the Ryan family was the fact that two weeks before Francis went missing Maurice threatened to kill him. Things became heated when Francis refused to lend his brother $5. To get even, Maurice threatened to tell his mother that Francis was keeping a bawdy house. That, he told everyone within listening distance, would kill her, "and I will kill him."[15]

In late March 1909, Maurice went on trial for murder. The proceedings were a formality. Witness after witness testified that just about everything Maurice did following the disappearance of Francis made them suspicious that something was amiss. Even the alibi Maurice offered investigators did not hold up. The accused killer said he was not the person who drove his brother to the train station the night he disappeared. The driver, he said, was James Driscoll. When Driscoll was called to the stand he brought with him a copy of his work record, which proved beyond a shadow of a doubt that in the months before and after the killing he was nowhere near North Bay.

Because Maurice did not testify at his trial, all his lawyer could do was suggest to jurors that his client should not be convicted because (a) the Crown failed to show that Francis was dead, and (b) the Crown failed even to prove that the skeleton discovered in the bush was that of a man. Neither of the arguments did anything to change the minds of jurors, and twenty-five minutes after they began deliberating they returned to court with their verdict. A little over two months later Maurice paid the price for his crime.

June 3, 1909, dawned bright and beautiful in North Bay, and it was a day of great promise, for everyone except Maurice Ryan. He spent the previous evening in quiet conversation with his spiritual adviser, taking time to converse with a few of the newspaper reporters on hand to witness his execution.

> I am not guilty of the crime which I have been convicted of, nor do I know anything about it, and I thank Mr. Bull, my lawyer, for what he has done for me, as I did not have one dollar to pay him for fighting my case. If I had another trial I could have proved where I got the money, but I did not know I would have to account for it; and, not being able to see my lawyer until the last few days, I was unable to give him the information I wanted, consequently he had nothing to work on for a new trial, nor had he any money to work with. I had several witnesses, but did not have money to get them here, and I did not know where they were before the trial, finding out afterwards, but too late. I hope that people will soon learn that I died an innocent man. I forgive my enemies, and die with a clear conscience, so help me God.[16]

During his last hours Ryan did not appear troubled by what was to come. He slept soundly until thirty minutes before he was to be hanged. Then things passed in a blur. After his spiritual adviser woke the sleeping killer the two talked for a little more than ten minutes, and then the hangman arrived. He quickly pinioned Ryan's arms behind his back, and with the local sheriff leading the way, the small group milling about the death cell departed for the scaffold. Behind the sheriff came a turnkey, followed by the condemned man, his executioner, and reciting prayers as he walked, Ryan's spiritual adviser.

As soon as Maurice caught sight of the scaffold he began to cry, and for a time appeared to be on the verge of collapse. With every step up the stairs to the platform of the gallows his panic grew. By the time he was guided to the trap door, he was almost shouting, "I am innocent!" The hangman quickly pulled the death hood over the killer's head, but as he started to bend to pinion his legs, realized that Ryan was about to collapse. The executioner immediately stood, and as he did he pulled the lever. One moment Ryan was there, and in the next he was gone.

The drop did not break his neck, but it instantly rendered him unconscious. It took Ryan almost twelve minutes to strangle to death, his body hanging motionless as his oxygen-starved brain slowly stopped functioning.[17]

Marcel Bernier: The Bodies Came Back

Quebecker Denise Therrien was a sixteen-year-old honour student at South Shawinigan High when she went missing in August 1961. Like her mother, she was pretty, petite, and a hard worker. In fact, with only two weeks of her summer holidays left, she was determined to earn a few more dollars so that she could add to her back-to-school wardrobe. With that in mind she registered with the Provincial Employment Bureau in Shawinigan for work as either a housekeeper or babysitter.

On August 7, she had a stroke of luck. Micheline, her sister, was a receptionist at the Bureau, and when a man phoned inquiring about a babysitter, Micheline immediately thought of Denise. She told the man she had someone in mind for the job, and she would call him back to get more details later. No, that wouldn't do, he said. He would call back. With that he hung up, and Micheline called her sister to see if she wanted the $25 a week job. A couple of hours later the man phoned, identifying himself as Claude Marchand. Micheline told him someone would be able to start the following day, and took down instructions for where the babysitter would be picked up.

When Micheline got home after work she again talked to Denise about the job, and sensed that her sister was a little hesitant about taking it. In the end the sixteen-year-old shook off her sense of foreboding and admitted she needed the money. The next morning Denise put on a green dress, matching shoes, black socks, and a black sweater. From her summer savings she took $3 to pay for her bus fare to the spot where she would be picked up. On the way she asked the driver to drop her off near the Caribou Motel, about two miles distant. When the bus arrived at her stop no one was waiting. Denise stayed in her seat for almost another mile, and then decided to get off and find a phone to call home. But no sooner had the bus pulled to a stop than a truck pulled up. After a brief conversation with the man behind the wheel, Denise got into the vehicle.

No one in the Therrien residence slept that night. When Denise did not return from her appointment by 7:00 p.m. relatives and family friends began searching for her. Their first stop was the address given to the employment agency by the man who called himself Claude Marchand. It turned out to be an empty chalet, already shuttered for the winter. Early the next morning the telephone rang. As luck would have it, the phone was answered by Micheline, who realized at once to whom she was speaking. "I recognized the voice. He was the same person who called on Monday. He said Denise would be returned safely on Thursday if we didn't call the police."[18] Then he hung up. Before he did, she got the distinct impression that there was someone in the background whispering to the caller.

Despite instructions not to do so, Henry Therrien, the father of Micheline and Denise, called the police. It was their belief that Denise had been kidnapped, a suspicion that grew stronger when seven more calls were received over the next day and a half. Thursday evening the calls stopped. Even at this stage in the investigation, however, a number of police officers involved in following up leads thought there was more to the disappearance of Denise than a kidnapping. What concerned them was that at least twice over the summer other women responded to similar requests for a babysitter, and one of the women was sexually assaulted. Another assault likely was avoided when a woman showed up at the Caribou Motel with a friend.

A couple of days after their daughter went missing the Therriens were sitting on their porch. The couple was frantic with worry and exhausted by the constant searching. This afternoon was warm and sunny and the two decided to sit for awhile. Suddenly a truck drove up. Beside the male driver sat two women. The man walked over to the Therriens and introduced himself. He said his companions were his wife and his mother-in-law. The Therriens were a little taken aback, since they had never seen the three before. When the driver began speaking to the distraught parents, he used vulgarities not normally tolerated in the deeply conservative home. Looking directly at them, the man said "It takes a real s.o.b. to do a thing like that."[19] What startled the Therriens more than the language was the implication behind his words. Their daughter was missing for less than a week, and there was no official indication that anything bad might have happened to her. Mrs. Therrien recalled being upset by the comment of their visitor. "We had had no news whatsoever from her or about her since she disappeared."[20]

Denise was gone barely a week when the police began receiving sightings of young women believed to be the missing girl. One of the first came from North Bay, where a girl registered at an area motel using the name Denise Therrien, giving Shawinigan as her home address. The same day Quebec Provincial Police received a report that someone who looked just like Denise was standing in front of a Hull theatre. A third call came from a trucker, who said one of the female hitchhikers he picked up near Shawinigan looked a lot like the missing youth. The most promising of the false leads involved a nineteen-year-old male said to have been the missing girl's lover. When investigators received the report they sensed they may finally be making progress. The man was located in Toronto, and brought to Montreal under police escort. It turned out that although he did know Denise, the two had never met — they were pen pals. While these reports were troubling, the Therriens were more concerned by comments they were reading in local newspapers, to the effect that police were now convinced that Denise was dead.

With nothing to show after weeks of searching, the mayor of Shawinigan called a public meeting to discuss what should be done. The consensus was that Denise was either dead, or had been kidnapped. Those attending the meeting agreed that if she was taken, they should do something while there was still time. The mayor agreed, and called on the missing girl's abductors to name their price. The first ransom note arrived at the Therrien residence on August 19. The five page letter was written in French and printed on sheets torn from a small, 1961 calendar. Although not dated, the note was postmarked "Shawinigan — August 18," and addressed to Henry Therrien. It instructed Denise's father to wrap up $5,000 in $10 bills, and suspend the package from a railing at the north end of a bridge on Montreal Island. "As soon as we got the money, five hours later we will bring her down to your home unharmed."[21] The note also contained a warning not to seek the help of either the police or civilians, and on a separate sheet, printed in large letters, the words "$5,000 in exchange for Denise. She is well." The letter was signed "Claude Marchand." Henry Therrien followed the instructions to the letter, but five hours after hanging the package from the

Charlemagne Bridge his daughter was still missing. When he returned to Montreal the following morning, the money was where he left it.[22]

A second ransom note was received six days later, again by mail. This one demanded $8,000, and instructed Mr. Therrien to place the money under a rock behind a local bus station by no later than midnight the day the note was received. Once again Therrien did what he was told to do, and once again the money went unclaimed. Although both notes were hand printed, investigators concluded they were produced by different people. But written ransom requests were not the only demands received by the Therriens. Every day for almost a week they answered a telephone demand for money. The first two callers wanted $5,000, while subsequent ransomers asked for a different amount. Police suspected that more than one of the calls were likely from the same person, and an investigator was stationed in the Therrien home in case further calls came in. When the telephone finally rang, the waiting officer instructed Therrien to keep his caller on the line, and headed into Shawinigan, where he located a man standing in a phone booth. The officer casually walked over, and when he heard reference to a $5,000 ransom, he placed the caller under arrest. Well before Denise was found the would-be fraudster completed his three-year jail sentence for trying to extort money from her parents.

By the end of August the entire Therrien family was worn out and desperate for news. Henry's brother placed a newspaper ad offering $10,000 for a picture, or even a negative, showing Denise either dead or alive. Interviewed by reporters about the ad, Henry made no apologies. "The negative must show my daughter so that she can be recognized. It may be a picture of her dead or alive. Either is acceptable."[23] Therrien told reporters that out of desperation he and his brother also visited a mystic living near Shawinigan, and hired a team of private detectives from Montreal, to assist the Quebec Provincial Police in their investigation.

When Denise Therrien went missing Marcel Bernier was a grave digger employed by the St. Michel Cemetery. Because the cemetery and Bernier's small house were just across the highway from the spot where Denise was picked up by the mysterious Claude Marchand, he initially came under suspicion. Although police questioned him at length about the disappearance of the young woman, Bernier denied knowing anything, and even agreed to take a lie detector test to prove his innocence.

With nothing to hold him, he was released. A more thorough investigation may have turned up something that would have helped investigators solve not one, but two murders.

The exact nature of Bernier's relationship with Laurette Beaudoin was never made clear, but at the very least the two were drinking friends, and likely more intimate than that. About a week before Beaudoin went missing in April 1962, the pair were socializing. Bernier reached into his pocket for some money, and when he took his hand out a woman's wallet fell onto the ground. Beaudoin did not make much of it at the time, even after Bernier told her that the wallet once belonged to Denise Therrien. But the more she thought about it, and drank, the more determined she was to profit from what she had learned. She began telling just about any-one who would listen that what she knew about the missing Shawinigan girl could convict someone of murder. Bernier heard about her claims, and eight months after Therrien disappeared, he met Beaudoin for drinks at a local hotel. The two then drove to Bernier's house in the St. Michel Cemetery. There Beaudoin demanded that Bernier pay her $150, or she would go to the authorities with what she knew about Therrien. Bernier agreed to pay, but asked for time to raise the money. Beaudoin refused, and as the ensuing conversation grew heated, she threw a jug at him and tried to hit him with a shoe. Bernier went to the garage, found a piece of pipe, and returned to the house. Minutes later Beaudoin lay dead, her skull fractured in multiple places.

Bernier later claimed that the murder was not planned, that it was a spur of the moment thing. But there was more to his story than he initially let on. After killing Beaudoin he put her body in his truck and drove to a grave he dug the previous day. When he was asked whether he opened the grave for a funeral, Bernier's one word response sealed his fate: "No."[24] Not satisfied to merely bury the body of his victim, the killer soaked it in gasoline and then set it on fire.

For the next two and a half years the investigation into the deaths of Denise Therrien and Laurette Beaudoin went nowhere. Bernier left his job after assaulting the priest responsible for administering the affairs of the St. Michel Cemetery, and he moved to Montreal to work for a con-struction company. Shortly after Claude Wagner became Quebec's new attorney-general he held a press conference to announce his priorities.

He was going to overhaul the administration of justice in the province; he was going to kick off his war on criminals by taking down the leaders of organized crime; and, he said, he would be reopening the Therrien case. He told reporters that in the past few days his office received new and very precise information about what happened to the missing youth.

Within two months of Wagner's announcement it was obvious to even casual observers that something indeed had happened to reinvigorate the search for Therrien. In a January 1965 article, the *Shawinigan Standard* noted that "Indications are the mystery surrounding the 1961 disappearance of Denise Therrien from her home at Shawinigan South will be solved within a matter of days. Police now believe she is dead."[25] A day after the article appeared, another newspaper began discussing the case. According to the *Montreal Gazette*, a Quebec chemico-legal expert and three provincial police detectives were digging on private property in the Shawinigan area, looking for articles of clothing. "Shortly after daybreak each day since Tuesday the four men, equipped with shovels, drive from their motel accompanied by a uniformed police escort and disappear into the hilly countryside in the Shawinigan area. They return to their motel late at night, between 9 and 10 p.m. and almost immediately go to bed."[26]

By the end of January investigators decided they would wait until spring for the ground to thaw, and then resume their digging. In early April officers took Bernier into custody, charging him with attempted murder for his 1962 assault on the parish priest. A day or two later they began another digging operation, this time in the St. Michel Cemetery. Almost immediately they hit the jackpot, albeit not the one they were searching for originally. The skeleton unearthed was not that of Therrien, but of Laurette Beaudoin. Her skull was so badly battered that officers first believed she was shot multiple times in the head. Not found in the cemetery was the body investigators were looking for. That discovery, however, was not long in coming.

With Bernier in custody, the police had all the time they needed to question the former grave digger. To ensure that they were not interrupted, they moved him from jail to jail, keeping the suspected killer away from both the press and his lawyer. Whatever one may think of the interrogation techniques employed by the Quebec Provincial Police, they worked.

Three weeks after his arrest, Bernier cracked. He told officers that he killed Therrien when she rejected his advances and buried her body in a heavily wooded spot about ten miles north of Shawinigan. They would find her remains on a small hill, lying face up under about a foot and a half of dirt, her head pointing towards the St. Maurice River. If officers wanted her personal effects, they would have to look elsewhere. With that he drew a map of St. Michel Cemetery, putting an "X" on the spot where he buried Therrien's gloves, address book, and prayer beads.

As of April 30, 1965, Denise Therrien was no longer missing. Bernier led officers directly to the spot he told them about. It was obvious that she had been brutally beaten prior to being murdered. Four days later an inquiry into her death got underway. Shortly before it did, Quebec's chief pathologist warned reporters about what they would hear. The dead girl's skull, he said, showed multiple fractures, likely caused by an iron bar, and, he added, "When I say multiple … I use it in the strongest sense of the word."[27]

When the inquiry was convened it was, for the first time in Quebec history, presided over by a judge rather than a coroner. Bernier testified under protection of the *Canada Evidence Act*, which meant that nothing he said could be used against him in any subsequent proceeding. What he had to say made it clear that he had been a predator for years. He admitted that yes, he was the Claude Marchand registered at the Shawinigan employment agency, but he had used other names to lure young women into his clutches, always with the offer of a babysitting job. Asked specifically about Denise Therrien, he recalled that he met her just as she got off a bus. "I told her Mr. Marchand had been unable to make it and had asked me to drive her to his cottage." There he tried to kiss her, and when she resisted, he struck her. Did he mean to kill her? "I don't know. There was a helicopter overhead. It all happened very quickly." When the pathologist who examined Therrien's body was asked if the young woman had been sexually assaulted, he said there was nothing to suggest she had been. All that was left of her were bones, and what clothing remained was so badly decomposed he could not tell for sure whether it was rearranged during a rape.[28]

Bernier's trial started on February 14, 1966, and lasted ten days. Testimony by investigating officers made it clear that while Bernier admitted knowing where Therrien's body was buried, he actually never confessed to killing the teenager. Not to someone in uniform, that is. Bernier did confess to the murder during a series of talks he had with a bank robber lodged in the cell next to his while he was awaiting trial. Only the man was not a criminal — he was an undercover policeman. In testimony he gave at trial, the officer said Bernier not only told him he murdered Therrien, he also spelled out where he buried her. The officer asked the killer if it bothered him to talk about the murder. No, Bernier replied, not too much. Even before that conversation, Bernier confessed to being involved in Therrien's disappearance. During a conversation with his wife and mother-in-law about five months after the Shawinigan girl went missing, he told the women that he alone knew where Therrien's body was buried. "On my deathbed I will say where she is buried — not before."[29]

It took jurors just forty minutes to find the former grave digger guilty of murder, and another fifteen to agree that he should be hanged, rather than have his sentence commuted to life imprisonment. But the killer did not hang. When the federal Liberal party took office in 1963, it refused to allow anyone to be executed, and in January 1968, the federal government officially commuted all outstanding death sentences. So Bernier was not executed, and if we are to believe former Liberal Member of Parliament Jacques Lavoie, that was a very fortunate thing. In 1977 the politician started to lobby the Quebec justice department to reopen its investigations into the murders of Laurette Beaudoin and Denise Therrien. Bernier, he said, was innocent. Even though the convicted killer died in a British Columbia prison in May 1976, the MP said he deserved the right to have his name cleared, at least with regard to the murder of Therrien.

According to Lavoie, Bernier was in love with Beaudoin, who plotted the kidnapping with her boyfriend, a man whose name Bernier refused to divulge, out of concern for the safety of his children. Bernier said Therrien was drugged and kept in a house near Shawinigan. She was going to be released in due course, but one day she stumbled as she came down a staircase. As a result of the fall, she fractured her skull and died. Lavoie said Bernier was not even present when Therrien died, and only agreed to bury the young woman's body because of his love for Beaudoin. That love, however, died with Therrien, and from that day forward Bernier grew increasingly determined to get even with Beaudoin and her boyfriend.

For better or worse, Lavoie was not able to clear Bernier of the Therrien murder.

Appendix: Timelines

1: They Got Away with It Before

FRED STAWYCZNYK AND PAULINE YATCHUK:
BABIES IN BOXES

1918	Wife of Fred Stawycznyk dies, leaving him with three children.
1921	Yatchuk family arrives from the U.S., settles on farm near Stawycznyk.
circa 1925	Yatchuk returns to the United States to work.
June 1927	Stawycznyk and Pauline Yatchuk begin affair.
September 1, 1929	Illegitimate child born to Stawycznyk and Yatchuk; strangled and buried.
October 1929	Nicola Yatchuk returns, leaves with couple's three oldest children.
July 18, 1930	Birth of second illegitimate child; strangled and buried in yard.
September 1930	Yatchuk's three oldest children move back home to live with her.
June 21, 1931	Twins born to Stawycznyk and Yatchuk; they too are strangled and buried.
June 27, 1932	Fifth baby born to Stawycnyk and Yatchuk stillborn; Yatchuk buries it.

1932	Stawycznyk accuses Yatchuk of burning down a stable on his farm.
November 1932	Justice of the peace receives anonymous letters about death of babies.
November 28, 1932	Police discover bodies of five babies buried in Yatchuk's garden.
November 28, 1932	Stawycznyk and Yaychuk arrested and charged with murder.
December 10, 1932	Stawycznyk committed to trial for murder at end of preliminary hearing; murder charges against Yatchuk reduced to charge of concealment of birth.
December 26, 1932	Tachuk overheard admitting her allegations against Stawycnyk are untrue.
April 5, 1933	Murder trial gets underway; charge of concealment of birth added.
April 7, 1933	Stawycznyk found guilty, sentenced to hang July 12, 1933.
April 1933	Yatchuk guilty of concealing birth; sentenced to two years in jail.
June 30, 1933	Manitoba Court of Appeal turns down appeal by vote of 2–1.
July 5, 1933	Federal cabinet turns down application for clemency.
July 12, 1933	Stawycznyk executed.

WILLIAM BAHREY:
THE BROTHERS IN THE HAYSTACKS

1907	William born in Rosthern, Saskatchewan; two years younger than Alex.
circa 1931	William begins affair with Dora Bahrey, wife of his brother Alex.
June 1931	Nestor Tereschuk marries Annie Bahrey, already married to a wife in Poland, few months later Annie separates from her husband, moves in with brothers.

October 31, 1932	William Bahrey murders his brother-in-law, Nestor Tereschuk.
April 10, 1933	Annie and Dora leave to visit Ambrose Bahrey, William murders Alex.
April 11, 1933	William Bahrey returns to Alex's body, drags it to haystack, burns haystack.
April 12, 1933	Dora Bahrey returns home; William tells her he killed Alex.
April 16, 1933	Dog belonging to owner of land where Alex burned discovers his remains.
April 17, 1933	Police arrive, move body to church hall, invite people to identify it.
April 19, 1933	Horse allegedly ridden by Alex when he disappeared found tied to a tree.
April 21, 1933	Father of William and Alexander identifies Alexander's body.
April 24, 1933	Coroner's inquest convened; adjourned; body turned over to pathologist.
April 25, 1933	William taken into custody on a coroner's warrant.
May 8, 1933	Bahrey confesses to both murders.
May 11, 1933	Preliminary hearing; Bahrey charged with two murders, pleads not guilty by reason of insanity.
September 1933	Skull of Teresczuk found half a kilometre from where his body discovered.
October 2, 1933	Special jury finds Bahrey mentally fit to stand trial.
October 5, 1933	Bahrey stands trial for murdering his brother
October 7, 1933	Bahrey found guilty; sentenced to hang on February 23, 1934.
October 1933	Crown decides not to proceed with a trial for Teresczhuk murder.
December 19, 1933	Saskatchewan Court of Appeal reserves judgment on Bahrey's appeal.
February 21, 1934	Executioner arrives in Prince Albert to prepare for double hanging.

February 22, 1934	Double execution becomes single hanging when second killer reprieved.
February 23, 1934	Bahrey executed in Prince Albert, Saskatchewan, at 6:00 a.m.

WILLIAM LAROCQUE AND EMMANUEL LAVICTOIRE:
MURDER FOR INSURANCE

October 4, 1930	Athanase Lamarche allegedly drowns, with Larocque and Lavictoire.
October 7, 1930	Larocque and Lavictoire only witnesses at coroner's inquest; verdict of accidental death returned.
February 2, 1931	Larocque and Lavictoire defraud father of Lamarche out of $3,868.
July 1931	Larocque says Leo Bergeron asked to be insured for $2,500; Bergeron warned by his father Larocque will do him in if he takes out policy.
December 4, 1931	Bergeron increases policy to $5,000, makes Larocque beneficiary.
1931–1932	Larocque and Lavictoire ask three other young men to take out insurance.
February 1932	Larocque and Lavictoire try to get Bergeron hired out to cut ice.
March 18, 1932	Leo Bergeron allegedly trampled to death on Larocque farm; post-mortem carried out; police begin their investigation.
March 28, 1932	Police announce they are considering exhuming body of Lamarche; body eventually exhumed.
March 30, 1932	Inquest into Bergeron's death convened by coroner, then adjourned.
April 5, 1932	Larocque and Lavictoire arrested for defrauding Felix Lamarche.
April 5, 1932	Coroner's jury conclude Bergeron's death caused by person or persons unknown, or by being trampled by horses.

April 12, 1932	Lacrocque and Lavictoire charged with murder; remanded to custody.
April 28, 1932	Preliminary hearing ends; accused committed to stand trial.
December 8, 1932	Murder trial of Larocque and Lavictoire gets underway.
December 15, 1932	Accused murderers convicted; sentenced to hang March 15, 1933.
March 15, 1933	First Lavictoire, and then Larocque hanged at L'Orignal jail.
July 20, 1933	Company that insured life of Bergeron refuses to pay proceeds to father.

2: Murdering Neighbours

MICHAEL FARRELL:

FIFTEEN YEARS BETWEEN MURDERS

1860s/70s	Farrell kills his neighbour.
August 25, 1878	Farrell murders Francis Conway.
August 27, 1878	Inquest into the murder of Conway; Farrell not allowed to attend.
November 2, 1878	Murder trial gets underway.
November 5, 1878	Jury returns a verdict of guilty.
January 10, 1879	Farrell hanged in Québec Gaol.

EMERSON SHELLEY:

A NEIGHBOUR KILLS AGAIN

| August 16, 1909 | Shelley kills Michael Hall. |
| August 17, 1909 | Shelley arrested and charged with murdering Hall; coroner's inquest begins its deliberations. |

August 19, 1909	Inquest reconvenes, concludes Shelley shot Hall accidently and charges of murder previously laid against Shelley are withdrawn.
December 7, 1909	Shelley convicted of stealing a gun; receives a suspended sentence.
June 12, 1913	Shelley burns neighbour's house; charged with theft and arson.
June 27, 1913	Shelley acquitted of arson; sentenced to two years in jail for theft.
May 10, 1915	Shelley tells friends of his plans to rob and murder Shoup.
May 11, 1915	Fifty-seven-year-old Christian Shoup robbed and murdered near Simcoe.
May 11, 1915	Shelley and an accomplice break into general store.
May 11, 1915	Warrant issued for arrest of Shelley on charge of rape in Norwich.
May 12, 1915	Shelley arrested for rape of thirteen-year-old girl; questioned about Shoup's murder.
May 14, 1915	Shelley pleads guilty to the sex charge; sentenced to two years in jail.
May 19, 1915	Inquest into Shoup's death concludes Shelley likely responsible.
June 5, 1915	Preliminary hearing into Shoup's murder begins; reconvenes on June 12, Shelley committed to stand trial.
September 23, 1915	Shelley's two-day murder trial in Simcoe ends with verdict of guilty; Shelley sentenced to hang on December 18.
October 5, 1915	Shelley blames accomplice in store break-in for murder of Shoup; a month later the accomplice is sentenced to five years in jail.
December 18, 1915	Shelley executed.

LARRY HAROLD HANSEN:

KILLED BY HIS BEST FRIEND

November 19, 1976	Hansen and his neighbour, Joseph Baraniuk, argue about trees cut by Baraniuk.
November 20, 1976	Hansen murders Baraniuk.
November 22, 1976	Hansen charged with murder; remanded to custody.
June 6, 1977	Pleads guilty to second degree murder; sent to Stony Mountain Penitentiary.
January 1987	Hansen released from prison on full parole.
1995	McKay becomes RCMP informant in Operation Decode; paid $250,000.
1996	McKay's work as informant for RCMP comes to an end.
1997	McKay returns to Manitoba; moves into acreage next to Hansen.
mid-January 1998	McKay receives death threats; reports them to RCMP.
April 16, 1998	John McKay shot as he drives out of his farm yard.
April 21, 1998	Hansen soloist at McKay's funeral; sings *I Have A Friend*.
June 12, 1998	Manitoba M.P. accuses RCMP of gross negligence in death of McKay.
June 1998	Hansen charged with driving offences; violates parole terms; sent back to prison.
September 18, 1998	Hansen hangs himself in his cell at Stony Mountain Penitentiary.
September 20, 1998	RCMP confirm that Hansen was suspect in shooting of McKay.

3: Reprieved to Kill Again

GARY RICHARD BARRETT:
ONE SECOND CHANCE TOO MANY

1852	Garry Richard Barrett born in Michigan.
1872	Barrett marries; by 1882 he is father of eight children.
1905	Barrett marries Johnson, and converts to Mormonism; moves to Egg Lake, Saskatchewan.
October 14, 1907	Barrett shoots his stepson Brunell Johnson; stepson dies.
June 3, 1907	Barrett sentenced to hang on July 17, 1908; jury recommends clemency.
June 2, 1908	Barrett's trial for murder begins in Prince Albert, Saskatchewan.
August 5, 1908	Sentence commuted to life imprisonment.
January 1909	Deputy Warden Richard Stedman refuses to let Barrett see prison doctor.
April 15, 1909	Barrett kills deputy warden at the Alberta Penitentiary in Edmonton.
April 24, 1909	Preliminary hearing held at the Alberta Penitentiary; Barrett to stand trial.
May 17, 1909	Barrett's trial for murder of Stedman begins in Edmonton; jury deliberates for five minutes before rejecting Barrett's plea of insanity and finding him guilty of murder; sentenced to be hanged on July 14, 1909; jury makes no recommendation for mercy.
July 14, 1909	Barrett executed at the Alberta Penitentiary by an unknown hangman.

JOHN BOYKO:

MARRY ME OR DIE

March 1941	Boyko meets Thekla "Tessy" Oliansky; two weeks later she asks him to be her man; they go into business together.
spring 1946	Boyko wants to make business arrangement official, she refuses.
June 1946	Boycko advised his wife was murdered by Russian soldiers.
November 1946	Boyko proposes marriage to Oliansky, she rejects him as too old.
November 24, 1946	Boyko moves out of Oliansky's house.
November 25, 1946	Oliansky's new boyfriend moves into her house.
November 28, 1946	Boyko murders his business partner/lover.
November 28, 1946	Boyko walks into police station and confesses to the murder.
November 29, 1946	Coroner's jury holds Boyko responsible for murder of Oliansky; remanded to custody December 6 for preliminary hearing.
December 6, 1946	Preliminary hearing for murder; Boyko committed to trial.
February 24, 1947	Murder trial begins.
February 25, 1947	Boyko convicted of murder; sentenced to hang on June 6, 1947.
May 29, 1947	Sentence commuted to life imprisonment.
November 24, 1948	Boyko murders fellow inmate at St. Vincent de Paul; confesses to the murder.
November 26, 1948	Boyko arraigned; preliminary hearing set for December 4.
December 4, 1948	Boyko found criminally responsible at coroner's inquest.
May 6, 1949	Jurors find Boyko guilty; sentenced to be hanged on August 26, 1949.

August 18, 1949	Federal cabinet confirms that Boyko is to be hanged.
August 26, 1949	Boyko hanged in Montreal's Bordeaux Jail.

ALBERT VICTOR WESTGATE:
FASCINATION LEADS TO MURDER

1901	Westgate born in Kent, England.
1916	Westgate arrives in Winnipeg, and lies about age to enlist in army.
1918	Westgate receives honourable discharge from army.
1921	Marries.
1924	Westgate's wife introduces him to her co-worker, Lottie Adams
1927	Westgate admits to friends his fascination for Lottie.
1928	Lottie refuses to see Westgate, and ends their relationship.
February 16, 1928	Lottie agrees to see Westgate one last time; he murders her.
February 28, 1928	Body of Lottie Adams found in snow bank; Westgate arrested.
November 16, 1928	Westgate convicted of murder; sentenced to be hanged.
December 20, 1928	Manitoba Court of Appeal orders that Westgate be re-tried.
March 22, 1929	Westgate again convicted of murder; sentenced to hang June 5, 1929.
June 3, 1929	Sentence commuted to life imprisonment.
June 3, 1943	Westgate paroled; returns to Winnipeg.
August 1943	Sixteen-year-old Edith Cook moves into rooming house where Westgate lives.
December 4, 1943	Westgate strangles Cook in a Winnipeg hotel room.
December 5, 1943	Police detain Westgate on Coroner's warrant.

| May 8, 1944 | Westgate's convicted of murder for a third time; sentenced to death. |
| July 24, 1944 | Westgate executed at Manitoba's Headingley jail. |

4: Loved Ones Tell All

OLIVER PRÉVOST:
THE PIGGERY MURDERS

February 11, 1897	Two bodies discovered in ruins on pig farm near Port Arthur, Ontario.
February 11, 1897	Coroner's inquest called; hears witnesses then adjourns.
February 13, 1897	Coroner's inquest reconvenes to hear more witnesses; adjourns.
February 25, 1897	Coroner's inquest reconvenes to hear more witnesses; adjourns.
February 26, 1897	Coroner's inquest ends; two fire victims murdered by an unknown person.
March 5, 1897	Coroner's inquest reconvenes; concludes that fire victims were murdered.
November 24, 1897	Prévost sentenced to prison for theft of furs and pork at Renfrew, Ontario.
November 26, 1897	Prévost tells authorities his wife murdered two men in Port Arthur.
November 1897	Prévost held in the insane ward in Kingston Penitentiary.
November 1897	Rosanna Gauthier charged with the two Port Arthur murders.
December 7, 1897	Preliminary hearing; Gauthier committed to trial; transferred to Port Arthur.
1898	Charges against Gauthier withdrawn and Prévost charged with murder.

December 6, 1898	Murder trial of Prévost gets underway in Port Arthur.
December 7, 1898	Jury returns with a verdict of guilty; Prévost to hang March 17, 1899.
March 1899	Psychiatrists who examine Prévost advise the government that he is sane.
March 15, 1899	Federal cabinet refuses to commute sentence to life imprisonment.
March 15, 1899	Canada's official executioner arrives in Port Arthur.
March 17, 1899	Oliver Prévost executed.

JOHN "COBALT" IVANCHUK:
TOO MUCH TO SAY

1887	Ivanchuk born in Austria.
1914	Ivanchuk immigrates to Canada; settles in northern Ontario.
October 15, 1926	Liquor inspector Thomas Harry Constable murdered.
October 15, 1926	Ivanchuk leaves murder weapon with fifteen-year-old Sophia Dincorn.
October 19, 1926	Ivanchuk spends two days with acquaintance; confesses to the murder.
October 1926	Ivanchuk discusses opening brothel; admits shooting Constable.
October 23, 1926	Coroner's jury concludes Constable murdered by an unknown person.
October 23, 1926	Ivanchuk meets Dincorn in Empress Café; takes back gun he left with her.
November 5, 1926	Reward for apprehension of killer raised from $2,000 to $5,000.
November 1928	Police investigators speak to Sophia Dincorn in Kapuskasing.
November 15, 1928	Ivanchuk arrested in a Cochrane drinking club.

November 17, 1928	Police confirm Ivanchuk's identity; charge him with murder.
November 29, 1928	Ivanchuk committed to stand trial for Constable's murder.
April 12, 1929	Ivanchuk found guilty after three-day trial; sentenced to hang on June 21.
May 1929	Federal department of justice postpones execution for one month.
July 17, 1929	Ivanchuk executed at Haileybury Jail.

STANLEY DONALD MCLAREN:

A FATAL MISTAKE

August 26, 1926	Stanley McLaren born in Portage la Prairie, Manitoba.
August 1945	McLaren moves to Calgary one month before Lum murder.
September 24, 1945	McLaren robs and beats Lum severely about the head.
September 25, 1945	Lum dies from his head wounds.
August 1946	McLaren marries Marie Kayter; couple ends up in northern Ontario.
July 1949	Stanley and Marie McLaren move to Toronto.
August 28, 1949	McLaren charged common assault; Marie tells police her husband is a murderer.
August 29, 1949	McLaren questioned by police; confesses to Calgary murder.
September 1949	Returned to Calgary.
October 13, 1949	Committed to trial following a two-day preliminary inquiry.
November 1, 1949	*Criminal Code* amended to allow appeal on question law; comes into effect.
November 20, 1949	Found guilty after six day trial; McLaren sentenced to hang on March 30, 1949.

November 21, 1949	Transferred to death cell at Lethbridge jail to await execution.
March 10, 1949	Alberta Court of Appeal denies McLaren's request for a new trial.
March 28, 1949	Justice Kerwin denies request to appeal to the Supreme Court of Canada.
March 29, 1949	Federal cabinet rejects McLaren's application for clemency.
March 30, 1949	McLaren executed in Lethbridge; body is interred in jail yard; Lum buried.

ARTHUR KENDALL:

KILLING IN FRONT OF FAMILY

June 1952	Kendall moves his wife and five children into a one-room cabin.
August 2, 1952	Thirty-three-year-old Helen Kendall disappears.
August 2, 1952	Kendall begins living with a woman with her own five children.
September 5, 1952	Kendall children lie to police about what happened to their mother.
September 1952	Kendall children placed in foster homes, where they remain for two years.
1954	Beatrice Hogue divorced by her husband
1959	Helen Kendall declared dead; less than a year later Kendall marries Hogue.
January 1961	Kendall's oldest daughter tells the police her father murdered her mother.
January 27, 1961	Kendall arrested and charged with murdering his wife.
September 1, 1961	*Criminal Code* section imposed, dealing with capital murder.
October 27, 1961	Kendall guilty of murder; sentenced to hang January 23, 1962.

January 23, 1962	Ontario Court of Appeal dismisses Kendall's appeal.
February 5, 1962	Stay of execution to April 17, 1962, granted to allow appeal to SCC.
March 14, 1962	Supreme Court hears Kendall's appeal; on March 26, it is dismissed.
April 10, 1962	Federal cabinet commutes Kendall's sentence to life imprisonment.
April 12, 1962	Bayfield Cemetery trustees vote against allowing Kendall to be buried.
February 13, 1971	Kendall fails to return from a one-day pass from his jail.
February 25, 1971	Kendall recaptured.

5: Suspicions Linger

WILLIAM JASPER COLLINS:

TOO MUCH MONEY

1912	Braymer, Missouri lawyer John Benson defends William Jasper Collins.
August 1912	John Benson leaves Missouri to file homestead claim near Cereal, Alberta.
1913–1914	Benson sells off his holdings in Missouri.
April 4, 1913	Benson and Collins return to Canada to improve Benson's claim.
April 27, 1913	The pair finish building a small shack and barn.
May 1, 1913	Collins murders Benson, burns house to hide evidence of his crime.
May 3, 1913	Not aware her husband is dead, Clara Benson leaves Missouri for Canada.
May 5, 1913	Clara arrives in Saskatoon; informed that her husband has died in a fire.

May 6, 1913	Clara meets up with Collins; he tells her about the accident.
May 1913	Clara and Collins return to Braymer with body of John Benson.
June/July 1913	Collins begins spending money lavishly.
July/August 1913	Rumours circulate about source of money; friends of Benson hire detective.
August 1913	Body of Benson exhumed; cause of death determined to be criminal act.
August 10, 1913	Collins arrested; his home searched and large amount of money found.
August 10, 1913	Collins confesses to the murder of John Benson.
September 1913	Collins returned to Alberta to stand trial for murder.
November 24, 1913	Preliminary hearing into the murder of Benson begins in Calgary.
November 25, 1913	Preliminary ends; Collins formally charged with the murder of Benson.
November 27, 1913	Murder trial of William Jasper Collins gets underway in Calgary.
February 11, 1914	Federal cabinet turns down the application of Collins for clemency.
February 23, 1914	Collins hanged; his execution badly botched.
February 24, 1924	Arthur Ellis contacts the press to deny he took part in the execution.

MARIE BEAULNE AND PHILIBERT LEFEBVRE:
POISON DOES THE TRICK

1929	Marie Beaulne begins affair with Philibert Lefebvre.
January 22, 1929	Zephyr Viau dies under mysterious circumstances; buried immediately.
late January 1929	Parish priest grows suspicious that death wasn't natural; contacts police.

February 7, 1929	Body of Viau exhumed and an autopsy performed; strychnine found.
February 1929	Preliminary hearing holds Beaulne and Lefebvre responsible for Viau's death.
June 1929	Beaulne and Lefebvre murder trial gets underway.
June 12, 1929	Lefebvre and Beaulne guilty of murder; to hang August 23.
June 27, 1929	Beaulne advised no one will support her bid for clemency.
July 1929	Lawyers approach federal cabinet for pardon; clients too ignorant to know murder is wrong.
August 1, 1929	Lawyer for the couple formally seek clemency from department of justice.
August 1929	Announced that reporters will not be allowed to attend execution.
August 20, 1929	Federal cabinet refuses to commute sentences; confirm order following day.
August 20, 1929	Carpenters begin erecting gallows in yard of Hull, Quebec, jail.
August 22, 1929	Couple transferred to death cells in Hull; Lefebvre collapses.
August 22, 1929	Beaulne asks to visit with her lover; Lefebvre refuses to see her.
August 22, 1929	Reporter sneaks into jail; caught shortly before midnight and thrown out.
August 23, 1929	Hangman ordered not to hang couple at midnight as planned.
August 23, 1929	Lefebvre writes father; breaks down; Beaulne unemotional in her cell.
August 23, 1929	Lefebvre hanged at 8:00 a.m. in pouring rain; father claims body.
August 23, 1929	Beaulne hanged at 8:21 a.m.
August 24, 1929	Beaulne's body not claimed; buried in pauper's grave in Hull.

MARIE LOUISE CLOUTIER AND ACHILLE GRONDIN:

MARRIED TOO SOON

1916	Seventeen-year-old Marie Louise Cloutier marries Vilmond Brochu.
February 1936	Brochu hires Achille Grondin to help Clouiter operate family farm.
1936	Clouiter and Grondin begin affair; Cloutier also affair with Adolphe Gilbert.
late 1936	Brochu suspects wife's affair with Grondin, fires him; Cloutier leaves husband.
late 1936	Brochu obtains permission to sue Grondin for alienation of affections.
November 1936	Cloutier begins lacing Brochu's food with arsenic.
January 1, 1937	Brochu complains of severe stomach pains.
July 16, 1937	Brochu again becomes ill; diagnosed with indigestion.
July 21, 1937	Brochu hospitalized for five days after complaining about stomach pains.
July 1937	Gilbert and Grondin place curse on Brochu.
August 16, 1937	Brochu becomes seriously ill.
August 19, 1937	Brochu dies.
August 20, 1937	Cloutier applies for life insurance benefits payable under husband's policy.
August 21, 1937	Days before marrying Grondin, Cloutier has sexual encounter with Gilbert.
August 22, 1937	Grondin moves into Brochu residence to live with Cloutier.
September 2, 1937	Grondin asks permission of local priest to marry Cloutier; denied.
September 1937	Cloutier and Grondin ask permission of another priest to marry; denied.
October 1937	Cloutier and Grondin marry.
October 1937	Brochu's sister contacts police about her suspicion that her brother was poisoned.

October 1937	Police order Brochu's body exhumed; pathologist finds traces of arsenic
October 1937	Cloutier and Grondin taken into custody while on their honeymoon.
November 29, 1937	Cloutier and Grondin held in custody following coroner's inquest.
December 4, 1937	Cloutier and Grondin committed to stand trial at end of preliminary hearing.
September 21, 1938	Murder trial of Cloutier gets underway at St. Joseph de Beauce.
October 8, 1938	Jury returns a verdict of guilty; Cloutier to hang March 3, 1939.
October 24, 1938	Lawyer for Cloutier seeks permission to appeal verdict.
November 3, 1938	Grondin's murder trial gets underway before judge who tried Cloutier.
November 10, 1938	Quebec Court of Appeal agrees to hear Cloutier's appeal.
November 26, 1938	Grondin found guilty; sentenced to hang on April 21, 1939.
November 29, 1938	Cloutier and Grondin transferred from St. Joseph de Beauce to Quebec City.
January 1939	Quebec Court of Appeal dismisses Cloutier's appeal.
February 19, 1939	Execution of Grondin stayed pending hearing by Quebec Court of Appeal.
June 2, 1939	Grondin's execution postponed to allow appeal to Quebec Court of Appeal.
June 13, 1939	Cloutier's execution date postponed to allow appeal to Supreme Court of Canada.
June 1939	Court of Appeal dismisses Grondin's appeal; executions stayed to appeal to SCC.
October 30, 1939	Supreme Court of Canada hears Cloutier's appeal; dismiss appeal.

February 1940	Site of double execution moved from St. Joseph to Montreal.
February 15, 1940	Grondin moved from Quebec City jail to death cell at Bordeaux Jail.
February 22, 1940	Federal cabinet denies applications for clemency by condemned couple.
February 22, 1940	Cloutier moved from Quebec City.
February 23, 1940	Grondin hanged at 6:45 a.m.; declared dead sixteen minutes later.
February 23, 1940	Cloutier hanged at 7:10 a.m.; declared dead fifteen minutes later.

6: The Two Rolands

ROLAND ASSELIN:
FIFTY-FIVE WEEKS BETWEEN MURDERS

November 9, 1946	Ulric Gauthier murdered.
November 10, 1946	Body of Gauthier found on dirt road thirty-two miles west of Montreal.
November 1946	Coroner's inquest into death of Gauthier comes to no decision.
Nov/Dec 1946	Second inquest decides Gauthier committed suicide; investigation officially ends.
February 1947	Marie Blanche Alice Gauthier, widow of Ulric, commits suicide.
February 1947	Investigation in death of Ulric Gauthier officially reopened.
Fall 1947	Roland Asselin gives statement about death of Ulric Gauthier.
December 30, 1947	Asselin taken into custody.
December 31, 1947	Third inquest finds Asselin responsible for death of Ulric Gauthier.

January 5, 1948	Asselin arraigned on charge of murder.
January 9, 1948	Preliminary hearing into murder of Ulric Gauthier.
June 9, 1948	Murder trial of Asselin gets underway.
June 15, 1948	Asselin guilty of murdering Gauthier; sentenced to hang on October 1, 1948.
September 15, 1948	Asselin's execution postponed until January 14, 1949.
November 25, 1948	Asselin's execution postponed a second time, until March 25, 1949.
March 15, 1949	Asselin's execution postponed third time, until June 10, 1949.
March 31, 1949	Request for another postponement denied by Quebec Court of Appeal.
June 10, 1949	Roland Asselin executed.

ROLAND GENEST:

HE NEVER MURDERED A WOMAN HE DIDN'T LOVE

May 29, 1951	Charred body of Rita Genest discovered in burning bed.
May 30, 1951	Inquest finds that woman was murdered before being set on fire.
May 31, 1951	Police announce they have no leads.
February 18, 1953	Roland Genest beats his girlfriend to death.
February 19, 1953	Nude body of badly beaten woman found in farmer's field.
February 20, 1953	Public view body of woman; picture published in Montreal newspapers.
February 22, 1953	Body tentatively identified.
February 23, 1953	Mother of Marie Paule Langlais identifies body; Genest arrested.
February 25, 1953	Genest confesses to murdering Langlais.

February 27, 1953	Genest appears at coroner's inquest investigating death of Langlais.
February 27, 1953	Genest formally charged with murdering Langlais.
May 19, 1953	Murder trial gets underway; Genest again admits murder.
May 21, 1953	Genest found guilty of murder and sentenced to hang on August 28.
August 28, 1953	Genest executed.

7: Confessions and Presumptions of Guilt

PORAL STEFOFF:
LAST MINUTE CONFESSION OF A SERIAL KILLER

circa 1904	Poral Steffoff murders Englishman in Indiana.
circa 1906	Steffoff allegedly murders two Macedonians in New York state.
October 1908	Poral Steffoff arrives in Canada.
April 22, 1909	Simoff murdered in Toronto; Steffoff held as material witness.
April 23, 1909	Coroner's inquest held.
April 26, 1909	Steffoff charged with murder.
May 7, 1909	Steffoff committed to stand trial.
September 23, 1909	Elia Petroff placed in a cell next to the one occupied by Steffoff.
October 18, 1909	Blood stains on Steffoff's clothes determined to be human.
October 27, 1909	Steffoff found guilty of murder at end of a two-day trial.
October 28, 1909	Sentenced to hang December 23, 1909.
December 23, 1909	Between 10:00 and 11:00 p.m. Steffoff confesses to various murders.
December 23, 1909	Steffoff executed in Don Jail.

JOHN BARTY:

THE COLD-SET KILLER

June 25, 1925	Triple murder, almost certainly committed by John Barty.
June 10, 1926	Barty assaults clerk during robbery; held until police arrive; arrested.
June 12, 1926	Clerk dies after being operated on.
June 18, 1926	Barty committed to stand trial at end of preliminary hearing.
October 7, 1926	Convicted of murder; sentenced to hang on December 13, 1926.
December 22, 1926	Court of Appeal allows stay after court turned down the request.
January 18, 1927	Barty executed at Hamilton jail.

JOHN KOOTING:

CONFESSIONS ON THE PRAIRIES, PART I

November 5, 1921	Kooting murders friend, and builds pig pen over place body buried.
January 1922	Police arrest Kooting for the murder of his friend.
spring 1923	Charges against Kooting stayed because body of victim not found.
February 1925	Kooting falls ill, believes he is dying.
April 26, 1925	Believing he is about to die, Kooting confesses to murder of friend.
April 27, 1925	Police locate remains of murder victim.
November 25, 1925	Kooting convicted of murder.
February 19, 1926	Kooting executed; buried in unmarked grave in jail yard.

JOHN PAWLUCK:
CONFESSIONS ON THE PRAIRIES, PART II

November 4, 1935	John Pawluk murders wife Julia; buries her under a manure pile.
November 8, 1935	Pawluk tells wife's family that Julia ran away.
November 1935	Pawluk tells several neighbours that he murdered his wife.
March 23, 1936	Pawluk murders neighbour.
March 1936	Neighbour of Pawluk tells police Pawluk confessed to murder of Julia.
March 27, 1936	Police start searching for Julia Pawluk in manure pile.
March 28, 1936	Police find remains of Julia Pawluk; arrest John for firearms offence.
March 30, 1936	John Pawluk charged with murdering his wife.
March 31, 1936	Pawluk tells cellmate he murdered his wife.
June 12, 1936	Pawluk convicted of murder; sentenced to death.
August 21, 1936	Executed; body buried in yard of Manitoba's Headingley jail.

JAMES ALFRED KELSEY:
A TENDENCY TO TALK TOO MUCH

December 9, 1949	Kelsey and his brother murder cab driver Sam Delibasich.
December 10, 1949	Killers attempt to sell cab in Toronto; abandon it.
December 14, 1949	Toronto police tow cab to their compound.
December 17, 1949	Body of Delibasich discovered by a hunter near St. Catharines.
1951	Kelsey confesses his part in murder to his girlfriend.
September 1951	Kelsey confesses his part in murder to a childhood friend.
January 1952	Childhood friend tells police of Kelsey's confession.
January 31, 1952	Brothers arrested and charged with murder.

March 10, 1952	At his preliminary hearing Kelsey confesses to the murder.
September 18, 1952	Kelsey convicted; to hang January 6, 1953; jury does not recommend mercy.
December 1952	Court of Appeal dismisses appeal; stays execution to March 10.
January 13, 1953	Brother of Kelsey found not guilty at his murder trial.
February 19, 1953	Supreme Court of Canada reserves judgment on Kelsey's appeal.
March 16, 1953	Supreme Court dismisses Kelsey's request for a new trial.
April 9, 1953	Federal cabinet commutes Kelsey's sentence to life imprisonment.

8: Killers on the Run

HENRY SÉGUIN:

FROM ONTARIO TO BRITISH COLUMBIA

July 30, 1925	Henry Séguin born in Cornwall, Ontario.
March 16, 1935	Séguin's first arrest; he was ten years old.
March 25, 1939	Séguin released from reformatory; returns home to his parents.
September 27, 1939	Convicted of theft; returned to reformatory.
January 28, 1942	Convicted of break and enter; sentenced as adult to seven months in jail.
December 16, 1942	Sentenced to six months in jail for theft.
July 12, 1943	Convicted escaping lawful custody and other offences; given two more years.
August 25, 1944	Escapes from jail and goes on crime spree.
September 29, 1944	Joins Canadian Armed Forces to avoid being recaptured.

November 1, 1944	Séguin recaptured and sentenced to two years more.
January 22, 1945	Séguin dishonourably discharged from the Canadian Armed Forces.
December 7, 1946	Released from Kingston Penitentiary.
May 29, 1947	Convicted of break and enter; sentenced to two years in penitentiary.
February 8, 1952	Released from Kingston Penitentiary.
April 12, 1952	Burns house trailer; steals some of its contents, including a .22 calibre rifle.
August 16, 1952	Séguin murders Leonard Hurd.
August 22, 1952	Warrant issued for arrest of Séguin.
August 28, 1952	Séguin hired by lumber company; near Williams Lake, British Columbia.
October 2, 1952	Séguin, calling himself Henry Godin, meets Fred and Jean Labie.
October 25, 1952	Séguin's unusual looking car found in a bush near Quebec border.
November 3, 1952	Jean leaves Fred.
November 7, 1952	Police begin questioning people around Williams Lake about Séguin.
November 8, 1952	Séguin, a.k.a. Godin, leaves Williams Lake with Labie for Kamloops.
November 14, 1952	Séguin and the Labies move into a duplex together.
November 17, 1952	Last time the Labies seen alive.
December 13, 1952	Séguins packs up and leaves Kamloops.
December 15, 1952	Séguin arrives in Williams Lake; robs bank.
December 16, 1952	Séguin shot and captured.
December 22, 1952	Police in B. C. learn than man in custody is Henry Séguin, not Godin.
January 8, 1953	Séguin released from hospital; placed in police cell.
January 12, 1953	Séguin appears at preliminary hearing.

January 17, 1953	Pleads guilty to three charges related to robbery; sentenced to five years.
March 16, 1953	British Columbia Court of Appeal dismisses Séguin's appeal.
April 26, 1953	Transferred from B.C. to Kingston Penitentiary to appear on murder charge.
August 19, 1953	Preliminary hearing; bound over for trial.
October 26, 1953	Murder trial begins in Cornwall.
October 28, 1953	Found guilty and sentenced to hang on January 19, 1954.
December 15, 1953	Ontario Court of Appeal rejects Séguins appeal.
January 6, 1954	Asks Supreme Court for permission to appeal; justice of that court says no.
January 16, 1954	Stay sought; denied; B.C. officer questions Séguin about the missing Labies.
January 18, 1954	Federal government rejects application for clemency.
January 19, 1954	Minutes before being taken to scaffold Séguins commits suicide.
September 18, 1955	Remains of Labies and their dog found in British Columbia by worker.
February 15, 1956	Inquest into deaths of the Labies held; Séguin held to be their killer.
April 9, 1956	Remains of Fred and Jean Labie buried in Kamloops.

WALTER PAVLUKOFF:

FROM BRITISH COLUMBIA TO ONTARIO

1929	Pavlukoff's father dies.
1933	Nineteen-year-old Pavlukoff commits first crime.
1938	Twin sisters die of tuberculosis after long illnesses.
July 11, 1938	Arrested in Chicago on five counts of robbery; deported to Canada.

August 2, 1938	commits armed assault in Vancouver; sent to prison.
1940	Paroled; almost immediately commits robbery; sent to jail for three years.
March 9, 1944	Arrested with holster, mask, ammunition; gun found within a few days.
1945	Pavlukoff sentenced by Vancouver court to three years on gun charge.
August 25, 1947	Vancouver bank manager shot during bank robbery.
August 25, 1947	Clothes worn by Pavlukoff during robbery found; hat found in a different location.
August 26, 1947	Police find tailor who made suit; Pavlukoff charged with murder; warrant issued.
August 27, 1947	Pavlukoff shows up unannounced at shack near rural C.P.R. right of way.
August 28, 1947	Reward of $5,000 for arrest of Pavlukoff offered by bankers association.
August 29, 1947	Largest manhunt in history of British Columbia underway.
August 31, 1947	Revolver found on beach; a hotel key found in a different location.
September 2, 1947	Search comes up empty; authorities locate room occupied before bank robbery.
January 1, 1952	Sick and hungry, Pavlukoff taken to hospital; known as Ralph McRae.
May 23, 1952	Magazine runs photo of Pavlukoff; Toronto police receive tip he is in the city.
June 1952	Anonymous tipster tells police he has seen Pavlukoff on a Toronto street.
January 8, 1953	Pavlukoff Canada's second most wanted man; arrested on Toronto street.
January 9, 1953	Killer breaks down in tears when advised he was being charged with murder.
January 11, 1953	Arrives in Vancouver; allowed to speak with his mother and sister.

January 12, 1953	Makes first appearance in Vancouver courtroom; remanded one week.
January 24, 1953	Pavlukoff identified in police lineup by a witness to the robbery.
January 26, 1953	Preliminary hearing begins; defence lawyer agrees to holding him for trial.
April 1, 1953	Pavlukoff found guilty of murder; sentenced to hang June 23, 1953.
July 8, 1953	British Columbia Court of Appeal denies Pavlukoff's appeal.
July 8, 1953	Pavlukoff stabs himself to death after being advised; appeal rejected.
July 14, 1953	Inquest into Pavlukoff's suicide adjourned for one week.
July 28, 1953	Pavlukoff's execution date.

9: Pictures on the Dash

OWEN "MICKEY" FEENER

1926	Cathy Essers born in Belgium.
1934	Kay Chouinor born.
1937	Mickey Feener born in Bridgewater, Nova Scotia.
1942	Dolly Woods born.
1945	Feener shot in the head; three months in hospital; given up by his parents.
1957	Twenty-year-old Feener marries a fifteen-year-old young woman.
1958	Cathy Essers immigrates; establishes a dress business in Nova Scotia.
March 26, 1959	Feener becomes father to a baby girl.
April 14, 1959	Dolly Woods disappears from Kirkland Lake rooming house.

October 1959	Feener receives careless driving ticket, which he does not pay.
October 1959	Feener's wife charges him with not supporting her and their daughter.
June 1960	Skeleton of Woods discovered near Ontario-Quebec border; not identified.
July 1960	Essers moves to Toronto, where she meets Conrad Walther.
September 20, 1960	Thirty-four-year-old Essers disappears on way from Toronto to New Glasgow, Nova Scotia.
October 1, 1960	Essers reported missing by fiancé, Conrad Walther of Bradford.
October 1, 1960	Unidentified person attempted to cash a cheque drawn Esser's account.
October 4, 1960	Feener appears at home of Kay Chouinor; she agrees to go out that evening.
October 4, 1960	Last time red-haired twenty-six-year-old Kay Chouinor seen alive.
October 5, 1960	Unidentified body (Essers) found in ditch near Fredericton.
October 5, 1960	Chouinor's employers reports her missing.
October 5, 1960	Feener arrested in Kirkland Lake for failing to pay careless driving fine.
October 1960	Police reopen missing person investigation of Dolly Woods.
October 8, 1960	Investigators from Timmins interview Feener in his cell in Kirkland Lake.
October 8, 1960	RCMP in Fredericton charge Feener with offering an indignity to a body.
October 9, 1960	Badly beaten body of Kay Chouinor found near Timmins.
October 9, 1960	Feener charged with murdering Chouinor.
October 12, 1960	Feener remanded to October 26, 1960, for a preliminary hearing.

October 26, 1960	Feener remanded to trial in spring 1961.
December 1960	Feener granted a new preliminary hearing.
January 20, 1961	Feener remanded to trial at second preliminary hearing.
March 6, 1961	Feener's trial in Cochrane, Ontario gets under way.
March 8, 1961	Jury convicts Feener of murder after deliberating fifteen minutes.
March 9, 1961	Two local newspapers found in contempt for coverage of trial.
May 15, 1961	Ontario Court of Appeal dismisses appeal from Feener's conviction.
June 12, 1961	Feener confesses to murdering Dolly Woods.
June 13, 1961	Feener hanged at Haileybury Jail.
June 13, 1961	Police begin searching for the body of Dolly Woods.
June 14, 1961	Body of Dolly woods located on Quebec side of Ontario-Quebec border.

10: Skeletons Resurface

JOHN MUNROE:
NOBODY ASKED ABOUT MOTHER AND DAUGHTER

1839	John Munroe born in Ireland.
1840s	Munroes arrive in Canada, where father operates a lumberyard.
1849	Sarah Margaret Vail born.
1849	Mother of Sarah Margaret Vail dies.
1862	Munroe marries Annie Potts.
1862	Munroe and Annie become parents of their first child, a son.
1865	Munroe meets Vail at a community event near Vail's home in Caledon.

1866	Munroe and his wife have their second child.
1867	Sarah Margaret Vail's father dies; leaves her the family home.
1867	Munroe's affair with Sarah Margaret Vail commonly acknowledged.
February 4, 1868	Sarah Margaret Vail gives birth to a baby girl, Ella May Munroe.
Summer 1868	Munroe visits Vail every Sunday in her home, remaining one hour each time.
Fall 1868	Munroe purchases a .22 calibre revolver.
early October 1868	Vail sells family home for $500; gives some of the money to Munroe.
late October 1868	Sarah travels with Munroe to Boston.
October 23, 1868	Vail checks into Brunswick Hotel as Mrs. Clarke; trunks arrive.
October 26, 1868	Vail goes for drive with Munroe; on return checks into the Union Hotel.
October 29, 1868	Vail and her baby scheduled to depart on a steamer for Boston.
October 30, 1868	Munroe and wife travel to Fredericton; begins planning murder of Vail.
October 31, 1868	Vail goes for drive with Munroe; Munroe murders Vail and their baby.
November 2, 1868	Munroe checks Vail's trunks onto *New England*, a Boston-bound steamer.
September 12, 1869	Berry-pickers discover skeletons of Sarah Vail and her baby.
September 21, 1869	Munroe sentenced to hang for the murder of Vail and her baby.
September 29, 1869	Steamer *New York* returns Vail's trunks to Saint John; were unclaimed in Boston.
late fall 1869	Munroe arrested and charged with Vail's murder.
December 7, 1869	Munroe's murder trial gets underway.
February 14, 1870	Munroe confesses to committing the two murders.

February 15, 1870	Munroe executed.
1870s	Annie Munroe changes her surname and that of her children to Potts.
1878	Annie remarries.
1924	Munroe's son Frank Potts elected mayor of Saint John; dies in office.

MAURICE RYAN:
BONES OF A BROTHER

October 1, 1907	Nora McKeown agrees to manage brothel in North Bay for Francis Ryan.
October 1907	Francis refuses to loan $5 to brother Maurice.
November 17, 1907	Francis charged with keeping bawdy house; decides to leave North Bay.
November 1907	Francis closes one of his bank accounts; receives $550.
November 18, 1907	Maurice Ryan murders his brother Francis.
November 24, 1907	Ryan pays off debts in North Bay; no one knows where money came from.
1908	James Ryan receives letters from brother Francis; but Francis cannot write.
1908	Farmer clearing bush discovers skeleton.
1909	Inquest finds Maurice killed his brother; Ryan committed to stand trial.
March 28, 1909	Maurice Ryan found guilty of murdering brother; to hang June 3, 1909.
May 20, 1909	Federal cabinet turns down Ryan's request for clemency.
June 2, 1909	Court of Appeal refuses to hear Ryan's request for new trial.
June 3, 1909	Ryan hanged in Nipissing District jail; denied he murdered his brother.

MARCEL BERNIER:

THE BODIES CAME BACK

August 8, 1961	Denise Therrien disappears on way to job interview.
August 13, 1961	Therrien's killer shows up at family home; offers condolences.
August 19, 1961	Therrien family receives ransom note; postmarked previous day.
August 24, 1961	Second ransom note received; man telephones demanding money.
August 26, 1961	Man charged with trying to extort money; third telephone ransom received.
August 27, 1961	Father and uncle of missing girl consult mystic.
August 28, 1961	Uncle of missing girl offers $10,000 for proof she is alive or dead.
September 11, 1961	Father hires team of private detectives hired to help police in their search.
November 2, 1961	Investigation into disappearance reopened; new information received.
January 1962	Bernier tells wife and mother-in-law only he knows where Therrien is.
January 18, 1965	Police begin digging in countryside around Shawinigan.
January 22, 1965	Police stop digging; frozen ground makes progress too difficult.
April 6, 1965	Body of Laurette Beaudoin found; Bernier arrested for attempt murder.
April 13, 1965	Police begin digging for Therrien; tell public have new information.
April 30, 1965	Police find Therrien's skeleton in shallow grave near river in bush area.
May 4, 1965	Autopsy indicates that Therrien died from multiple skull fractures.

May 11, 1965	Coroner's inquest holds Bernier criminally responsible for death of Therrien; Bernier arraigned on murder charges; Bernier confesses.
May 12, 1965	Bernier sentenced to three months in jail for assaulting priest.
May 19, 1965	Preliminary hearing in charge of murder held for Bernier.
June 2, 1965	Bernier confesses; tells undercover police officer he murdered Therrien.
February 14, 1966	Bernier brought from Bodeaux Jail for beginning of murder trial.
February 24, 1966	Bernier found guilty of murder; sentenced to hang July 22, 1966.
January 4, 1968	Bernier's death sentenced commuted to life imprisonment.
April 16, 1969	Lawyer for Bernier announces his client wrote book about the murder.
February 24, 1970	Bernier sentenced to twenty-five years in jail for murder of Beaudoin.
May 1977	Bernier dies of heart attack while imprisoned in British Columbia.
November 8, 1977	Member of Parliament writes book on murders; wants inquest reopened.

Notes

1: They Got Away With It Before

1. *Winnipeg Free Press* (13 July 1933) 1.
2. *Saskatoon Star-Phoenix* (12 May 1933) 3.
3. *Ibid.*
4. *Ibid.*
5. *Ibid.*
6. *Ibid.*
7. *Ibid.*
8. *Saskatoon Star-Phoenix* (5 October 1933) 3.
9. Dr. Frances McGill, "She Solved Murders in the Morgue" in *Ottawa Citizen* (22 October 1955).
10. *Saskatoon Star-Phoenix* (10 May 1933) 3.
11. *Ottawa Citizen* (22 March 1932) 1.
12. *Ibid.*
13. *Ibid.* (12 December 1932) 13.
14. *Ibid.* (9 December 1932) 20.
15. *Ibid.* (12 December 1932) 13.
16. *Ibid.* (15 December 1932) 1.
17. *Ibid.*
18. *Ibid.* (16 December 1932) 28.

2: Murdering Neighbours

1.   The Conway Murder. *www.pbalkcom.com/valcartier/Biographies/conway_murder.htm*

2.   *Ibid.*

3.   *Ibid.*

4.   *Ibid.*

5.   *Ibid.*

6.   *Ibid.*

7.   *Ibid.*

8.   *Ibid.*

9.   *Ibid.*

10. *Ibid.*

11. *Ibid.*

12. *Ibid.*

13. *Ibid.*

14. *Ibid.*

15. *Ibid.*

16. *Ibid.*

17. *Ibid.*

18. *Ibid.*

19. *Ibid.*

20. *Ibid.*

21. *Ibid.*

22. *British Canadian* (25 August 1909) 1.

23. *Ibid.*

24. *Ibid.* (9 June 1915) 1.

25. *Ibid.* (26 May 1915) 7.

26. *Ibid.*

27. *The Globe* (20 May 1915) 2.

28. *British Canadian* (22 December 1915) 7.

29. *Ibid.*

30. *Ibid.*

31. *Ibid.*

32. *Ibid.*

33. *Ibid.*

34. *Ibid.*

35. *Ibid.*

36. *Ibid.*

37. *Brandon Sun* (17 April 1998) 1.

38. *Ibid.* (18 April 1998) 1.

39. *Ibid.*

40. *Brandon Sun* (7 June 1977) 1.

41. Dale Brawn, *Every Stone A Story II* (Great Plains: Winnipeg, 2009) 131.

42. *Brandon Sun* (23 April 1998) 3.

43. *Ibid.*

44. *Ibid.*

45. *Ibid.* (21 September 1998) 1.

3: Reprieved to Kill Again

1. "Crime Reporter" by Jana Pruden: *Edmonton Journal, www.edmonton journal.com/news/hanged/upcoming/barrett.html.*

2. *Ibid.*

3. *Ibid.*

4. *Ibid.*

5. *Ibid.*

6. *Montreal Gazette* (29 November 1946) 13.

7. *Ibid.*

8. *Ibid.*

9. *Ibid.*

10. *Ibid.* (25 February 1947) 3.

11. *Ibid.*

12. *Ibid.*

13. *Ibid.*

14. *Ibid.*

15. *Ibid.*

16. *Ibid.*

17. *Ibid.* (26 February 1947) 11.

18. *Ibid.* (25 February 1947) 3.

19. *Ibid.*

20. *Ibid.* (26 November 1948) 3.

21. *Ibid.* (25 November 1948) 11.

22. *Ibid.* (27 November 1948) 3.

4: Loved Ones Tell All

1. *Daily Journal* (27 February 1897) 3.

2. *The Globe* (7 December 1897) 2.

3. *Ibid.*

4. Toronto *Daily Mail and Empire* (8 December 1898) 2.

5. *Daily Journal* (8 December 1898) 1.

6. *Ibid.* (17 March 1899) 1.

7. *Ibid.*

8. Cochrane *Northland Post* (5 November 1926) 1.

9. *Ibid.* (12 April 1929) 1.

10. *Northern News* (25 July 1929) 13.

11. *Calgary Herald* (25 September 1945) 1.

12. *Ibid.* (18 November 1948) 1.

13. *Ibid.*

14. *Ibid.*

15. *Ibid.* (19 November 1948) 1.

16. *Ibid.* (15 November 1948) 1.

17. *Ibid.*

18. *Ibid.*

19. *Ibid.*

20. *Ibid.* (20 November 1948) 1.

21. *Ibid.* (19 November 1948) 1.

22. *Ibid.*

23. *Ibid.* (22 November 1948) 1.

24. *Ibid.*

25. *Ibid.*

26. *Saskatoon Star-Phoenix* (26 March 1949) 4.

27. *Globe and Mail* (25 October 1961) 3.

28. *Saskatoon Star-Phoenix* (4 March 1961) 6.

29. *Globe and Mail* (25 October 1961) 3.

30. *Ibid.* (27 October 1961) 31.

31. *Ibid.*

32. *Ibid.*

33. *Ibid.* (26 October 1961) 9.

34. *Ibid.* (16 April 1962) 6.

35. *Windsor Star* (25 February 1971) 34.

5: Suspicions Linger

1. *Calgary Herald* (25 November 1913 7; and (28 November 1913) 1.

2. *Ibid.* (28 August 1913) 1.

3. *Ibid.* and (29 November 1913)1.

4. *Ibid.* (29 November 1913) 1.

5. *Ibid.* (19 January 1914) 1.

6. *Saskatoon Phoenix* (18 February 1914) 1.

7. *Quebec Daily Telegraph* (24 February 1914) 5.

8. *The Deseret News* (26 August 1929) 4.

9. *Montreal Gazette* (27 September 1938) 4.

10. *Ibid.* (23 September 1938) 13.

11. *Ibid.* (4 October 1938) 11.

12. *Ibid.* (5 October 1938) 21.

13. *Ibid.* (24 September 1938) 3.

14. *Ibid.*

15. *Ibid.*

16. *Ibid.* (27 September 1938) 4.

17. *Ibid.* (29 September 1938) 11.

18. *Ibid.* (7 October 1938) 3.

19. *Ibid.*

20. *Ibid.* (10 October 1938) 3.

21. *Ibid.* (15 November 1938) 11.

6: The Two Rolands

1. *Montreal Gazette* (15 June 1948) 13.

2. *Ibid.* (20 February 1953) 1

3. *Ibid.* (21 February 1953) 17.

4. *Ibid.* (20 May 1953) 12.

5. *Ibid.* (21 May 1953) 23.

6. *Ibid.*

7. *Ibid.* (26 September 1981) 4.

8. *Ibid.*

9. *Ibid.*

7: Confessions and Presumptions of Guilt

1. *Globe and Mail* (23 April 1909) 12.

2. *Ibid.* (27 October 1909) 4.

3. *Ibid.* (28 October 1909) 7.

4. *Ibid.*

5. *Ibid.* (8 October 1926) 3.

6. *Manitoba Free Press* (24 November 1925) 3.

7. *Winnipeg Free Press* (4 April 1936) 1.

8. *Ibid.* (11 June 1936) 1.

9. *Ibid.*

10. *Ibid.* (22 August 1936) 3.

11. *Globe and Mail* (13 January 1953) 1.

12. *Ibid.* (18 September 1952) 3.

13. *Ibid.* (14 January 1953) 2.

8: Killers on the Run

1. *Ibid.* (20 January 1954) 1.

2. *Ibid.*

3. *Ibid.* (21 January 1954) 1.

4. Frank W. Anderson, *The Henry Seguin Murder Case* (Saskatoon: Frontiers Unlimited, 1979) 73.

5. *Vancouver Sun* (9 January 1953) 2.

6. *Ibid.* (26 August 1947) 1.

7. *Ibid.*, 2.

8. *Ibid.*

9. *Ibid.*

10. *Ibid.*

11. *Ibid.*

12. *Ibid.* (27 March 1953) 18.

13. *Ibid.*

14. *Ibid.* (29 August 1947) 3.

15. *Ibid.* (30 August 1947) 1.

16. *Ibid.*

17. *Ibid.* (9 January 1953) 1.

18. *Ibid.*

19. *Ibid.*

20. *Ibid.*

21. *Ibid.* (8 January 1953) 1.

22. *Ibid.* (28 March 1953) 3.

23. *Ibid.*

24. *Ibid.* (27 March 1953) 1.

25. *Ibid.* (12 January 1953) 1.

26. *Ibid.*

27. *Ibid.*

28. *Ibid.* (27 January 1953) 1.

29. *Ibid.* Ian Macdonald and Betty O'Keefe, *Canadian Holy War: A Story of Clans, Tongs, Murder, and Bigotry* (Surrey, B.C.: Heritage House, 2000) 206.

30. *Ibid.*

31. *Vancouver Sun* (9 July 1953) 1.

32. *Ibid.*

33. *Ibid.*

34. *Ibid.* (10 July 1953) 23.

9: Pictures on the Dash

1. Neil Boyd, *The Last Dance: Murder in Canada* (Scarborough, Ont.: Prentice-Hall, 1988) at 270.

2. *Ibid.*

3. *Ibid.*, 277.

4. *Globe and Mail* (14 June 1961) 12.

5. *Last Dance* at 271.

6. *Globe and Mail* (11 October 1960).

7. *Last Dance* at 272–73.

8. *Ibid.*, 273.

9. *Ibid.*

10. Ruth Reynolds, *Reading Eagle* (28 April 1963) 96.

11. *Last Dance* at 274.

12. *Ibid.*, 274–75.

13. *Ibid.*

14. *Globe and Mail* (9 March 1961) 1.

15. *Last Dance* at 276.

16. *Ibid.*

17. *Reynolds.*

18. *Ibid.*

19. *The Man I Knew* at *http://mfather.blogspot.ca/*.

10: Skeletons Resurface

1. *The Black River Road Tragedy*, CIHM no. 11172. Testimony of William Douglas, 44.

2. *Ibid.*, 67.

3. *Ibid.*, 67–68.

4. *Ibid.* Testimony of Robert Worden, 45.

5. *Ibid.*

6. *Ibid.* Testimony of Edward Price, 103.

7. *Ibid.* Closing argument of W.H. Tuck, 104.

8. *Ibid.*, 108.

9. *Ibid.*, 105.

10. *Ibid.*, 107.

11. *Ibid.*, 108.

12. *Ibid.* Confession of John Munroe, 130.

13. *Ibid.*, 130.

14. *Ibid.* The Execution, 130.

15. *Globe and Mail* (24 March 1909) 1.

16. *Ibid.* (4 June 1909) 7.

17. *Ibid.*

18. *Montreal Gazette* (14 August 1961) 3.

19. *Ibid.* (16 February 1966) 37.

20. *Ibid.*

21. *Shawinigan Standard* (23 August 1961) 1.

22. *Ibid.*

23. *Saskatoon Phoenix* (29 August 1961) 1.

24. *Regina Leader-Post* (11 May 1965) 10.

25. *Shawinigan Standard* (20 January 1965) 5.

26. *Montreal Gazette* (21 January 1965) 13.

27. *Quebec Chronicle-Telegraph* (3 May 1965) 3.

28. *Montreal Gazette* (10 October 1981) 4.

29. *Ibid.* (19 February 1966) 3.

Bibliography

1: They Got Away With It Before

FRED STAWYCZNYK ABD PAULINE YATCHUK:

BABIES IN BOXES

Winnipeg Free Press (30 November 1932) 1; (1 December 1932) 10; (10 December 1932) 1; (4 April 1933) 5; (5 April 1933) 3; (6 April 1933) 6; (7 April 1933) 3; (8 April 1933) 1; (11 July 1933) 6; (13 July 1933) 1.

WILLIAM BAHREY:

THE BROTHERS IN THE HAYSTACKS

Anderson, Frank W. "The William Bahrey Murders" in *Outlaws of Saskatchewan: Strange Tales of Crime and Criminals from Our Storied Past* (Humbolt, Saskatchewan: Gopher Books, 1999) 65.

McGill, Dr. Frances. "She Solved Murders in the Morgue" in *Ottawa Citizen* (22 October 1955).

Regina *Leader-Post* (12 May 1933) 13; (3 October 1933) 5.

Montreal Gazette (24 February 1934) 4.

Saskatoon Star-Phoenix (21 April 1933) 3; (27 April 1933) 3; (10 May 1933) 3; (11 May 1933) 3; (12 May 1933) 3; (4 October 1933) 3; (5 October 1933) 3; (7 October 1933) 3; (22 February 1934) 3; (23 February 1934) 7; (4 December 1982) C7.

Vancouver Sun (10 May 1933) 11.

WILLIAM LAROCQUE AND EMMANUEL LAVICTOIRE:

MURDERS FOR INSURANCE

Windsor *Border Cities Star* (26 September 1934) 10.

Calgary Herald (6 April 1932) 18.

Globe and Mail (13 April 1932) 2.

Montreal Gazette (16 December 1932) 7; (15 March 1933) 1.

Ottawa Citizen (19 March 1932) 9; (22 March 1932) 1; (29 March 1932) 11; (12 April 1932) 8; (26 April 1932) 20; (27 April 1932) 9; (9 December 1932) 20; (12 December 1932) 13; (14 December 1932) 15; (15 December 1932) 1; (16 December 1932) 28; (17 December 1932) 5; (30 December 1932) 1; (15 March 1933) 3; (20 July 1933) 3.

Vancouver Sun (21 March 1932) 16.

2: Murdering Neighbours

MICHAEL FARRELL:

FIFTEEN YEARS BETWEEN MURDERS

Conway Murder: *www.pbalkcom.com/valcartier/Biographies/conway_murder.htm*.

Montreal Gazette (27 August 1878) 3; (28 August 1878) 3; (29 August 1878) 3; (4 November 1878) 3; (5 November 1878) 3; (6 November 1878) 3; (11 January 1879) 2.

Lawrence, Kansas, *Western Home Journal* (16 January 1879) 2.

EMERSON SHELLEY:

A NEIGHBOUR KILLS AGAIN

British Canadian (18 August 1909) 1; (25 August 1909) 1; (19 May 1915) 1, 7; (26 May 1915) 7; (9 June 1915) 1; (16 June 1915) 1; (29 September 1915) 1; (22 December 1915) 7.

Globe (14 May 1915) 11; (15 May 1915) 5; (20 May 1915) 2; (7 June 1915) 5; (14 June 1915) 3; (22 September 1915) 3; (23 September 1915) 9; (24 September 1915) 1; (5 November 1915) 10; (17 November 1915) 14.

LARRY HAROLD HANSEN:

KILLED BY HIS BEST FRIEND

Brandon Sun (22 November 1976) 1; (7 June 1977) 1; (17 April 1998) 1; (18 April 1998) 1; (20 April 1998) 1; (22 April 1998) 1; (23 April 1998) 3; (21 September 1998) 1.

Winnipeg Free Press (23 November 1976) 8; (11 June 1998) A7; (13 June 1998) A5; (19 September 1998) A3.

3: Reprieved to Kill Again

GARRY RICHARD BARRETT:

ONE SECOND CHANCE TOO MANY

www.telusplanet.net/dgarneau/alberta11.html.

Anderson, Frank. "Death of a Gloomy Little Man" in *Crimes Across the Nation* (Saskatoon: Frontier Publishing) 62.

Edmonton Journal (17 May 1909) 7.

Globe and Mail (3 June 1908) 5.

Manitoba Free Press (16 April 1909) 1.

New York Times (17 April 1909). Officer Down Memorial Page, Inc., *http://canada.odmp.org/officer/31-deputy-warden-richard-h.-stedman.*

Pruden, Jana, "Crime Reporter" in *Edmonton Journal, www.edmontonjournal.com/news/hanged/upcoming/barrett.html.*

Warden of Alberta Penitentiary: *http://en.wikipedia.org/wiki/Matthew_McCauley_(politician).*

JOHN BOYKO:

MARRY ME OR DIE

Fred Rose, *en.wikipedia.org/wiki/Fred_Rose_(politician).*

Montreal Gazette (29 November 1946) 13; (30 November 1946) 3; (7 December 1946) 15; (25 February 1947) 3; (26 February 1947) 11; (25 November 1948) 11; (26 November 1948) 3; (27 November 1948) 3; (4 December 1948) 7; (22 October 1960) 37.

ALBERT VICTOR WESTGATE:

FASCINATION LEADS TO MURDER

Brookside Cemetery: A Celebration of Life, v. 1 (Winnipeg: E.R. Publishing) 55.

Cook v. Westgate (1944) Man. R. 227 (C.A.).

Globe and Mail (13 December 1928) 21.

John Burchill, "Wordless Westgate," *http://winnipeg.ca/police/History/story9. stm.*

Morriss, W.E., *Watch the Rope* (Winnipeg: Watson Dwyer, 1996).

4: Loved Ones Tell All

OLIVER PRÉVOST:

THE PIGGERY MURDERS

Fort William *Daily Journal* (11 February 1897) 3; (16 February 1897) 1; (24 February 1897) 3; (27 February 1897) 3; (7 December 1897) 1; (8 December 1898) 1; (15 March 1899) 1; (16 March 1899) 3; (17 March 1899) 1, 4.

Daily Mail and Empire (8 December 1898) 2.

Globe (12 February 1897) 1; (27 February 1897) 17; (25 November 1897) 1; (27 November 1897) 23; (7 December 1897) 2; (9 December 1897) 1; (6 December 1898) 2; (7 December 1898) 9; (8 December 1898) 1; (16 March 1899) 2.

JOHN "COBALT" IVANCHUK:

TOO MUCH TO SAY

Windsor *Border Cities Star* (17 November 1928) 13.

Fort William *Daily Times-Journal* (25 August 1919) 1.

Edmonton Journal (3 May 1928) 19.

Kenora Daily Miner and News (27 August 1919) 1; (30 August 1919) 1; (3 September 1919) 1.

Montreal Gazette (18 October 1926) 15.

Cobalt, Ontario *Northern News* (18 April 1929) 1; (25 July 1929) 13.

Cochrane *Northland Post* (22 October 1926) 1; (29 October 1926) 8; (5 November 1926) 1; (12 April 1929) 1; (19 July 1929) 1.

Sudbury Star (20 July 1929) 1.

STANLEY DONALD MCLAREN:

A FATAL MISTAKE

Calgary Herald (25 September 1945) 1; (26 September 1945) 1; (27 September 1945) 1; (28 September 1945) 1; (30 August 1948) 1; (31 August 1948) 1; (2 October 1948) 1; (13 October 1948) 1; (14 October 1948) 1; (15 November 1948) 1; (16 November 1948) 1; (17 November 1948) 1; (18 November 1948) 1; (19 November 1948) 1; (20 November 1948) 1; (22 November 1948) 1; (28 March 1949) 1; (29 March 1949) 1; (30 March 1949) 1.

Saskatoon Star-Phoenix (26 March 1949) 4.

ARTHUR KENDALL:

KILLING IN FRONT OF FAMILY

Globe and Mail (24 October 1961) 12; (25 October 1961) 3; (26 October 1961) 9; (27 October 1961) 31; (28 October 1961) 2; (23 January 1962) 5; (6 February 1962) 4; (15 March 1962) 8; (16 March 1962) 41; (27 March 1962) 8; (5 April 1962) 25; (11 April 1962) 3; (13 April 1962) 23; (16 April 1962) 6.

Regina *Leader-Post* (28 January 1961) 29; (27 October 1961) 32.

Saskatoon Star-Phoenix (4 March 1961) 6.

Windsor Star (27 January 1961) 1; (25 February 1971) 34; (26 February 1971) 6.

5: Suspicions Linger

WILLIAM JASPER COLLINS:

TOO MUCH MONEY

Boston Transcript (4 March 1914) 20.

Calgary Herald (28 August 1913) 1; (11 November 1913) 1; (22 November 1913) 13; (25 November 1913) 7; (26 November 1913) 10; (28 November 1913) 1; (29 November 1913) 1; (19 January 1914) 1; (10 February 1914) 1; (17 February 1914) 15; (18 February 1914) 1, 6.

Nelson, New Zealand, *Colonist* (20 February 1914) 5.

Quebec *Daily Telegraph* (24 February 1914) 5.

St. Joseph, Missouri, *News-Press* (25 November 1913) 1.

Pfeifer, Jeffrey and, Ken Leyton-Brown. *Death By Rope*, v. 1: *1867–1923* (Centax Books: Regina, 2007) 172.

Saskatoon Star-Phoenix (19 February 1914) 6.

Toronto Sunday World (15 February 1914) 12.

MARIE BEAULNE AND PHILIBERT LEFEBVRE:

POISON DOES THE TRICK

Anderson, Frank W. "Marie Viau: Too Much Haste" in *A Dance with Death: Canadian Women on the Gallows, 1754–1954* (Saskatoon: Fifth House, 1996) 20.

Windsor *Border Cities Star* (1 August 1929) 12; (24 August 1929) 3.

Salt Lake City, Utah, *Desert News* (26 August 1929) 4.

St. Petersburg, Florida, *Evening Independent* (23 August 1929) 1.

Sarasota, Florida, *Herald-Tribune* (23 August 1929) 1.

Miami News (23 August 1929) 1.

Montreal Gazette (13 June 1929) 6; (21 August 1929) 3; (23 August 1929) 13; (24 August 1929) 3.

Pittsburg Press (27 June 1929) 11; (22 August 1929) 1.

Reading Eagle (24 August 1929) 1.

Vancouver Sun (20 August 1929) 4; (23 August 1929) 1.

MARIE LOUISE CLOUTIER AND ACHILLE GRONDIN:

MARRIED TOO SOON

Anderson, Frank W. "Marie Cloutier: A First-Class Embalming" in *A Dance with Death: Canadian Women on the Gallows, 1754–1954* (Saskatoon: Fifth House, 1996) 28.

Lewiston Evening Journal (10 February 1940) 2.

Montreal Gazette (30 November 1937) 10; (4 December 1937) 3; (21 September 1938) 11; (22 September 1938) 11; (23 September 1938) 13; (24 September 1938) 3; (27 September 1938) 4; (28 September 1938) 21; (29 September 1938) 11; (30 September 1938) 21; (1 October 1938) 3; (3 October 1938) 15; (4 October 1938) 11; (5 October 1938) 21; (6 October 1938) 10; (7 October 1938) 3; (8 October 1938) 21; (10 October 1938) 3; (3 November 1938) 11; (4 November 1938) 9; (8 November 1938) 11; (9 November 1938) 3; (10 November 1938) 14; (11 November 1938) 2; (15 November 1938) 11; (18 November 1938)

2; (19 November 1938) 9; (22 November 1938) 4; (23 November 1938) 4; (25 November 1938) 2; (26 November 1938) 23; (28 November 1938) 3; (30 November 1938) 4; (20 February 1939) 3; (3 June 1939) 4; (14 June 1939) 3; (23 February 1940) 10; (24 February 1940) 13.

Vancouver Sun (23 February 1940) 4.

Windsor Daily Star (31 October 1939) 14.

6: The Two Rolands

ROLAND ASSELIN:

FIFTY-FIVE WEEKS BETWEEN MURDERS

Edmonton Journal (5 January 1948) 16.

Montreal Gazette (1 January 1948) 3; (5 January 1948) 11; (9 June 1948) 3; (10 June 1948) 11; (11 June 1948) 3; (15 June 1948) 13; (16 June 1948) 3; (10 June 1949) 3.

Ottawa Citizen (31 December 1947) 10.

"Ranger, Marie Blanche Alice," Quebec, Vital and Church Records (Drouin Collection), various records.

ROLAND GENEST:

HE NEVER MURDERED A WOMAN HE DIDN'T LOVE

Montreal Gazette (30 May 1951) 2; (31 May 1951) 3; (1 June 1951) 3; (20 February 1953) 1; (21 February 1953) 17; (23 February 1953) 3; (24 February 1953) 1; (25 February 1953) 3; (26 February 1953) 1; (27 February 1953) 17; (28 February 1953) 17; (20 May 1953) 12; (21 May 1953) 23; (22 May 1953) 1; (26 September 1981) 4.

Ottawa Citizen (27 August 1953) 3.

7: Confessions and Presumptions of Guilt

PORAL STEFOFF:

LAST MINUTE CONFESSION OF A SERIAL KILLER

Globe (23 April 1909) 12; (8 May 1909) 23; (19 October 1909) 14; (25 October 1909) 14; (27 October 1909) 14; (28 October 1909) 7; (30

October 1909) 28; (4 November 1909) 14; (24 December 1909) 5; (25 December 1909) 6.

Montreal Gazette (27 April 1909) 5.

Warsaw Daily Union (24 December 1909) 1.

JOHN BARTY:

THE COLD-SET KILLER

Ayre, John D. "John Barty, 1927" in *Felons of Hamilton, Haldimand and Brant, 1828–1953* (Simcoe, Ont.: Ayre, 2000) 94.

Globe and Mail (27 June 1925) 1; (7 July 1925) 3; (11 June 1926) 1; (14 June 1926) 1; (17 June 1926) 3; (19 June 1926) 3; (22 June 1926) 3; (7 October 1926) 3; (8 October 1926) 3; (13 January 1927) 3.

Montreal Gazette (23 December 1926) 17.

Morning Leader (7 October 1926) 3.

Nevada Daily Mail (13 January 1927) 5.

Saskatoon Phoenix (23 December 1926) 1.

JOHN KOOTING:

CONFESSIONS ON THE PRAIRIES, PART I

Manitoba Free Press (27 April 1925) 1; (19 November 1925) 2; (20 November 1925) 11; (24 November 1925) 3; (25 November 1925) 6; (26 November 1925) 1; (27 November 1925) 9.

JOHN PAWLUK:

CONFESSIONS ON THE PRAIRIES, PART II

Winnipeg Free Press (26 March 1936) 1; (27 March 1936) 1; (28 March 1936) 3; (30 March 1936) 1; (31 March 1936) 3; (1 April 1936) 4; (4 April 1936) 1; (10 June 1936) 1; 11 June 1936) 1; (12 June 1936) 1; (13 June 1936) 1; (22 August 1936) 3.

JAMES ALFRED KELSEY:

A TENDENCY TO TALK TOO MUCH

Globe and Mail (18 September 1952) 3; (19 September 1952) 1; (22 November 1952) 2; (13 January 1953) 1; (14 January 1953) 2; (20 February 1953) 32.

Kelsey v. R., 1953 1 S.C.R. 220.

Sam Delibasich. *www.taxi-library.org/canada/1-d04.htm.*

8: Killers on the Run

HENRY SÉGUIN:

FROM ONTARIO TO BRITISH COLUMBIA

Anderson, Frank. *The Henry Seguin Murder Case* (Frontiers Unlimited: Saskatoon, 1979).

Calgary Herald (31 October 1953) 9.

Edmonton Journal (18 March 1953) 20.

Globe and Mail (18 August 1952) 1; (19 August 1952) 5; (23 August 1952) 2; (28 April 1953) 5; (27 October 1953) 10; (15 December 1953) 5; (18 January 1954) 2; (19 January 1954) 1; (20 January 1954) 1; (21 January 1954) 1; (28 January 1954) 7; (2 February 1954) 5.

Montreal Gazette (21 August 1953) 12.

Ottawa Citizen (23 May 1947) 16; (18 August 1952) 1, 7; (20 August 1952) 1; (22 August 1952) 1; (29 December 1952) 16; (19 January 1953) 2; (27 April 1953) 1; (28 April 1953) 5; (5 May 1953) 20; (18 August 1953) 14; (20 August 1953) 18, 34; (23 November 1953) 34; (15 December 1953) 20; (20 September 1955) 1.

Quebec Chronicle Telegraph (15 December 1953) 16.

Saskatoon Star-Phoenix (28 April 1953) 12; (21 August 1953) 2; (30 October 1953) 2; (14 January 1954) 4; (21 January 1954) 1.

Henderson, North Carolina, *Times-News* (20 January 1954) 1.

Vancouver Sun (14 January 1953) 2; (20 January 1953) 13; (21 February 1953) 1; (28 February 1953) 8; (22 April 1953) 1; (24 September 1955) 48.

Windsor Daily Star (24 December 1952) 15; (22 November 1955) 6.

WALTER PAVLUKOFF:

FROM BRITISH COLUMBIA TO ONTARIO

Macdonald, Ian and Betty O'Keefe. *Canadian Holy War: A Story of Clans, Tongs, Murder, and Bigotry* (Surrey, B.C.: Heritage House, 2000) at 204–07.

Montreal Gazette (9 July 1953) 1.

Vancouver Sun (26 August 1947) 1, 2; (27 August 1947) 1; (28 August 1947) 1; (29 August 1947) 1, 3; (30 August 1947) 1; (2 September 1947) 1; (3 September 1947) 8; (4 September 1947) 2; (5 September 1947) 3; (8

January 1953) 1; (9 January 1953) 1, 2; (10 January 1953) 1; (12 January 1953) 1; (26 January 1953) 1; (27 January 1953) 1; (24 March 1953) 2; (25 March 1953) 9; (26 March 1953) 1; (27 March 1953) 1, 18; (28 March 1953) 1, 3; (30 March 1953) 1; (31 March 1953) 2; (1 April 1953) 1; (4 July 1953) 10; (8 July 1953) 1; (9 July 1953) 1; (10 July 1953) 23; (14 July 1953) 3; (21 July 1953) 34.

Windsor Daily Star (10 July 1953) 25.

9: Pictures on the Dash

OWEN "MICKEY" FEENER

Boyd, Neil. *The Last Dance: Murder In Canada* (Toronto: Prentice-Hall, 1988) 269–278.

Globe and Mail (8 October 1960) 5; (10 October 1960) 1; (11 October 1960) 1; (12 October 1960) 4; (13 October 1960) 1; (14 October 1960) 8; (27 October 1960) 9; (3 November 1960) 9; (10 December 1960) 5; (21 January 1961) 4; (7 March 1961) 9; (8 March 1961) 4; (9 March 1961) 1; (10 March 1961) 3; (16 May 1961) 1; (13 June 1961) 38; (14 June 1961) 12; (15 June 1961) 37.

The Man I Never Knew. *http://mfather.blogspot.ca.*

Ottawa Citizen (14 June 1961) 18.

Reynolds, Ruth. *Reading Eagle* (28 April 1963) 96.

Sudbury Star (11 October 1960); (28 October 1960) 2.

10: Skeletons Resurface

JOHN MUNROE:

NOBODY ASKED ABOUT MOTHER AND DAUGHTER

Black River Road Tragedy, 1869 (Saint John: G.W. Day, 1870), CIHM no. 11172.

Lawton Family. "Murder of Sarah Vail" at *www.lawtonfamilynb.com/page/Murder+of+Sarah+Vail.*

Little, Peter. "Ghost Stories: The Sad Tale of Maggie Vail" at: *http://new brunswick.net/newbrunswick/ghoststory/ghost2.html.*

MAURICE RYAN:

BONES OF A BROTHER

Globe and Mail (24 March 1909) 1; (3 June 1909) 5; (4 June 1909) 7.

Montreal Gazette (25 March 1909) 11; (4 June 1909) 8.

Pfeifer, Jeffrey and Ken Leyton-Brown. *Death by Rope*, v. 1: *1867–1923* (Centax Books: Regina, 2007) 144.

MARCEL BERNIER:

THE BODIES CAME BACK

Montreal Gazette (14 August 1961) 3; (26 August 1961) 3; (28 August 1961) 3; (12 September 1961) 21; (8 August 1964) 3; (12 August 1964) 14; (3 November 1964) 1; (21 January 1965) 13; (11 May 1965) 17; (15 February 1966) 3; (16 February 1966) 37; (17 February 1966) 3; (19 February 1966) 3; (22 February 1966) 3; (25 February 1966) 1; (10 October 1981) 4.

Ottawa Citizen (15 August 1961) 1.

Quebec Chronicle Telegraph (3 May 1965) 3.

Regina Leader-Post (18 August 1961) 35; (6 September 1961) 34; (11 May 1965) 10; (9 November 1977) 8.

Saskatoon Phoenix (29 August 1961) 1; (1 May 1965) 2; (3 May 1965) 12.

Shawinigan Standard (23 August 1961) 1; (20 January 1965) 5; (7 April 1965) 1; (14 April 1965) 17; (5 May 1965) 1; (12 May 1965) 1; (19 May 1965) 4; (2 March 1966) 1; (16 April 1969) 1; (25 February 1970) 2.

Windsor Star (8 April 1965) 62; (10 January 1968) 18; (8 November 1977) 18.

Index

Numbers in italics refer to images and their captions.

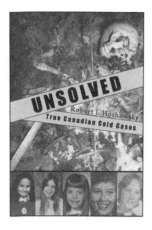

Unsolved
True Canadian Cold Cases
by Robert J. Hoshowsky
978-1554887392
$24.99

Despite advances in DNA testing, forensics, and the investigative skills used by police, hundreds of crimes remain unsolved across Canada. With every passing day trails grow colder and decades can pass before a new lead or witness comes forward if one comes forward.

In *Unsolved*, Robert J. Hoshowsky examines twelve crimes that continue to haunt us. Some cases are well-known, while others have virtually disappeared from the public eye. All of the cases remain open, and many are being re-examined by police using the latest tools and technology. Hoshowsky takes the reader through all aspects of the crimes and how police are trying to solve them using three-dimensional facial reconstructions, DNA testing, age-enhanced drawings, original crime scene photos, and more.

None of the individuals profiled in *Unsolved* deserved their fate, but their stories deserve to be told and their killers need to be brought to justice.

Justice Miscarried
Inside Wrongful Convictions in Canada
by Helena Katz
978-155488874
$24.99

Former bank manager Ronald Dalton never got to watch his three young children grow up. In 1989 he was convicted for a crime that never happened. His wife, Brenda, was later ruled to have choked to death on breakfast cereal, not strangled as a pathologist had initially claimed. Dalton's daughter, Alison, was in kindergarten when he was charged with second-degree murder in 1988. He attended her high school graduation on June 26, 2000, two days after his conviction was finally overturned.

Behind the proud facade of Canada's criminal justice system lie the shattered lives of the people unjustly caught within its web. *Justice Miscarried* tells the heart-wrenching stories of twelve innocent Canadians, including David Milgaard, Donald Marshall, Guy Paul Morin, Clayton Johnson, William Mullins-Johnson, and Thomas Sophonow, who were wrongly convicted and the errors in the nations justice system that changed their lives forever.

DUNDURN

VISIT US AT
Dundurn.com
Definingcanada.ca
@dundurnpress
Facebook.com/dundurnpress